THE
MANAGER'S
GUIDE TO
ISO 9000

KENNETH L. ARNOLD

THE MANAGER'S GUIDE TO ISO 9000

THE FREE PRESS

New York   London   Toronto   Sydney   Singapore

The Free Press
A Division of Simon & Schuster Inc.
1230 Avenue of the Americas
New York, N.Y. 10020

Manufactured in the United States of America

10 9 8 7 6 5 4 3 2

Library of Congress Cataloging-in-Publication Data

Arnold, Kenneth L.
    The manager's guide to ISO 9000 / Kenneth L. Arnold.
        p.   cm.
    Includes index.
    ISBN 0–02–901035–7
    1. Quality control—Standards.   2. Manufactures—Quality control—
Evaluation.   I. Title.
TS156.A75   1994
658.5'62'0218—dc20   94–4413
                                                                      CIP

I would like to dedicate this effort to my parents, the Rev. Forest L. Arnold MEd. and the Rev. Virginia L. Arnold MA. They have provided me with physical, emotional, and financial support during this and many other projects. Beyond this support, they have given me love without bounds, without reservations, and without expectations of anything in return. This unconditional love and support have set the example for my life.

To all who know you, your lives are living examples of what it means to be a man and woman of God. While you are my parents by heredity, you are my best friends by choice. For that, I love you both very much.

CONTENTS

FOREWORD

This book was written as a road map to guide the reader past all the pitfalls, U-turns, road hazards, and dead ends that were experienced by one company in its quest for certification to the ISO-9001 standard. As the terrain is constantly changing and viewed differently by each traveler undertaking the journey, it is impossible to anticipate every obstacle. This book attempts to provide enough information so that the reader will be able to cope effectively with situations as they arise.

The beauty of the ISO 9000 series standard is that it is conceptual—it allows the reader to determine the most effective way in which to implement the stated requirements. The downside, however, is that this conceptualist approach leaves the standard open for potential abuse.

The ISO 9000 series standards received thorough analysis by the International Organization for Standardization in Europe prior to being released. But the same sort of analysis and organization has not existed in the United States with regard to certification activities. The European Community exhibited far more forethought and concern in establishing registration boards to verify the qualification of agencies performing certification activities to the standard. The United States is only now coming up to speed in controlling, verifying, and promoting consistency among certification agencies. For this reason, many companies in the United States have opted to collaborate with European organizations to provide them with certification.

The basic intent and requirement of the standard have been coordinated within the European Community. Certification agencies use a similar base for analysis ensuring that verification activities will not vary substantially from one agency to another. No amount of coordination and control will ensure that each certification audit will proceed exactly as any other performed. However, enough attention has been concentrated in this area in the European Community to minimize the likelihood of certification agencies performing audits with radically different perceptions of the standard due to their own personal bias.

Unfortunately, this assurance does not exist with American certification agencies. American history is long and steadfast in the implementation of military and industry standards which focus solely on the product produced while allowing the process to run uncontrolled. It is deplorable that many American agencies will audit a company and audit to the ISO 9000 series standard with the same mentality used to evaluate a product-only oriented standard. Additionally, an excessive amount of money is wasted each day in the United States on consultants with the same product-oriented mentality and military standard bias. These exercises serve only to try to force an existing MIL-STD, product-oriented program into compliance with an International Standard that requires nothing at all of this nature. In light of this, companies pursuing certification should thoroughly investigate the certification agency they intend to use.

If an organization's intent is only to force its existing product-oriented program into compliance with and certification to the ISO 9000 series standard, the certification agency chosen should exhibit the same philosophy. The importance of the certification must also be determined. Currently, reciprocity agreements exist between many countries in the European Community regarding certification by specific agencies. If international recognition of the certification is a factor, it is imperative that the certifying agency have credibility in the market where the company participates. What good is certification if it will not be accepted by the potential customer because of the certifying agency? In this case, it would be wise to verify that the potential marketplace will accept certification by a local agency promoting certification to ISO 9000. Additionally, if an agency is not certified by a recognized registration body, the focus, understanding, and basis on which the audit is performed may or may not be in line with the orginal intent of the standard and focus of this text.

Americans are experienced in determining percentages and creating paperwork to outweigh the product as a means of verifying the system. This mind-set must be broken if effective implemetation of the ISO 9000 Series Standard and execution of good business sense are ever again to be achieved in the United States.

To support the American approach, the standard was not adopted in the United States as issued. Time, money, and effort were wasted to "republish" the standard in an American form. Even now, at the writing of this Foreword, efforts are still being wasted in an attempt to prove that the ISO 9000 Series is not a unique document but bears its formation in a previously issued American military standard. And for what purpose is all of this activity being conducted? The European approach, as fortified by the standard, is "If it's good, accept it. Don't waste the effort to reinvent the wheel." In all fairness, America cannot claim sole rights to the nationalization of the ISO standard. The Germans, Japanese, and British all rejected adoption of ISO 9000 in favor of creating their own national standards which bear their identification systems but with verbiage directly from ISO 9000.

This book's approach may well be criticized for its "European" mentality. And justly, why not? It is a European Standard whether one calls it ISO 9000, BS 5750, or Q90. But far more than that, it is a good standard. It breaks the rules of focusing solely on the product and, if properly implemented, establishes a program to provide product acceptablity with process control.

Linda I. Laird

ACKNOWLEDGMENTS

I wish to acknowledge the assistance of the following people in helping me to complete this work. I would like to thank my daughters Beth, Maggie, and Ginny for allowing me the time needed to work on this project. They experienced many days and nights in which I was locked away from them writing and editing the manuscript. Completing that job would have been impossible without their love and support.

I would like to express my deepest appreciation to Linda I. Laird CQE, CQA for the technical edit of this book. Linda was involved in developing the quality systems in the companies from which the implementation strategies detailed in the text were taken. Because of her input, through her technical competence and unique insight to the standard, the qualtiy of this product is greatly improved.

I would also like to express my sincere thanks to Susan Adamski for her help in proofreading and correcting the manuscript. Her many hours of work have helped make this book possible.

Finally, I extend my appreciation to the American National Standards Institute for allowing me to reprint portions of ISO 9001 and ISO 9004 1987 version and the ISO/DIS 9000 series draft standard.

THE MANAGER'S GUIDE TO ISO 9000

1

WHAT IS ISO 9000, AND WHERE DID IT COME FROM?

ISO 9000 is one of the more misunderstood series of standards in common use today. After leading a manufacturing facility into compliance with and certification to ISO 9001 and providing direction and resources to bring a chemical manufacturing facility into compliance with ISO 9002, I can say without hesitation that the ISO 9000 series of standards is *not* solely a quality control standard.

But if ISO 9000 is not a quality control standard, what is it? The standard is a guideline for the design, manufacture, sale, and servicing of a product. For the purpose of this book, a product can be defined as either hard (for example, a car, computer, or sheet of paper) or soft (such as the service provided by a bank, information provided by a computer, or a design file or specification). To implement this standard successfully, the team working to establish the system must view the ISO 9000 series as a complete design, manufacturing, sales, and servicing standard. The system developed must concentrate on consistency of purpose and focus on the requirements of doing business well. In summary, ISO 9000 is nothing more than a checklist for doing business on a world-class level.

The ISO 9000 standard is a unique document. It was written in such a way that it can be successfully implemented in almost any type of business without modification or change. It has been implemented in health care institutions, banks, chemical manufacturing companies, heavy blacksmith-type manufacturing shops, pharmaceutical manufacturers, and food processing plants. The ISO 9000 standard is different from many of the existing quality standards in that it does not require specific actions to be carried out. Many standards state in exacting detail the amount of NDE required, the amount and type of incoming inspection required, how to document in-process or final inspection, or what is required in an inspection and test plan. ISO 9000 does not take this approach.

For this reason, ISO 9000 encourages each company to determine how best to meet the intent and requirement of the standard. This allows for flexibility and individualization of a company's method of operation. The underlying philosophy suggests that each business must address specific elements (design control, purchasing, product qualification, and so forth) in order to be successful. The authors of this standard have effectively defined the areas of business that must be properly addressed for a company to produce a consistent product. The list of these areas was compiled into a group of documents called ISO 9000, 9001, 9002, 9003, and 9004. These documents define the requirements within each area that must be satisfied before a program can be certified.

A Word of Warning

It is only fair that I explain my viewpoint of ISO 9000 very early in this text. While working on this project I received two criticisms from a national quality society. The first was that I have taken a very "European" view of the standard. To this criticism, I plead guilty. I have been involved in directing the efforts of a manufacturing facility making oil-field stimulation equipment certified to the European standards BS 5750: Part 1, ISO 9001, EN 29001; 1987. I have also helped a chemical manufacturing plant develop a quality system certified to BS 5750: Part 2, ISO 9002, EN 29002; 1987. The certification body in each activity was the Norwegian firm Det Norske Veritas Quality Assurance LTD, and the audit team did its work within the guidelines of the British scheme. I have developed this view as the certification program was initiated to allow both companies to compete better in Europe. As a result, I do have a European view of this standard.

I feel the approach outlined by ISO 9001 (be it European or American) is one that allows a company to use the standard as an improvement tool. The standard can be used as the structure through which to implement a Total Quality Management (TQM) program. The standard will allow a company to truly have a quality program that will pay for itself instead of being a drain.

If this is a European view, so be it. It is about time someone determined that quality programs must be custom fit to a company instead of the one-size-fits-all approach that many of the existing standards try to take.

This leads us to the second criticism made by the quality society, which was that this book was not written to describe in detail exactly how a program must be implemented to pass the certification audit. In other words I have not tried to develop a generic program that, if followed, might result in a certification. To this criticism, I also plead guilty. This book does not detail a program down to the percentage of parts that have to be inspected using military standard 105D, nor does it define who is required on a material review board, or how many copies of a form must be made. After having spent three years dissecting the ISO 9000 series standard, I can say without reservation that this series is one of the most forward-thinking approaches that has ever been taken for a quality system document. This series of standards has not taken a cookie-cutter approach to implementation, where everyone must do the same things and have the same programs. It provides overall direction while allowing the creativity generated from within each company to determine how best to implement the standard.

The International Organization for Standardization has taken the innovative approach that ISO 9001, 9002, and 9003 are minimum guidelines that should be followed for a company to do business well. This group of professionals understood that to dictate the detail of implementation would in itself doom this standard to a state of obsolescence before the ink dried on the paper. Why should anyone override this effort by publishing a work that tries to push a personal view of how a quality program should function? The standard allows for innovation and improvement; a generic program can be neither cost-effective nor certifiable in all industries. The lack of specific program structure is the strong point of this standard.

What this book will do is look at each element of the standard, outline the intent, list the requirements, and give an example of an implementation strategy that has worked. I stress that the implementation strategy is an *example* of how the standard was implemented in a certified program, not a mandate for how it must be implemented. Find out what works well for your company and decide if what you are doing meets the intent of the standard, fulfills the requirement, and makes sense. If you can answer yes to each area, the program will probably pass a certification audit.

What About the 1994 Version?

This text was written in relation to the 1987 version of the ISO 9000 series standard. In March 1993, the first recommended revisions to the European series standard were presented to the member countries for possible ratification. The draft standard was referred to as ISO/DIS 9000 through ISO/DIS 9004. The member countries evaluated the standard and in September 1993 voted to accept the content of the modifications to the ISO 9000 standard. The modified standard will be issued in the spring of 1994 with the U.S. version being issued through the American National Standards Institute in late spring of 1994.

The American National Standards Institute has given us permission to reprint the 1987 version of ISO 9001 and 9004 along with reprinting any portions of the ISO/DIS 9000 series that we felt necessary to adequately present this topic. The verbiage of ISO 9001 and 9004 as cited in this book will be that of the 1987 versions as the revisions incorporated by the 1994 version have not altered the intent or basic requirements of the standard. The major revisions have provided further clarification of the 1987 standard or added requirements exceeding those originally issued.

Throughout the text, the additional requirements of the 1994 version will be identified and discussed. The terminology and requirements that will be discussed in this text will be taken directly from the ISO/DIS 9001 standard. Although some minor editorial changes are expected to occur between the ISO/DIS and the formal issue of the ISO 9000 1994 series standard, no major content changes or additional requirements are expected.

In theory, the standard has been modified to stress even further the purpose of customer satisfaction. The introduction in ISO 9001 has been modified to state "for the purpose of a supplier demonstrating its capability, and for the assessment of such supplier capability by external parties." Where the 1987 version stated that the scope was ". . . aimed primarily at preventing nonconformances at all stages . . . ," the 1994 version states ". . . aimed primarily at achieving customer satisfaction by preventing nonconformity at all stages. . . .

There has also been expansion in the introduction to further define the purpose of this standard. This definition includes that the ISO 9000 series standards are to ". . . specify requirements which determine what elements quality systems have to encompass but it is not the purpose to enforce uniformity of quality systems." The standards are designed as ". . . generic, independent of any specific industry or economic sector." The introduction stresses that each organization must develop its quality system in regard to its specific needs, objectives, products, and services.

Where Did ISO 9000 Come From?

During World War II many countries (including the United States, Great Britain, and France) came together to stop the march of Germany, Italy, and Japan. The problem was that as the soldiers of countries fought side by side, major differences existed. Not only did the Allied countries have different languages, customs, and religious beliefs with which to contend, they also had differing munitions, vehicles, and units of measure. These differences prevented supplies (such as bullets) from being shared by forces fighting on the same side.

To keep this incompatibility of components from becoming a future issue, the first military standards were developed. Industry soon realized the merit of standardization and followed the lead of the military; unfortunately, industries in each different country developed their own standards. The following is a list of a few of the standards that were developed over the years.

Year	Standard	Source
1963	MIL-Q-9858A	U.S. military
1969	AQAP	NATO
1971	ASME Boiler Code	American Society of Mechanical Engineers
1973	Defstan 05	U.K.
1973	API 14A	American Petroleum Institute
1975	CSA Z299	Canadian Standard
1975	AS 1821/22/23	Australian Standard
1979	BS 5750	British Standard
1985	API Q1	American Petroleum Institute

Many of the standards that are used today are direct descendants of these early standards. One element that was common among many of the military, petroleum, and government standards was heavy inspection focused solely on the end product, rather than the processes used to create it. The standards tried to fit everyone into the same mold, with armies of inspectors looking over people's work.

During the 1970s and 1980s the science of quality control evolved from reactive (inspection-dominant) to proactive (system-oriented) organizations. The focus changed from the end result (the product) and centered on the process by which it was produced. The theory behind this change was that if the process used to produce the product was developed and maintained properly, the product would be consistent and the quality could be improved. This theory was set forth by such leaders in quality as Juran, Deming, Crosby, and Feigenbaum, and it was the manufacturing approach taken by Japan in its efforts to become an industrial power.

The problem was that many existing standards did not make the transition from product orientation to process orientation. Some countries saw the need and attempted to make the change in their own requirements. As markets became global, companies thus found themselves having to meet many standards for different countries that were sometimes conflicting and usually confusing. In an effort to eliminate some of the confusion, the International Organization for Standardization convened to develop, among other standards, an international quality system standard. In March 1987, the ISO 9000 series was issued.

The ISO 9000 series standards have become the most widely recognized and accepted standards in the world. In 1993 it became mandatory in some industries to possess certification to the ISO 9000 series to participate in the European Community (EC), the largest consumer market in the world. The type of industries that require certification to participate in the EC market are quite limited and deal with health, public safety, and environmental issues. A greater push for companies to become certified, however, comes from consumers. Many countries have adopted ISO 9000, often writing national standards that follow it word for word. Some of the national standards that mirror ISO 9000 are ANSI Q-90, BS 5750 (revision), AS 3900, and the NZS 5600 series.

What Is ISO 9000?

The ISO 9000 standard is a five-part standard that was written to address the areas that are considered good business practices for every part of a company. The standard, as written, is not industry specific; it is a general guideline for good, efficient business operation. As noted earlier, the unique part of the standard is that it allows each company to evaluate each element of the standard and decide how to meet the intent of that element effectively. This means that two companies may look at an element such as design control and decide to implement programs that are radically different in content and documentation. Although the programs are different, however, both meet the intent and requirement of design control.

The standard is a guide to world-class business practices. The manner in which the elements are addressed is decided on by the individual company. Use of the ISO 9000 series standards can also provide companies some assurance that a certified supplier follows sound business practices and has systems in place that will provide consistent quality of goods or services. Companies gaining certification are awarded a certificate attesting to their conformance to the requirements of the standard.

How Is the Standard Structured?

The ISO 9000 series is produced in five parts: ISO 9000, 9001, 9002, 9003, and 9004. ISO 9000 and 9004 are guidelines. ISO 9001, 9002, and 9003 are the categories (each with detailed requirements) for which companies may apply for certification. The following summary will describe each part. Due to their similarities, ISO 9000 and 9004 will be discussed first, followed by 9001, 9002, and 9003.

ISO 9000, "Quality Management and Quality Assurance Standards—Guidelines for Selection and Use," is an advisory document. It explains how the overall standard is divided, gives guidelines to use in determining which of the three classifications (9001, 9002, or 9003) is applicable to the business, and gives guidelines on how the systems may be implemented.

ISO 9004, "Quality Management and Quality Systems Elements—Guidelines," is also an advisory document. Although ISO 9004 is very helpful, implementation of its guidelines is not mandatory for certification. It provides detailed advice to businesses on overall quality management and the quality system elements within the ISO 9000 series. In other words, this section will help a company determine the intent of the elements of 9001, 9002, or 9003. In addition to the information relevant to the requirements of the three standards, ISO 9004 provides guidance in such other areas as marketing, quality costs, and product safety and liability. As of late 1993, it includes subsections 9004.1, which explains the ISO 9000 series for manufacturing, and 9004.2, which explains the same standards for service companies.

ISO 9003, "Quality Systems—Model for Quality Assurance in Final Inspection and Test," is used when conformance to specified requirements is to be assured by the supplier solely by a final inspection and test. Generally, an ISO 9003 quality system will only be relevant to a fairly simple product or service. Certification to this standard is not widely accepted. ISO 9003 stipulates requirements for the following system elements:

Management responsibility
Quality system
Document control
Product identification
Inspection and testing
Inspection, measuring, and test equipment
Inspection and test status
Control of nonconforming product
Handling, storage, packaging, and delivery
Quality records
Training
Statistical techniques

ISO 9002, "Quality Systems—Model for Quality Assurance in Production and Installation," is used when conformance to specified requirements is to be assured by the supplier during production and installation. ISO 9002 incorporates the final inspection and test requirements of ISO 9003 but significantly expands the detail of the ISO 9003 clauses. In addition, ISO 9002 defines elements that are not addressed in ISO 9003, adding the following requirements:

Internal auditing
Contract review
Purchasing
Process control
Corrective action
Purchaser-supplied product

ISO 9001, "Quality Systems—Model for Quality Assurance in Design/Development, Production, Installation, and Servicing," is the most complete model for quality assurance systems. The wording of the clauses in ISO 9001 is identical to that found in ISO 9002, but it adds two more quality system elements—design control and servicing—to the mandatory requirements.

The entire collection of standards is identified as the ISO 9000 series standards. As noted above, ISO 9000 and 9004 are basic guidelines; ISO 9001, 9002, and 9003 are the categories for which companies may apply for certification. Which of these categories applies to a company is totally dependent on the nature of its business. Certification to ISO 9003 is not widely accepted, and many registrars will not consider a request for 9003 certification. Certification to ISO 9002 is for companies that do not design the product being produced and do not contract for the service of the product on an ongoing basis (for example, service on a copier or large mainframe computer) after the sale. Certification to ISO 9001 is for companies that have the design function and/or service of the product after the sale.

ISO 9001 is not better than 9002 or 9003; it simply is written for companies having control of design and/or service. One major misconception of the three classifications is that a company starts at ISO 9003 and, as the quality system improves, moves to 9002 and then to 9001. The intent of the standard is for a company with no control of the design and service function to certify under 9002 and a company having control of the design and/or service function to certify to 9001.

In summary, the sections of the ISO 9000 series are as follows:

ISO 9000—Guidelines for the selection and use of 9001, 9002, or 9003

ISO 9001, 9002, 9003—Models for programs, the applicability of which is dependent on the activity present in the organization

ISO 9004—Handbook for implementation of quality management and quality system elements

What About the 1994 Version?

The 1994 version of ISO 9002 will incorporate the element of servicing. Previously in the 1987 version of the standard, any company performing *either* the design of the product or the service after the sale, was required to certify to ISO 9001. With issuance of the 1994 version, a company performing the service after the sale but with no design responsibility will certify to ISO 9002. This is one of the major changes to be experienced with the 1994 version of the standard. Companies already certified to ISO 9001 who perform the servicing without design responsibility should contact their registrar to see how this will affect the maintenance of their certificate.

What About the Twenty Elements?

ISO 9001 consists of twenty elements that make up the quality system. ISO 9002 consists of eighteen of these twenty elements while ISO 9003 consists of twelve of the elements. The twenty elements can be divided into three categories based on the implementation activities. Categorization depends on the responsibility and method of implementation, as detailed below:

Management Activities

Section 4.1 Management responsibility
Section 4.2 Quality system

Companywide Activities

Section 4.5 Document control
Section 4.8 Product identification and traceability
Section 4.12 Inspection and test status
Section 4.13 Control of nonconforming product
Section 4.14 Corrective action
Section 4.16 Quality records
Section 4.17 Internal quality audits
Section 4.18 Training

Specific Requirements

Section 4.3 Contract review
Section 4.4 Design control
Section 4.6 Purchasing
Section 4.7 Purchaser-supplied product

Section 4.9 Process control
Section 4.10 Inspection and testing
Section 4.11 Inspection, measuring, and test equipment
Section 4.15 Handling, storage, packaging, and delivery
Section 4.19 Servicing
Section 4.20 Statistical techniques

With the elements properly divided, responsibility for each activity can be easily defined. The implementation process from this point becomes an individually structured exercise that must be adjusted to fit the organizational environment.

The remainder of this book will be dedicated to looking at the content of each of the twenty elements of ISO 9001. I will evaluate what ISO 9004 has to say about the standard's intent, presenting the true intent from the experience of going through the certification process for two plants in two years. Strategies for implementation will be presented for each of the elements. The strategies discussed will be from experience as to what has worked in different situations. These are to be viewed as examples that are presented to help companies quickly and effectively implement the standard, not rigid prescriptions that must be followed to the letter. Each company is different, and the method for compliance will also be different.

Since its introduction in 1987 I have had the pleasure of presenting several seminars on the implementation of this standard. I have collected the thirty most common questions about ISO 9000 and will attempt to answer each of them in the last chapter of this book. My intent is to provide you with a resource on which to rely when the intent of an element comes under question.

How to Use This Standard

Development of a quality system in accordance with ISO 9001 or 9002 typically occurs for one of two reasons. The first reason is to obtain company certification. In this type of approach, being awarded the certificate becomes the entire focus of the certification program; quality and efficiency improvement become secondary. This approach, while taken by many companies, does not follow the original intent or spirit of the standard. If gaining certification is the only desired result, purchasing a canned program will probably result in receipt of the certificate. The downside is that the return on investment may not be acceptable to many managers. With this approach, one of the only financial measures to calculate return on investment would be an increase in market share. A seldom-discussed problem is that the company will only be able to compete with other companies taking this same approach. It will *not* be able to compete with companies using the standard as a quality improvement tool.

The second reason companies implement ISO 9001 or 9002 is to use the standard as a quality improvement tool for better business. Following this approach, the standard is viewed as the minimum guidelines a company should follow to make sure that good business is being conducted. Receiving the certification is secondary in this instance. If the program is properly developed, using the standard as a quality improvement tool will provide a higher return and help the company become a world-class manufacturer. In this scenario, the process that creates the product will be evaluated and improved. This approach encourages development of a system to maintain product consistency and a mechanism to improve product quality. It is the approach that is followed through the remainder of this book.

How to Use This Book

This book is intended to help the reader gain a full understanding of the ISO 9000 standard. This understanding is required for a program to be efficiently implemented in a company. This book is not an attempt to outline how a program must be structured; ISO 9000 does *not* specifically call for a set of actions or programs to be in place prior to certification. The quickest way to implement this standard is to understand the reason behind each of the elements listed in it. After understanding why each is included, determine why it would be considered a good business practice to meet each element. A company should formulate a plan to decide what elements apply to its organization. After a determination has been made, decide the most efficient way to meet the intent and requirement of the standard for the given situation. With this approach to the standard, the program development should be smooth and cost-effective. Program development will also be shorter in duration than if an attempt was made to force a canned program into a company.

One last word of caution: one of the major problems faced during the implementation of ISO 9001 that I worked on was that time was wasted arguing the validity of the standard. Many argued that "the design control requirement will kill creativity of the engineers. The standard is asking for more than we need for our product any way." This sounds valid until the standard is understood. The standard is only asking that good engineering practices be followed. What part of good engineering is not valid? After hours of arguments, it was discovered that when the ISO 9001 standard was finally understood, every element was valid and made good sense. All the arguing accomplished was to waste valuable time that could have been used implementing the standard.

Appendix I of this book is a quality evaluation form that can be used as a checklist for internal audits to determine the baseline for compliance to the standard. By simply answering the questions and analyzing the responses, a company can determine where it stands as far as the ISO 9001 is concerned. The same form may be used to determine the baseline for compliance with ISO 9002 or 9003 by selecting only the applicable elements.

2

MANAGEMENT RESPONSIBILITY AND ORGANIZATION

Management responsibility and organization is one of the eighteen elements that is required by both ISO 9001 and 9002. The first section of the ISO 9001 standard covers the overall responsibility of management to the organization, which centers around providing direction or vision to the rest of the organization. The vision and dedication to quality should be spelled out in the policies and objectives of the company. Management should define responsibilities and authorities and provide the resources and personnel to perform the required functions within the organization, and it should provide a system by which a uniform high-quality product is produced. Management should consistently review this system to make sure it is effective.

These may seem like "motherhood" statements with regard to the responsibilities of upper management, but they are more than pie-in-the-sky concepts. These are the requirements of the management responsibility section in ISO 9001, 9002, and 9003, and they should be the vision that upper management has for the organization. Upper management should provide direction, empower the next level of management, help set goals, and measure results. It should avoid gathering power and making day-to-day operational decisions that should be made at a much lower level. The ISO standard should be viewed as a tool that can be used to implement Total Quality Management ("TQM") in an organization. The management responsibility section is a forward-looking, proactive TQM document that—if properly implemented—can provide a structure upon which a company can build a strong TQM philosophy.

As the requirements of the standard are explored, one thing to keep in mind is that the ISO standard can be used as a tool to develop a TQM program, but it will not (and should not) specifically spell out how to implement each of the elements. It is meant to be used as a guide that will provide structure to a quality system while making sure that critical areas are being addressed. The intent of each element of the standard should be identified so that a program or activity can be developed to meet the intent and requirement of the standard. The method that can be used to meet the intent and requirement of the standard is flexible. As long as the program meets the intent and requirement of the element and the program is effective in producing a consistent, high-quality product, the method is left to each organization.

Before lasting quality improvement can be made, the production must first be consistent. Otherwise, quality will constantly change from good to bad. Many times, a company must first make a product consistently bad before it can improve and make the product consistently good! The ISO 9000 standards are designed to create increased consistency of the process by which the product is produced.

The remainder of this chapter will compare section 4.1 of ISO 9001 (Management Responsibility) side by side with the explanation set forth in ISO 9004. The basic intent of each element of the section will be discussed. The requirements of each element will be listed, and several strategies for implementation will be discussed for each area. As stated in Chapter One, this book is not an attempt to outline how a program must be structured, as ISO 9000 has not specifically called for an exact set of actions or programs. The quickest way to implement this standard is to understand the purpose of each of the elements listed in the standard.

ISO 9001

4 Quality system requirements

4.1 Management responsibility

4.1.1 Quality policy

The supplier's management shall define and document its policy and objectives for, and commitment to, quality. The supplier shall ensure that this policy is understood, implemented and maintained at all levels in the organization.

ISO 9004

4 Management responsibility

4.1 General

The responsibility for and commitment to a quality policy belong to the highest level of management. Quality management is that aspect of the overall management function which determines and implements quality policy.

4.2 Quality policy

The management of a company should develop and state its corporate quality policy. This policy should be consistent with other company policies. Management should take all necessary measures to ensure that its corporate quality policy is understood, supplemented and maintained.

4.3 Quality objectives

4.3.1 For the corporate quality policy, management should define objectives pertaining to key elements of quality, such as fitness for use, performance, safety and reliability.

4.3.2 The calculation and evaluation of costs associated with all quality elements and objectives should always be an important consideration, with the objective of minimizing quality losses.

4.3.3 Appropriate levels of management, where necessary, should define specialized quality objectives consistent with corporate quality as well as other corporate objectives.

ISO 9001

4.1.2 Organization

4.1.2.1 Responsibility and authority

The responsibility, authority and the interrelation of all personnel who manage, perform and verify work affecting quality shall be defined; particularly for personnel who need the organizational freedom and authority to

a) initiate action to prevent the occurrence of product nonconformity;

b) identify and record any product quality problems;

c) initiate, recommend or provide solutions through designated channels;

d) verify the implementation of solutions;

e) control further processing, delivery or installation of nonconforming product until the deficiency or unsatisfactory condition has been corrected.

4.1.2.2 Verification resources and personnel

The supplier shall identify in-house verification requirements, provide adequate resources and assign trained personnel for verification activities (see 4.18).

Verification activities shall include inspection, test and monitoring of the design, production, installation and servicing

ISO 9004

5.2.2 Quality responsibility and authority

Activities contributing to quality, whether directly or indirectly, should be identified and documented, and the following actions taken:

a) General and specific quality responsibilities should be explicitly defined.

b) Responsibility and authority delegated to each activity contributing to quality should be clearly established; authority and responsibility should be sufficient to attain the assigned quality objectives with the desired efficiency.

c) Interface control and coordination measures between different activities should be defined.

d) Management may choose to delegate the responsibility for internal quality assurance and for external quality assurance where necessary; the persons so delegated should be independent of the activities reported on.

e) In organizing a well structured and effective quality system, emphasis should be placed on the identification of actual or potential quality problems and the initiation of remedial or preventive measures.

5.2.3 Organizational structure

The organizational structure pertaining to the quality manage-

ISO 9001

processes and/or product; design reviews and audits of the quality system, processes and/or product shall be carried out by personnel independent of those having direct responsibility for the work being performed.

4.1.2.3 Management representative

The supplier shall appoint a management representative who, irrespective of other responsibilities, shall have defined authority and responsibility for ensuring that the requirements of this International Standard are supplemented and maintained.

ISO 9004

ment system should be clearly established within the overall management of a company. The lines of authority and communication should be defined.

5.2.4 Resources and personnel

Management should provide sufficient and appropriate resources essential to the implementation of quality policies and the achievement of quality objectives. These resources may include

a) human resources and specialized skills;

b) design and development equipment;

c) manufacturing equipment;

d) inspection, test and examination equipment;

e) instrumentation and computer software.

Management should determine the level of competence, experience and training necessary to ensure the capability of personnel. (See clause 18.)

Management should identify quality factors affecting market position and objectives relative to new products, processes or services (including new technologies) in order to allocate company resources on a planned and timely basis.

Programmes and schedules covering these resources and skills should be consistent with the company's overall objectives.

ISO 9001

4.1.3 Management review

The quality system adopted to satisfy the requirements of this International Standard shall be reviewed at appropriate intervals by the supplier's management to ensure its continuing suitability and effectiveness. Records of such reviews shall be maintained (see 4.16).

NOTE—Management reviews normally include assessment of the results of internal quality audits, but are carried out by, or on behalf of, the supplier's management, viz management personnel having direct responsibility for the system. (See 4.17).

ISO 9004

5.5 Review and evaluation of the quality management system

Provision should be made by company management for independent review and evaluation of the quality system. Such reviews should be carried out by appropriate members of company management or by competent independent personnel as decided on by company management.

Reviews should consist of well structured and comprehensive evaluations which include:

a) findings of audits centered on various elements of the quality system (see 5.4.3);

b) the overall effectiveness of the quality management system in achieving stated quality objectives;

c) considerations for updating the quality management system in relation to changes brought about by new technologies, quality concepts, market strategies, and social or environmental conditions.

Findings, conclusions and recommendations reached as a result of review and evaluation should be submitted in documentary form for necessary action by company management.

Quality Policy

What Is the Intent of This Element?

The intent of this element is for a company to set up a program that will provide leadership and direction by upper management while assigning authority and responsibility throughout the organization. In other words, the standard sets out a structure for conducting business in a TQM environment.

This element specifically states that management should develop and publish a quality policy. The policy should define and state the commitment of upper management toward quality and define the quality objectives of the company. The last part of the element suggests that upper management should make sure the policy and objectives are understood by everyone.

What Is the Requirement of This Element?

The requirements of this element are specific, and they center around the quality policy and the objectives. The quality policy is to be (1) defined, (2) documented, (3) understood by everyone, (4) implemented at all levels, and (5) maintained. The quality objectives for the company are used to define further and support the policies. Like the policy, the objectives are to be: defined, documented, understood by everyone, implemented at all levels, and maintained.

For many people, the distinction between a policy and an objective is not clear. To confuse the issue further, the standard will soon call for procedures. Policies and objectives are broad, sweeping guides to action; they address what we intend to do, and to what level we intend to perform. Procedures, meanwhile, are the nuts and bolts of how we will accomplish the task so as to reach the objectives. An example of the difference between policies, objectives, and procedures is detailed below.

Policy Statement

Crash and Burn Airlines is committed to provide a comfortable and clean smoke-free environment on every flight for all of our passengers.

Objective

The objective of this policy is to eliminate customer complaints about exposure to secondhand smoke during the time the customer is on the aircraft.

Procedure

The following is the procedure to be followed on each flight covering the use of smoking material:

Announce to the passengers that smoking is prohibited anywhere on the airplane during the time they are on the airplane.

The following is the procedure to follow if a passenger starts to smoke after entering the airplane.

1. Explain the smoking policy and ask the passenger to extinguish the smoking material.

If the passenger refuses to comply:

2. Ask the first officer to accompany you to demand that the passenger extinguish the smoking material.

If the passenger still refuses to comply:

3. Have the copilot and the first officer toss the passenger from the aircraft and extinguish the smoking material.

The intent of this area is for management to decide in what direction they will lead a company and to write down their decisions using broad terms. Management should make sure everyone understands the direction and that it is consistent with other policies within the company. Management implements the policy and monitors whether objectives are maintained at all levels.

What About the 1994 Version? Quality Policy

ISO/DIS 9001 has expanded the policy requirement by stating that "... policy shall be relevant to the supplier's organizational goals and the expectations and needs of its customers." This addition further stresses the importance of customer satisfaction in the goals and policies of organizations complying with the ISO 9000 series standard.

The 1994 version has also included the terminology of "... supplier's management with executive responsibility for quality. ...." This statement appears to further elevate the importance of executive level involvement in the quality system. Companies attempting certification should contact their registrar for their definition of "executive responsibility."

Implementation Strategy

The best strategy for implementation is for upper management to follow the standard closely. Upper management should first make decisions as to the direction of the company. These decisions are then placed in a policy statement. This should occur at the highest level of management. The statement should give direction and vision without getting into the hands-on or the how-to areas. This document is about where we want to go, not how we will get there.

The following page contains a generic example of a quality policy. This statement provides direction by stating that quality is the principal factor in the success of the company. The goal of always meeting—and wherever possible exceeding—customer expectations is stated. It gives credibility to the quality manual and the ISO program by stating that the program has total management approval. It assigns responsibility and authority for the quality program to the quality manager, and it empowers employees to improve the system. Lastly, it provides specific direction that the program be implemented and outlines how conflicts will be resolved.

Quality Objective

What Is the Intent of This Element?

The next area of implementation is to develop objectives that provide specific direction to the program. This document in many ways will restate the quality policy. Greater detail is provided as to activities required to accomplish the stated goals of the policy

QUALITY POLICY

FACILITY POLICY

STATEMENT OF POLICY

The principal factor in the successful performance of the ABC Corp. is the incorporation of Quality into all our services, products and equipment.

Our policy is to always attain, and wherever possible, exceed the standards expected by our customers. This can only be achieved by developing, establishing and maintaining a Quality Management System that encompasses all of our personnel and activities.

The Quality Program, as described in this manual, has been approved by all levels of management for issue and implementation within the company. The purpose of this program is to assure that all products, services and equipment provided will meet or exceed the requirements specified by our customers, by appropriate controlling documents and as set forth by corporate management.

The Quality Manager, who reports directly to me, is hereby assigned the responsibility and the authority to organize, maintain and administer the Quality Program and to assure its effective implementation. Further, all ABC Corp. employees are given the responsibility and authority to identify problems, implement solutions to those problems, and to control further processing of affected product. This includes preventing shipment of nonconforming, deficient or unsatisfactory materials or products, until satisfactory corrective action has been taken.

Each department is required to implement the Quality Program in its area of responsibility. The Plant Manager shall resolve any conflicts which cannot be resolved by the Quality Manager and department managers. Resolution of such conflicts shall always be in accordance with the requirements of the controlling documents and this Quality Program Manual. I fully support and approve this program.

_____   _____

Plant Manager   Date

statement. In the traditional approach, the objectives will have a scope that outlines how far-reaching the document is or details the purpose of the document. References should be listed showing other documents with which this objective will interface. The objective should be stated in a policy-type statement. This level is not the place to provide specific, point-by-point detail on how to accomplish this task; that is better left to a statement of procedures.

What Is the Requirement of This Element?

As discussed earlier in this chapter, the requirements are the same for the policy and the objective. The quality objectives shall be (1) defined, (2) documented, (3) understood by everyone, (4) implemented at all levels, and (5) maintained.

Implementation Strategy

One strategy is for the objectives to be written into a manual called "Quality Policy and Objectives." This manual can be viewed as the guiding principles by which the quality system is developed and controlled. The objectives can be restatements of the required elements of the ISO 9001 or 9002 standard. The objectives can state that the company will develop, implement, and operate the programs required to meet the ISO standard. See Appendix II for an example of a complete quality policy and objectives manual; the format used basically restates the specific verbiage of the ISO standard for applicable elements. Where elements are not applicable, it is so stated in the document.

This is the typical approach that is taken with ISO-9000 quality manuals that are offered for sale on computer disk. The flexibility of the standard allows for almost any format to be used.

Organization

What Is the Intent of This Element?

This section states that the company must identify its organizational structure and make sure everyone understands that structure. The structure must include those people who have direct or indirect control over the quality of the product; in most cases, everyone will be involved. The standard goes on to require that the in-house verification functions (inspection, testing, auditing, and so forth) be provided adequate resources and staffed by trained personnel. This section closes with the requirement that a representative be appointed who will have responsibility to ensure that the requirements of this standard are met.

The basic intent of this element is for management to demonstrate proper development of the approach being followed. In other words, the intent of the standard is for upper management to take a systematic and logical approach to the quality system. The lines of responsibility should be drawn, and everyone should know their areas of responsibility. This element also intends to show that management has given authority along with responsibility and is committed to proper funding for activities that will verify the system is working.

The last section of this element requires management to nominate one person who is responsible for maintaining the system. This gives direct responsibility, accountability, and authority for the system to a single individual, which promotes a coordinated effort for administration of the program.

What Is the Requirement of This Element?

The requirements for this element are very simple, and basic to good business practice. The requirements for each area of the standard are as follows:

Responsibility and Authority

1. Responsibilities for the quality program shall be defined.
2. Authority for the quality program shall be defined.
3. The interrelations of individuals who manage, perform, or verify work affecting quality shall be defined.

What About the 1994 Version? Responsibility and Authority

The 1987 version references only the prevention of occurrence of product nonconformity. ISO/DIS 9001 has expanded this requirement to include both process and quality system nonconformances in addition to those occurring with product. The same intent has been incorporated further in this element with ". . . identify and record any product, process and quality system problems" where the 1987 versions referenced only the product.

Verification Resources and Personnel

1. In-house verification requirements must be defined, including the following:
    a. Inspection
    b. Testing
    c. Monitoring of design
    d. Monitoring of production
    e. Monitoring installation
    f. Servicing processes and/or products
    g. Design reviews
    h. Audits of the quality system/processes and/or products
2. In-house verification activities shall be properly funded.
3. Trained personnel shall be assigned to carry out verification activities.
4. In-house verification must be carried out by personnel independent of those having direct responsibility for the work being performed.

What About the 1994 Version? Verification Resources and Personnel

This section has been modified from the original section to resources only. The standard now includes a requirement for the assignment of ". . . trained personnel for management, performance of work . . . including internal audits." The requirement of trained personnel for management functions was not specifically addressed in the 1987 version.

The 1987 version of 9001 stated that design reviews and audits of the quality system, process, and/or product were required to be carried out by personnel independent of those having direct responsibility for the work being performed. ISO/DIS 9001 has moved the independence requirements from the resources element and into the applicable elements themselves.

Management Representative

This section requires management to appoint a "management representative" who has authority and responsibility to ensure that requirements of the standard are implemented and maintained.

Contrary to common belief, this representative does not have to be the quality manager. This position may not even be a full-time one; keep in mind the standard states "irrespective of other responsibilities" (implying that such responsibilities may exist).What ISO 9001 does require is a responsible person to make sure the requirements are implemented and maintained.

What About the 1994 Version? Management Representative

This entry has been modified to state ". . . supplier management with executive responsibility for quality shall appoint a member of its own management . . . to have defined authority for the quality system." This is the second instance in which the term "executive responsibility for quality" has been added. The exact definition of "executive" should be determined with each organization's registrar. This representative now has the responsibility of "reporting on the performance of the quality system to the supplier's management for review and as a basis for improvement of the quality system." This further encourages the proactive approach to the quality system in review and improvement. By placing increased responsibility for the reporting with the management representative, the importance of analyzing the quality system and its conscious control is again stressed by the standard. A note has also been added to this section regarding the representative's responsibility for liaison with external bodies regarding the quality system.

Implementation Strategy

The strategy for the implementation of this element will, for the most part, be directed at the highest levels of upper management. Management must decide how the quality program will be structured and who will be responsible for its maintenance. The efforts should be focused on addressing each of the areas that were listed in the requirements section. Questions that must be answered include the following: (1) Who is going to be given the responsibility for directing the quality program? (2) What authority will the responsible person have to assure the program is implemented?

(3) What are the interrelationships of the people responsible for implementation of the program?

The organization for program implementation should be identified; an organizational chart is usually provided in the policy and/or the procedures manual. Jobs and responsibilities for the quality system are described and assigned. In most cases, existing job descriptions can be modified to list the quality system responsibilities assigned to each position.

Verification Resources and Personnel

Beyond these administrative decisions, responsible management levels should identify the product and process verification requirements. This is commonly accomplished and documented in the operating procedures and associated flowcharts. Once these activities are identified, it is management's responsibility to evaluate the funding needed for proper performance of each activity. Once it is determined that the activity is properly funded, the next step is to decide if the personnel are adequately trained to perform the verification activities. This step will require identifying the skills and knowledge needed to perform the function. These skill and knowledge requirements are usually listed in a document such as a job description.

The next step is to evaluate the staff to determine if the skills and knowledge are available; the results of this evaluation are usually documented in a personnel file for each person. The last step is the development of training programs. These provide employees an opportunity to gain the needed knowledge and skills if deficiencies are identified. This plan is usually also documented in the employee's personnel file.

One of the more obvious requirements is to ensure that persons verifying the product or processes are independent of the people directly responsible for the product or processes being verified. For example, the product inspection should be conducted by someone other than the individuals who performed the work. The traditional method is for the product inspection to be conducted by the quality control department. One method that has been proven effective calls for the worker to check his or her own work, after which the shop supervisor signs off on a check sheet showing that the work was evaluated. Manufacturing then conducts a controlled final inspection of the completed product, and quality control audits the results to ensure conformance. This approach is being used in an ISO 9001 certified program and has proven to be cost-effective, has improved the quality of the product, and has been accepted by a European registrar for a certified program.

The area of internal quality auditing also falls under this requirement. The team used to audit each department should have no responsibility over the elements being audited. In one company, the audit teams are made up of representatives from all areas of the company; the auditors are welders, engineers, planners, purchasing agents, secretaries, and truck mechanics. These team members were provided classroom and on-the-job training. In this situation, it is easy for the quality department to be audited and meet this element. This is also one of the smoothest and most effective ways to conduct legitimate quality audits. A second way to meet this requirement is to use auditors from a different division or from outside the company. In this area, a company should develop a program that makes sense and will promote quality improvement within a company. After determining the program, the company should stick to the audit schedule.

Management Representative

To comply with this area, many companies assign the responsibility and authority to one of the managers, usually the quality manager. This manager's authority and responsibility are outlined in the quality policy. The final action is for management actually to give this manager the necessary authority and responsibility for the program.

Management Review

What Is the Intent of This Element?

This portion of the standard states that the quality system be reviewed by "appropriate" levels of management at "appropriate" intervals. This statement requires that an organizational decision be made. Who would be considered appropriate management personnel, and what intervals should be used? The certification organization will determine whether the chosen representatives and intervals are effective. This will occur during the certification audit.

One issue that needs to be pointed out at this time is documentation. ISO 9001 specifically calls for documentation of management reviews to be maintained in a manner that satisfies the requirements of section 4.16 (Quality Records). Section 4.16 will be addressed in detail later in this book.

The intent of this element is to make the program a living, constantly growing program. The management review requirement is included to encourage upper management involvement in the quality system. This involvement should include the evaluation and identification of programs that are not working well. Management should participate in the development of new directions for these programs and recommend change. The goal is to have a constantly evolving program that involves more than just the quality assurance department.

The main reason for this requirement is to avoid writing a quality control manual that is put on a shelf to collect dust. That approach, which is typical, indicates that no one in management is concerned about or responsible for quality any further than purchasing binders and filling them with paper.

What Is the Requirement of This Element?

The requirements of this element are not as specific as some people would like. The exact requirement is for the program to be reviewed at "appropriate intervals by a supplier's management to ensure its continuing suitability and effectiveness." The second requirement is for the company to maintain records of this review. The frequency of the review process is left up to each company.

What About the 1994 Version? Management Review

Wording has been added to the management review section again referencing "... management with executive responsibility ..." to review the quality system at "defined intervals sufficient to ensure" continuing suitability. The inclusion of the word "defined" indicates that this activity may need to be documented by a schedule.

Implementation Strategy

One of the easiest ways to meet the intent of this element is to develop a procedure that establishes the method by which the entire system is reviewed by upper management on an ongoing basis. One strategy is for management to review the entire system and its effectiveness in an annual meeting. As long as the suitability and effectiveness is reviewed and direction is given for the program in the next year (as outlined in ISO 9004), the review is accepted. One company takes its upper management on a weekend retreat to perform this review; the meetings are documented, and the review is part of the certified program.

The management review may be broken up into four meetings that are held quarterly. The accepted time frame for a complete review appears to be once each year for most registrars. Annual cycles are common because the registrar must audit a certified program at least once a year. For many registrars, the system must complete a full cycle before the program can be effectively audited. Therefore, for a registrar to be able to verify that management review has been successfully accomplished, the review must have been conducted during the time frame between periodic audits.

Interpretation of this element would also allow for a single individual or department to prepare a report addressing each area of management review. The report would then be submitted to the most senior member of management. In this case, only the reviewing department and senior manager would be involved. Although meeting the requirements, this method may not be the most effective in addressing the intent of the element.

However the reviews are held, the activity must generate a documented record. This is one of the areas where documentation is required. As noted above, the record of review must be identified as a quality record and handled according to the quality records element. On the following page is a typical procedure for management review. This type of procedure will generally be included in the quality manual.

MANAGEMENT REVIEW

1.0 SCOPE

This document describes the requirements and responsibilities for management review of the quality system.

2.0 GENERAL

It is the responsibility of the Quality Assurance Manager under direction of the Plant Manager to assure that reviews of the various aspects of the Quality System are conducted annually as a minimum. This requirement may be satisfied by intermediate reviews held to address individual aspects.

3.0 SCHEDULING

It is the responsibility of the QA Manager to schedule reviews of the progress and effectiveness of the Quality System. Reviews will also involve the determination of the intent and direction of the Quality System for the upcoming year.

4.0 ATTENDANCE

Reviews of the Quality System will involve management representatives from appropriate departments. The QA Manager will assure that representatives are advised of meeting dates and times.

5.0 AGENDA

Areas to be addressed will include the following as appropriate.

- -Review of findings and follow-up corrective action, as necessary, identified through the internal audit program.

- -Review of the effectiveness of the quality management system in achieving stated quality objectives.

- -Considerations for updating the quality management system in relation to industry changes.

- -Determination of the intent and direction of the Quality System in the upcoming year.

6.0 DOCUMENTATION

Minutes of reviews will be taken and published to those in attendance and appropriate levels of management as determined necessary by the Quality Assurance Manager.

Summary

The Management Responsibility portion of ISO 9001 and 9002 is one of the more important areas to implement effectively. If management is providing direction, giving support, empowering people, financing the program, and monitoring and redirecting the system, all of the other elements will fall into place. If upper management is unconcerned and gives the impression that the ISO standard is the quality control department's job to implement, the effort will usually fail. If this is the attitude of a company's upper management, then a different standard should be identified for a company to implement. The ISO standard is structured to require that management be concerned about and active in the program.

As stated in the first chapter, ISO 9001 and 9002 are complete engineering and manufacturing standards. They are much more than a quality control standard and as such will require more than the quality control department to implement. This effort will take the direction of upper management and will require the input and dedication of everyone in the company.

3

QUALITY SYSTEM

The quality system is one of the eighteen elements detailed in both ISO 9001 and 9002. Even though it is one of the shorter elements in the standard, it reaches throughout the entire company. The implication is that a company should develop and implement a quality system that addresses each of the elements in a manner that is appropriate for that company.

The term *appropriate for that company* becomes key to the development of the system. This standard is not product oriented, as are many of the standards being imposed on companies in the 1990s. This standard is process oriented and therefore is not written in the traditional approach of "you will do step A and then step B and finally step C," whether the sequence works or not. The ISO 9000 standard allows—even encourages—a company to use the standard as a guideline to develop an effective quality program unique to each company. It also allows a company to decide if one or more of the elements do not apply to its organization. If a company can show that an element is truly not applicable to the operation, the company can state so in its policy. If this can be justified during the audit, the company will not be required to meet the requirements of that element. The key is proving that the element is not applicable. For example, some companies are not set up to provide service for a product after the sale. Element 4.19 (Servicing) thus can be exempted from the scope of the ISO 9001 audit. The company can, however, still be certified to ISO 9001 even with this exemption.

To address this element effectively, each company must customize the quality program to fit each application. Do not expect an off-the-shelf program to fit; it will not, no matter how hard you try. And do not expect the ISO 9001 standard to tell you in detail how to make the standard fit in a company; it will not. What it will do is provide the basic framework from which a company can make a checklist of minimum requirements for an effective system.

ISO 9001

4.1 Quality system

The supplier shall establish and maintain a documented quality system as a means of ensuring that product conforms to specified requirements. This shall include

a) the preparation of documented quality system procedures and instructions in accordance with the requirements of this International Standard;

b) the effective implementation of the documented quality system procedures and instructions.

NOTE—In meeting specified requirements, timely consideration needs to be given to the following activities:

a) the preparation of quality plans and a quality manual in accordance with the specified requirements;

b) the identification and acquisition of any controls, processes, inspection equipment, fixtures, total production resources and skills that may be needed to achieve the required quality;

c) the updating, as necessary, of quality control, inspection and testing techniques, including the development of new instrumentation;

d) the identification of any measurement requirement involving

ISO 9004

4.4 Quality system

4.4.1 A quality system is the organizational structure, responsibilities, procedures, processes and resources for implementing quality management.

4.4.2 Management should develop, establish and implement a quality system as the means by which stated policies and objectives might be accomplished.

4.4.3 The quality system should be structured and adapted to the company's particular type of business and should take into account the appropriate elements outlined in this International Standard.

4.4.4 The quality system should function in such a manner as to provide proper confidence that

a) the system is well understood and effective;

b) the products or services actually do satisfy customer expectations;

c) emphasis is placed on problem prevention rather than dependence on detection after occurrence.

5 Quality system principles

5.1 Quality loop

5.1.1 The quality system typically applies to, and interacts with, all activities pertinent to the quality of a product or service. It involves all phases from initial

ISO 9001

capability that exceeds the known state of the art in sufficient time for the needed capability to be developed;

e) clarification of standards of acceptability for all features and requirements, including those which contain a subjective element:

f) the compatibility of the design, the production process, installation, inspection and test procedures and the applicable documentation;

g) the identification and preparation of quality records (see 4.16).

ISO 9004

identification to final satisfaction of requirements and customers expectations.

These phases and activities may include the following:

a) marketing and market research;

b) design/specification engineering and product development;

c) procurement;

d) process planning and development;

e) production;

f) inspection, testing and examination;

g) packaging and storage;

h) sales and distribution;

i) installation and operation;

j) technical assistance and maintenance;

k) disposal after use.

See the figure for a schematic representation of the quality loop, which is similar in concept to the quality spiral.

5.1.2 In the context of interacting activities within a company, marketing and design should be emphasized as especially important for

a) determining and defining customer needs, expectations and the product requirements;

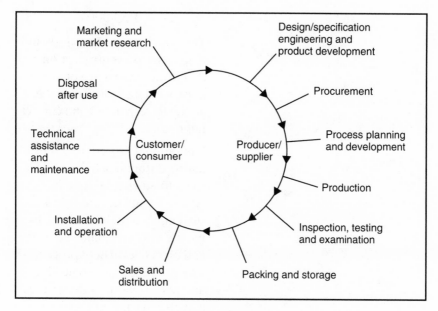

Quality Loop

b) providing the concepts (including back-up data) for producing a product or service to defined specifications at optimum cost.

5.2.1 General

Management is ultimately responsible for establishing the quality policy and for decisions concerning the initiation, development, implementation and maintenance of the quality system.

5.2.5 Operational procedures

The quality system should be organized in such a way that adequate and continuous control is exercised over all activities affecting quality.

ISO 9004

The management system should emphasize preventive actions that avoid occurrence of problems, while not sacrificing the ability to respond to and correct failures should they occur.

Operational procedures coordinating different activities with respect to an effective quality system should be developed, issued and maintained to implement corporate quality policies and objectives. These procedures should lay down the objectives and performance of the various activities having an impact on quality, e.g. design, development, procurement, production and sales.

All written procedures should be stated simply, unambiguously and understandably, and should indicate methods to be used and criteria to be satisfied.

5.3 Documentation of the system

5.3.5 Quality policies and procedures.

All the elements, requirements and provisions adopted by a company for its quality management system should be documented in a systematic and orderly manner in the form of written policies and procedures. Such documentation should ensure a common understanding of quality policies and procedures (i.e. quality programmes/plans/manuals/records).

ISO 9004

The quality management system should include adequate provision for the proper identification, distribution, collection and maintenance of all quality documents and records. However, care should be taken to limit documentation to the extent pertinent to the application. (See clause 17.)

5.3.2 Quality manual

5.3.2.1 The typical form of the main document used in drawing up and implementing a quality system is a "Quality Manual."

5.3.2.2 The primary purpose of a quality manual is to provide an adequate description of the quality management system while serving as a permanent reference in the implementation and maintenance of that system.

5.3.2.3 Methods should be established for making changes, modifications, revisions or additions to the contents of a quality manual.

5.3.2.4 In larger companies, the documentation relating to the quality management system may take various forms, including the following:

a) corporate quality manual;

b) divisional quality manuals;

c) specialized quality manuals (e.g., design, procurement, project, work instructions).

ISO 9004

5.3.3 Quality plans

For projects relating to new products, services or processes, management should prepare, as appropriate, written quality plans consistent with all other requirements of a company's quality management system.

Quality plans should define

a) the quality objectives to be attained;

b) the specific allocation of responsibilities and authority during the different phases of the project;

c) the specific procedures, methods and work instructions to be applied;

d) suitable testing, inspection, examination and audit programmes at appropriate stages (e.g. design, development);

e) a method of changes and modifications in a quality plan as projects proceed;

f) other measures necessary to meet objectives.

5.3.4 Quality records

Quality records and charts pertaining to design, inspection, testing, survey, audit, review or related results are important constituents of a quality management system (see 17.2 and 17.3).

Quality System

What Is the Intent of This Element?

The basic intent of this element is for the quality program to fulfill the requirements of the ISO standard. The program should have the understanding, support, and direction of the highest levels of management and incorporate a conscious decision-making process. In other words, the quality system should be directed by upper management and cover all aspects of the company.

The quality system outlined by this element is a model of a TQM approach to doing business. The standard in ISO 9004 discusses in great depth the "quality loop," which shows the quality program to be all encompassing, functioning as a continuous improvement cycle. This cycle is similar to many of the models used in quality assurance, such as the "spiral of quality" described by Dr. Joseph Juran in many of his publications.

The structure suggested by sections 5.1, 5.2, and 5.3 of ISO 9004 is a very traditional TQM structure. This structure calls for upper management to provide direction, support, and active participation. The program covers all activities, ranging from market research and design of the product through disposal after use. This approach is well beyond the scope of most traditional quality standards.

What Is the Requirement of This Element?

The requirement of this element is basic, but the ramifications are very far-reaching. The element requires a company to maintain a "documented quality system" that conforms to the specified requirements. This element specifically calls for "preparation of quality system procedures and instructions." The last requirement deals with the effective implementation of these procedures and instructions.

The standard calls for the "preparation of documented quality system procedures and instructions." ISO 9004 suggests that a quality manual be developed to house all of the information. Keep in mind that each company should decide what is best for the situation. Also note that the 1987 version of ISO 9001 does not require a company to have a quality assurance manual; the only requirement that procedures and instructions be documented. A second point is that procedures must be in accordance with the requirements of the standard.

What About the 1994 Version? Quality System

The standard calls for the "preparation of documented quality system procedures and instructions." Although suggested by ISO 9004, the 1987 version of ISO 9001 did not require a quality manual. ISO/DIS 9001, however, does require that a quality manual be developed and maintained to include or reference the documented procedures that form part of the quality system. The amount of documented procedures will be up to the discretion of the organization based on the skills and training of the affected work force. With both versions, the procedures must be developed in accordance with the requirements of the standard.

Quality planning has been addressed as a separate section in ISO/DIS 9001 and is required to be consistent with all other requirements of the quality system. Documented procedures are required to define how the requirements for quality will be met.

Implementation Strategy

Traditionally, the quality system is documented by a multilevel manual structure that houses the policies and procedures. In most traditional documented quality systems, the quality manual presides as the top-level manual. The ISO 9004 standard recommends this structure but is unique in that it allows for alternative approaches. The requirement is to document the system instead of requiring a quality manual. If will be easier for auditors to understand a system that is documented in the traditional quality manual style; each company should, however, develop and document the program that best fits its operation.

In one company certified to ISO 9001, it was decided that the best way to proceed with the documentation of the system was to develop a three-level manual structure but *not* a formal quality assurance manual. This was done because the management wanted the ISO 9001 system to belong to the entire organization, not just the quality assurance department. The top-level manual in this company was the quality policy manual, which gave the management philosophy and provided guides to action. The second-level manual was an operating procedures manual that was divided into departmental areas. This manual was filled with procedures for activities that crossed departmental boundaries. The third-level manuals were manuals in each department (engineering, quality assurance, manufacturing, and so forth) for procedures that affected only that department. If an activity did not cross department lines, the procedure went into the department manual.

In this situation, the procedures to maintain ISO 9001 certification were scattered throughout the policy manual and the different procedure manuals. Although it was hard to sell to the auditors, it has worked for this company. The idea behind this was to have the programs that met the requirements of the ISO 9001 standard become part of the everyday operation of the company. If the operating procedures were being followed all the time, the requirements of the standard were being met all the time.

In addition to the policies and procedures that are used to document the system, a company might decide to develop "quality plans" for use with one-time projects or special processes. These will be followed just as if they were quality policies. As described in ISO 9004, the plans should be specific and controlled for acceptance as quality documentation. Quality plans can (and in many cases should) be used when launching prototype or new products in which the process for production is still being developed. In each of these cases, the quality plan is the controlling document until the process and/or the product is developed to the point where formal procedures can be written to take precedence.

The implementation strategy for documentation of the quality system is for upper management to decide what makes best business sense for the company's needs. ISO 9001 allows for unique approaches to be taken provided they meet the intent of the standard and are proven effective. Whatever documentation method a company chooses, it must meet the basic elements of the standard, and it must work in practice. If the position taken is shown to be effective, then it will usually be accepted by the auditors.

A Word of Caution

A common approach to ISO 9000 is "Document what you do, and do what you document." This approach makes the quality system sound easy, but like most things that seem too good to be true, it is. The steps of process evaluation and improvement must first be in place before the processes are documented.

The first step is to evaluate procedures against the standard to make sure that the intent and requirement of each applicable element is being met. A system can be fully documented but fail the certification audit if it is missing one or more of the elements required by the standard. Even companies experienced in operating to government or industry regulations may miss one or more of the elements of ISO-9001, simply because this standard is process oriented. Since earlier standards have focused on the product, not the process, existing programs may not have been required to address elements specified in ISO 9001. For example, if a company did not control the process by which contracts were negotiated, or was not previously required to document that area, it would have a hard time convincing a registrar that it was meeting the standard. The documentation must address all applicable elements of the standard.

The second step in the documentation process is for the company to stand back and evaluate those areas in which it does not meet the intent or requirement of an element. The documentation of a system should be a journey of discovery for most companies; it is common for companies to operate for years and not have documentation on how work progresses through the organization. The documentation process could be the best improvement tool ever used in some facilities.

Do not fall into the trap of thinking that ISO 9000 is only an exercise in documentation. If bad business practices are documented and never improved or changed, a company will not receive certification. If the process is viewed as an improvement tool, the statement "Document what you do, and do what you document" can be applied with some added steps. "Address the element, document what you do, improve what you do, update the documentation, and then do what you document."

4

CONTRACT REVIEW

Contract review is another of the eighteen elements that is covered by ISO 9001 and 9002. The first step toward understanding this element properly is to define a contract. Within the boundaries of ISO 9000, a contract is any agreed sale of a product or service. In specific terms, if a company sells a product (no matter who they sell the product to), the act of selling constitutes a contract. This "contract" must therefore be reviewed.

In one company that was certified to ISO 9001, the requirements of this element had to be met for three different selling methods. The first method of selling products was the traditional contract-negotiation method. In this method a company would send out a tender and request for bid. The bid, once made, would spark contract negotiations; before the contract was signed, a formal contract review would occur. In the second method, a customer would order a standard product by phone using a catalog description, after which the product was assembled and shipped to the customer. The third method of sale allowed selected customers to order spare parts by directly accessing the company's computers. If the part was on hand, the computer would notify the parts department; the part would then be pulled and shipped that day.

Each of the referenced situations was studied to determine compliance with the requirements of the contract review element. The goal was to meet the requirements of the review element and still have a streamlined organization. After understanding the intent of the element, it became much easier to justify the changes needed in the method of processing orders.

ISO 9001

4.3 Contract review

The supplier shall establish and maintain procedures for contract review and for the coordination of these activities. Each contract shall be reviewed by the supplier to ensure that

a) the requirements are adequately defined and documented;

b) any requirements differing from those in the tender are resolved;

c) the supplier has the capability to meet contractual requirements.

Records of such contract reviews shall be maintained (see 4.16).

NOTE—The contract review activities, interfaces and communication within the supplier's organization should be coordinated with the purchaser's organization as appropriate.

ISO 9004

7 Quality in marketing

7.1 Marketing requirements

The marketing function should take the lead in establishing quality requirements for the product. It should

a) determine the need for a product or service;

b) accurately define the market demand and sector since doing so is important in determining the grade, quantity, place and timing estimates for the product or service;

c) accurately determine customer requirements by a review of contract or market needs: actions include an assessment of any unstated expectations or biases held by customers:

d) communicate all customer requirements clearly and accurately within the company.

7.2 Product brief

The marketing function should provide the company with a formal statement of outline of product requirements, e.g. a product brief. The product brief translates customer requirements and expectations into a preliminary set of specifications as the basis for subsequent design work. Among the elements that may be included in the product brief are the following requirements:

ISO 9004

a) performance characteristics (e.g. environmental and usage conditions and reliability);

b) sensory characteristics (e.g. style, colour, taste, smell);

c) installation configuration or fit;

d) applicable standards and statutory regulations;

e) packaging;

f) quality assurance/verification.

7.3 Customer feedback

The marketing function should establish an information monitoring and feedback system on a continuous basis. All information pertinent to the quality of a product or service should be analyzed, collated, interpreted and communicated in accordance with defined procedures. Such information will help to determine the nature and extent of product or service problems in relation to customer experience and expectations. In addition, feedback information may provide clues to possible design changes as well as appropriate management action. (See also 8.8, 8.9 and 16.3.)

Contract Review

What Is the Intent of This Element?

The basic intent of this element is for a company to establish a system to ensure that an understanding exists between the company and the customer. A common understanding must exist with regard to customer requirements; the company must determine whether those requirements can be met. Changes between the tender and the final contract must be identified and addressed by both parties. In other words, the intent is for the company to understand what the customer wants, assure that it can satisfy those needs, and implement a system that addresses changes in customer requirements. Most companies have some sort of contract review system in place for the big sales. Many, however, do not address the sale of small items (such as spare parts).

What Is the Requirement of This Element?

The contract review element has three simple requirements that must be met for any company to be able to deliver a satisfactory product to a customer:

1. The customer requirements must be adequately defined and understood.
2. Any requirements in the contract that differ from the tender must be resolved.
3. The company must be able to meet the requirements of the contract.

The first requirement of contract review is for the "supplier to review the contract to ensure that the requirements are adequately defined and documented." The most important part of dealing with a customer is making sure a common understanding exists regarding what he or she wants. On occasion, the customer may not be able to determine adequately in his or her mind exactly what is required. Part of defining the requirements is working with the customer to guarantee that at the time the contract is signed, both parties have the same understanding as to the expected result.

Once a common understanding is reached, the next requirement is to establish a mechanism that will identify and address differences between the tender and the contract. This requirement is to allow the contract to change as needed while still ensuring that both parties have a common understanding of the new requirements. For complex products, the requirements will continually be redefined as the contract is executed. Each of these changes should be evaluated to ensure that both parties have a common understanding of the change and that the company has the capability to meet the new requirements.

The third requirement is for the company to evaluate its ability to meet the agreed requirements. This requirement is simply good business. It is not in a company's best interest to contract for services or goods that it cannot deliver. It is common practice in some companies to commit to a contract without knowing whether the capability exists to meet each of the requirements; this could turn out to be disastrous for a company. To prevent this, an evaluation should be scheduled to determine if the company has the capability of meeting the contract.

What About the 1994 Version? Contract Review

The contract review element has been revised to address verbal orders. The same requirements are still applicable to written contracts in assuring a common understanding and ability to deliver.

The standard now requires that the mechanism addressing amendments to contracts and the manner in which such information is transferred to concerned functions be identified.

Implementation Strategy

In implementing this element, the first step is to identify all the ways a contract is executed in the course of doing business. As discussed earlier, after evaluating one certified program, it was discovered that contracts for the sale of products and services were made in one of three ways:

1. Formal bids were made in response to a tender.
2. Standard designs were assembled and sold (build to order).

3. Selected customers were allowed to place orders by computer; orders were taken, billed, and shipped without human intervention.

Each of these sales constituted a contract to which this element applied. The implementation strategy for each of these types of sales was unique and effective.

A very common type of sale that requires contract review is when a bid is prepared and submitted in response to a tender or request to bid on a project. In this situation, the traditional approach is to develop a system that will bring people from the appropriate departments together to review the tender and determine requirements of the contract. At this time, a checklist could be used to indicate that all areas of the tender have been evaluated by the appropriate departments.

This checklist could ask for the quality assurance department to list all specifications (for example, ASME, API, or CSA) the final design or production must meet. The checklist should address the areas of design criteria and specifications or standards to be followed, and specific manufacturing requirements (for example, certified welders to AWS or ASME) or SPC charts should be identified. The checklist should also include requirements for inspection and test plans, final testing, packaging, shipping and preservation. Every aspect of the contract needs to be evaluated and approved by the appropriate departments.

If a change is introduced in the requirements by either the customer or the company, the same approval process should be followed. If the change is small, the proposal is circulated to the appropriate departments for approval. If the change is significant, a meeting of the appropriate department heads should be convened and the change discussed and approved.

In the second type of sale, the customer orders a standard product from inventory or to be assembled to order. The contract review will usually be less extensive for this than for the engineer-to-order sale. The reason for a less extensive review is that the design criteria will not change, since the product is assembled from previously designed components. Critical portions of the contract that should be addressed include understanding the desired standard options desired by the customer, as well as the delivery time frame. When this understanding is reached, the next evaluation is to determine if the supplier can meet the requirements for optional equipment within the requested delivery time.

If a change is introduced to the standard product during the execution of the contract, the contract should be renegotiated to determine how the change will affect delivery time, functionality, and/or price. If the change is accepted by both the company and the customer, a new contract is executed. The change should receive the same level of attention as did the original contract.

In one certified company this was accomplished by a "build change order" (BCO). The change was detailed on the BCO form and circulated through all departments. Each department listed the effects of the change on how the product would look and function. The reliability was examined, along with the effects on cost and delivery. If the customer wanted the change after reviewing the updated information, a new contract was written and the change was implemented.

The third type of sale occurs when customers are directly linked into a company's information system. The customer can place orders directly into the company's materials requirements planning (MRP) system. In one ISO 9001 company the customer could place orders for standard spare parts directly into the MRP portion of the mainframe. The company's computer would check the inventory for the availability of unassigned inventory and print a shipping order if spares were available. But the specific requirements of the contract review element still had to be met. The system was designed so that the requirements were met without a great amount of effort and without human intervention. Even the records of this review were maintained on the computer electronically.

This was accomplished through a worldwide network link using the customer's personal computers as terminals to gain access to the company's mainframe. Because the customer had logged onto the system (and made it past the multilevel security system), the computer knew who the order was coming from and where it should be shipped. When the customer keyed in the part number that was being ordered, the computer checked to see that it was a valid number and returned the part description to the customer, asking if this was the part being ordered. If the customer agreed (through keyboard response), the computer checked to see if unassigned inventory was available. If no inventory was available, the order was sent to customer service as an exception to process by hand. If unassigned inventory was available, the computer would give an approximate ship date and ask the customer if this was acceptable. If yes, the order was accepted; if no, the order was sent to customer service for hand processing. The price was then displayed, and the customer was asked if this was acceptable. If yes, the order was accepted; if no, the order was sent to customer service for hand processing. If everything was accepted by the customer, an order was printed automatically in the shipping department, and the part was shipped. The customer was also automatically billed for the order.

In this type of automated order entry, all of the requirements of the contract review element were met. When the computer returned the description and asked if this was the part being ordered, the requirement of gaining understanding between the customer and the company was met. When the computer checked the availability of inventory, it met the requirement of determining if the company had the capability of meeting the contract. When the customer approved the ship date and price, the order was accepted, the contract was finalized, and all requirements of contract review were met.

The change mechanism was met when a message printed to the customer stating "If a change to this order is needed, please call ..." and directions were given for processing the change. In this case, it would be assumed that no change was needed if the customer did not initiate any change.

Provided the sales contracts are reviewed, the specific details of how the review requirements are met become less important. It makes good business sense to know what a customer is asking for, to know if the contract requirements are different from the tender, and to know if the company can meet the requirements of the contract before it is signed. Keep the process of contract review simple and efficient. The goal is to make good decisions about how to satisfy the customer; a simple process is the most efficient method of reaching this goal.

5

DESIGN CONTROL

Design control is one of the two elements that are found only in the ISO 9001 standard. (The second element is servicing after the sale.) Traditional quality standards do not address the concept of design control in the same depth as does ISO 9001. Most traditional standards are product oriented rather than system oriented; they do not properly address the system by which a product is designed. The ISO 9000 series is system oriented, in the belief that if the process used to control the design is effective, the design will be consistent. Using this concept, the probability of a quality design is high.

In implementing the ISO 9001 in companies, it often is the design control element that is the most hotly debated. The engineering departments of many companies feel that following specific steps during the design of a product will reduce or kill the creativity of designers. This has not been the case for most companies implementing the ISO 9001 standard. To the contrary, these companies have found that designs have been better overall as a result of the consistent and disciplined design approach. The standard merely requires a company to engineer and verify the design properly. The question then becomes this: what part of proper engineering, documentation, and verification of a design will kill creativity? If good engineering kills creativity, how creative should a company be?

The design control portion of the standard is divided into the following six basic parts.

4.4.1 General: This section states that a company should develop and maintain procedures that meet the requirements of this standard.

4.4.2 Design and Development Planning. This section calls for development of a plan that identifies all design activities to be completed.

4.4.3 Design Input. This section specifically requires that design input (user specifications) be identified and reviewed.

4.4.4 Design Output. This section requires the design output to be identified, documented and compared to the input.

4.4.5 Design Verification. This section calls for design verification to ensure that the design output meets the design input (user specifications).

4.4.6 Design Changes. This section calls for development of procedures to control design changes.

From this overview of the standard, it can be seen that the standard does not require steps that will kill creativity. It does ask, however, that the design work be accomplished with proper engineering documentation and verification. For a more comprehensive view of the standard, the ISO 9001 requirements should be compared to the 9004 explanation.

ISO 9001

4.4 Design control

4.4.1 General

The supplier shall establish and maintain procedures to control and verify the design of the product in order to ensure that the specified requirements are met.

4.4.2 Design and development planning

The supplier shall draw up plans that identify the responsibility for each design and development activity. The plans shall describe or reference these activities and shall be updated as the design evolves.

4.4.2.1 Activity assignment

The design and verification activities shall be planned and assigned to qualified personnel equipped with adequate resources.

4.4.2.2 Organizational and technical interfaces

Organizational and technical interfaces between different groups shall be identified and the necessary information documented, transmitted and regularly reviewed.

ISO 9004

8 Quality in specification and design.

8.1 Contribution of specification and design to quality

The specification and design function should provide for the translation of customer needs from the product brief into technical specifications for materials, products and processes. This should result in a product that provides customer satisfaction at an acceptable price that enables a satisfactory return on investment for the enterprise. The specification and design should be such that the product or service is producible, verifiable and controllable under the proposed production, installation, commissioning or operational conditions.

8.2 Design planning and objectives (defining the project)

8.2.1 Management should specifically assign responsibilities for various design duties to activities inside and/or outside the organization and ensure that all those who contribute to design are aware of their responsibilities for achieving quality.

8.2.2 In its delegation of responsibilities for quality, management should ensure that design functions provide clear and definitive technical data for procurement, the execution of work and verification of conformance of prod-

ISO 9004

ucts and processes to specification requirements.

8.2.3 Management should establish time-phased design programmes with checkpoints appropriate to the nature of the product. The extent of each phase and the stages at which design reviews or evaluations will take place may depend upon the product's application, its design complexity, the extent of innovation and technology being introduced, the degree of standardization and similarity with past proven designs.

8.2.4 In addition to customer needs, the designer should give due consideration to the requirements relating to safety, environmental and other regulations, including items in the company's quality policy which may go beyond existing statutory requirements.

8.2.5 The quality aspects of the design should be unambiguous and adequately define characteristics important to quality, such as the acceptance and rejection criteria. Both fitness for purpose and safeguards against misuse should be considered. Product definition may also include reliability, maintainability and serviceability through a reasonable life expectancy, including benign failure and safe disposability as appropriate.

ISO 9001

4.4.3 Design input

Design input requirements relating to the product shall be identified, documented and their election reviewed by the supplier for adequacy.

Incomplete, ambiguous or conflicting requirements shall be resolved with those responsible for drawing up these requirements.

4.4.4 Design output

Design output shall be documented and expressed in terms of requirements, calculations and analyses.

Design output shall

a) meet the design input requirements;

b) contain or reference acceptance criteria;

c) conform to appropriate regulatory requirements whether or not these have been stated in the input information;

d) identify those characteristics of the design that are crucial to the safe and proper functioning of the product.

ISO 9004

8.3 Product testing and measurement

The methods of measurement and test, and the acceptance criteria applied to evaluate the product and processes during both the design and production phases should be specified.

Parameters should include the following:

a) performance target values, tolerances, and attribute features;

b) acceptance and rejection criteria;

c) test and measurement methods, equipment, bias and precision requirements, and computer software considerations.

8.4 Design qualification and validation

The design process should provide periodic evaluation of the design at significant stages. Such evaluation can take the form of analytical methods, such as FMFA (Failure Mode and Effects Analysis), fault tree analysis or risk assessment, as well as inspection or test of prototype models and/or actual production samples. The amount and degree of testing should be related to the risks identified in the design plan (see 8.2). Independent evaluation may be employed, as appropriate, to verify original calculations, provide alternative calculations or perform tests.

ISO 9004

Adequate numbers of samples should be examined by tests and/or inspection to provide adequate statistical confidence in the results. The tests should include the following activities:

a) evaluation of performance, durability, safety, reliability and maintainability under expected storage and operational conditions;

b) inspections to verify that all design features are as intended and that all authorized design changes have been accomplished and recorded;

c) validation of computer systems and software.

The results of all tests and evaluations should be documented regularly throughout the qualification test cycle. Review of test results should include defect and failure analysis.

ISO 9001

4.4.5 Design verification

The supplier shall plan, establish, document and assign to competent personnel functions for verifying the design.

Design verification shall establish that design output meets the design input requirement (see 4.4.4) by means of design control measures such as:

a) holding and recording design reviews (see 4.16);

b) undertaking qualification tests and demonstrations;

c) carrying out alternative calculations;

d) comparing the new design with a similar proven design, if available.

4.4.6 Design changes

The supplier shall establish and maintain procedures for the identification, documentation and appropriate review and approval of all changes and modifications.

ISO 9004

8.5 Design review

8.5.1 General

At the conclusion of each phase of design development, a formal, documented, systematic and critical review of the design results should be conducted. This should be distinguished from a project progress meeting, which is primarily concerned with time and cost. Participants at each design review should include representatives of all functions affecting quality as appropriate to the phase being reviewed. The design review should identify and anticipate problem areas and inadequacies, and initiate corrective actions to ensure that the final design and supporting data meet customer requirements.

8.5.2 Elements of design reviews

As appropriate to the design phase and product, the following elements outlined below should be considered:

a) Items pertaining to customer needs

   1) comparison of customer needs expressed in the product brief with technical specifications for materials, products and processes;

   2) validation of the design through prototype tests;

   3) ability to perform under expected conditions of use and environment;

ISO 9004

4) considerations of unintended uses and misuses;

5) safety and environmental compatibility;

6) compliance with regulatory requirements, national and international standards, and corporate practices;

7) comparisons with competitive designs;

8) comparison with similar designs, especially analysis of internal and external problem history to avoid repeating problems.

b) Items pertaining to product specification and service requirements

1) reliability, serviceability and maintainability requirements;

2) permissible tolerances and comparison with process capabilities;

3) product acceptance/rejection criteria;

4) installability, ease of assembly, storage needs, shelf life and disposability;

5) benign failure and fail-safe characteristics;

6) aesthetic specifications and acceptance criteria;

7) failure modes and effects analyses, and fault tree analysis;

8) ability to diagnose and correct problems;

ISO 9004

9) labelling, warnings, identification, traceability requirements and user instructions;

10) review and use of standard parts.

c) Items pertaining to process specifications service

1) manufacturability of the design, including special process needs, mechanization, automation, assembly and installation of components;

2) capability to inspect and test the design, including special inspection and test requirements;

3) specification of materials, components and subassemblies, including approved supplies and suppliers as well as availability;

4) packaging, handling, storage, and shelf-life requirements, especially safety factors relating to incoming and outgoing items.

8.5.3 Design verification

Design verification may be undertaken independently or in support of design reviews by applying the following methods:

a) alternative calculations, made to verify the correctness of the original calculations and analyses:

b) testing, e.g. by model or prototype tests—if this method is adopted, the test programmes

ISO 9004

should be clearly defined and the results documented;

c) independent verification, to verify the correctness of the original calculations and/or other design activities.

8.6 Design baseline and production release

The results of the final design review should be appropriately documented in specifications and drawings that define the design baseline. Where appropriate, this should include description of qualification test units "as built" and modified to correct deficiencies during the qualification test programmes for configuration control throughout the production cycle. The total document package that defines the design baseline should require approval at appropriate levels of management affected by or contributing to the product. This "approval" constitutes the production release and signifies concurrence that the design can be realized.

8.7 Market readiness review

The quality system should provide for a review to determine whether production capability and field support are adequate for the new or redesigned product. Depending upon the type of product, the review may cover the following points:

a) availability and adequacy of

ISO 9004

installation, operation, maintenance and repair manuals;

b) existence of an adequate distribution and customer service
organization;

c) training of field personnel;

d) availability of spare parts;

e) field trials;

f) certification of the satisfactory
completion of qualification tests;

g) physical inspection of early
production units and their packaging and labeling;

h) evidence of process capability
to meet specification on production equipment.

*8.8 Design change control (Config-
uration management)*

The quality system should provide a procedure for controlling
the release, change and use of
documents that define the design
baseline (resultant product configuration) and for authorizing
the necessary work to be performed to implement changes
that may affect product during its
entire life cycle. The procedures
should provide for various necessary approvals, specified points
and times for implementing
changes, removing obsolete
drawings and specifications from
work areas, and verifications that
changes are made at the appointed times and places. This
control process is referred to as
"configuration management."

ISO 9004

These procedures should handle emergency changes necessary to prevent production of nonconforming product. Consideration should be given to instituting formal design reviews and validation testing when the magnitude, complexity or risk associated with the change warrant such actions.

8.9 Design requalification

Periodic re-evaluation of product should be performed in order to ensure that the design is still valid with respect to all specified requirements. This should include a review of customer needs and technical specifications in the light of field experiences, field performance surveys, or new technology and techniques. The review should also consider process modifications. The quality system should ensure that any production and field experience indicating the need for design change is fed back for analysis. Care should be taken that design changes do not cause product quality degradation and that proposed changes are evaluated for their impact on all product characteristics in the design baseline definition.

General

What Is the Intent of This Element?

This section basically states that a company should develop and maintain procedures that are identified as "good engineering practices." This is to ensure that designs and engineering decisions are consistent. The result of each is a design that is uniform, of high integrity, and focused on customer satisfaction. This system must be documented and usually takes the form of policies, objectives, and procedures. The key issue is how the design function is controlled rather than how it is documented. The purpose of design control is to inform everyone in the company on how the design function will operate. Design control also defines who is responsible for each phase of the design.

What Is the Requirement of This Element?

This section requires the supplier to establish and maintain procedures for design control. These procedures should provide control and verification of the design to ensure the specified design requirements are met.

Implementation Strategy

The best method to implement the requirements of this element effectively is to develop a policy covering design control activities. This policy should provide direction on procedures to address design control. At this point, flowcharting becomes an important step in determining how the design process works. The first time many companies develop flowcharts to map undocumented design departments, they are stunned. They find "black holes" that suck in information, perhaps never to be found again. This flowcharting exercise could save a company large amounts of money by finding inefficient and costly practices. From these flowcharts, procedures can be developed to control the flow of information and address all applicable areas of the design process.

Design and Development Planning

What Is the Intent of This Element?

This section calls for development of a plan that identifies all design activities requiring completion. This development plan at a minimum should include the following three areas:

1. Development planning
2. Activity assignment
3. Identification and control of organizational and technical interfaces

Development Planning

This area specifies that a development plan should be formulated to identify and assign responsibility for each step during the design and development phase. This plan should describe how a design project is initiated, what the design input is, and where it comes from. The plan should define activities conducted concerning design reviews and define how design changes will be documented. It should also list characteristics of design output and reference how the design output will be verified and compared to design input. Finally, this document should describe how the design will be documented and how it will be sustained with design changes. As described, this plan will be extensive.

Activity Assignment

Delegation is one important part of design planning. Management should assign responsibility for each step of the design and verification process to a department, position, or person. The next step is for management to make sure the assigned areas have sufficient qualified personnel and proper resources to perform the assigned responsibilities.

Organizational and Technical Interfaces

One of the last areas the design plan should address deals with interactions between departments. Procedures for timely and effective interaction between the design department and the other departments within the company should be established. The design plan attempts to eliminate the barriers that traditionally exist between the engineering and the manufacturing departments.

In many companies, the design team completes a design without the assistance of the manufacturing department. Sometime during the night, it often seems, the design file is thrown "over the wall" to land in the lap of manufacturing. The manufacturing department then must discover how to best produce the product. File transfer difficulties can be minimized, and the end product quality improved, if manufacturing is included in the design phase.

What Is the Requirement of This Element?

The requirements of this element center around the plan used to control the design process. The requirement calls for the supplier to draw up plans to accomplish the following:

1. Identify those responsible for development and verification activities
2. Assign activities to qualified personnel with adequate resources
3. Update the plan as the design evolves
4. Identify technical interfaces between the design team and other departments
5. Document, transmit, and review information needed by other departments on a regular basis

Implementation Strategy

One of the more effective implementation strategies is for a company to have written processes for the development of product. The document should include all the requirements of the design plan. In one company certified to ISO 9001, this document is called the "product development guideline." It has sections that address feasibility, development, field testing, commercialization, key meetings, technical reviews, and commercialization file transfer, each of which is treated as a separate phase. Interfaces are identified, and responsibilities are assigned to specific positions within the company. Guidelines are given describing activities required during each phase of the development cycle.

This document identifies the meetings that have to be held before the design can progress to the next phase of the development cycle. Also defined is the extent to which a design is to be documented and a detailed definition of a design file is provided. These processes were developed so that various teams working on unique projects would end up with a design that had progressed along a logical development path. The purpose of this document was to ensure that each design was properly evaluated and documented before being released to manufacturing.

If this type of document is to be developed, care should be taken to assure that each of the requirements of this element are properly addressed without putting the design team in a straightjacket. The design control element of ISO 9001 should be used as a guide by which the design activity progresses. This will result in a consistent output, instead of a control for its own sake.

A second strategy is to identify the flow of the design process. A flowchart should show such items as interactions with other departments and assignment of responsibility. After a comprehensive flowchart is developed, it can be released as the procedure to follow during the design process. The important issues are that (1) proper engineering is being performed on a product, and (2) a procedure is in place that will identify how to proceed with a design. The end result is for designs to be properly engineered, consistent, and manufacturable. The focus is on good design work, not good documentation.

Design Input

What Is the Intent of This Element?

The intent of this element is to make sure an understanding exists between the customer and the designer before the design is started. Everyone must understand what is expected from the design before the design team can start. This area is much like contract review in that a "meeting of the minds" must occur.

The design input becomes the design parameters the product will be engineered to meet. When details can be agreed to up front, the end product will have fewer problems. Good definition of the user specifications will also help when a design falls short of the design input. These differences can then be identified early and resolved with the customer. This process is a constant evolution and should be documented.

What Is the Requirement of This Element?

This element requires that procedures be developed to accomplish the following:

1. Identify and document the design input
2. Establish a method to resolve incomplete, ambiguous input or input that conflicts with other requirements
3. Review the design inputs with the customer

What About the 1994 Version? Design Input

In the design input portion, the 1994 version of the standard adds that "Design input shall take into consideration the results of any contract review activities."

Implementation Strategy

A meeting should occur between the customer and the designers to discuss the limitations and functionality of the proposed new product. One often neglected area of design control is the identification of the customer. In many companies, the customer is the marketing group; in other cases, it is the end user. Try to decide very early on in the design phase who the customer will be, and set up a meeting to start the definition process. The purpose of this meeting is to reach an agreement on parameters for a new product. After a decision is reached, the critical operating parameters should be documented.

In many cases, this is one of the toughest and time-consuming stages of a new product development cycle. This meeting, or series of meetings, should be documented (by way of published minutes) and involve as many design team members as possible. The result of these meetings should be as many specific operating/functional parameters as possible.

Typically, this type of design input (user specifications) will set the maximum and/or minimum ranges at which the product can be used. Additionally, they include the maximum weight, minimum cycle time, or maximum noise levels. An agreement should exist regarding functionality, cost estimates, and delivery time. These parameters, however, should be viewed as starting points. Many of the initial parameters will change as the design evolves and progresses from the ambiguous desire of a customer to a firm and functional product.

Once all of the parameters are agreed upon, a formal set of user specifications can be written for acceptance by both the customer and the design team. To document this acceptance, the user specifications are usually signed by both parties. The specifications then become the contract between the parties. To ensure that no information has been overlooked, a form can be developed to identify each design parameter. A formal mechanism for design changes should also be established. No change in a basic design input should occur unless it is reviewed and accepted in writing by both the customer and the design team. Change is a vital part of the design phase; the key issue is for the changes to be accepted in principle by the customer and the design team. This acceptance should occur long before the change has reached a nonreversible stage.

Design Output

What Is the Intent of This Element?

The intent of the design output element is to ensure that the output is properly documented and compared to the design input specification for compatibility. The design output is easily verified, provided the input is properly identified. For this reason, the design input should be stated in specific, measurable values (weight, physical size, color, shape, functionality, services required, temperature, noise levels, and so forth). The output should be expressed in the same units of measure.

In the absence of a way to measure the design output directly, calculations or other methods can be used for verification. As the user specifications are developed with the customer, an agreement should be reached regarding verification methods. An example of this type of output would be stress calculations for a bridge. The last thing someone would do is build a bridge and then test for design flaws by stressing it to the point that it collapses. In this case, stress calculations will be used to verify the design output.

In all cases, though, the output should be compared to the input to make sure they meet. Where the output has not met the input, the customer should be notified; then the user specification should be changed, the design changed, or the project scrapped. In every case, the customer is allowed to decide what to do before the design is released to manufacture. The output should have acceptance requirements listed in the user specifications, and output should be identified for compliance with appropriate regulations. Critical areas should be addressed as they are discovered.

What Is the Requirement of This Element?

The requirements of this section are specific and include the following:

1. The design output will be documented in terms of the requirements, calculations, or analyses.
2. The design output will be compared to the design input to make sure it meets the requirements.
3. The design output will reference the appropriate acceptance criteria.
4. The output will conform to appropriate regulatory agencies.
5. The design team will identify those characteristics that are crucial to the safe and proper functioning of the product.

What About the 1994 Version? Design Output

Under design output, the identification of characteristics crucial to the safe and proper functioning of the product have been detailed to include "operating, storage, handling, maintenance and disposal requirements." The design output is also required to "include a review of design output documents before release."

Implementation Strategy

The common approach to implementing this element is for the customer and the design team to meet periodically to perform a design review. These formal meetings should inform the customer of the progress made since the last meeting. Any problems that have been identified are discussed. Areas where the existing design does not meet the user specifications are identified, and areas where additional user specifications need to be developed are listed. During these meetings, the user specifications and the designs evolve into an effective and compatible set of documents. These meetings help prevent surprises at the end of the project.

Minutes or summaries of the meetings should be maintained. They will reflect that the outcome of the meeting has been understood and accepted by all parties. A checklist should be developed to identify all regulations that must be met (for example, Department of Transportation, Environmental Protection Agency, or industry regulations). All of this documentation should be maintained in a file that will be kept for the life of the product. This file (called a central product file) will document the evolution of the design and will follow the design to manufacturing. This file will be the collection place for all the information about the design, including the design output.

Design Verification

What Is the Intent of This Element?

The design should be verified to make sure it meets the input (user specifications) and that it is safe, reliable, and in compliance with other regulations. The design verification can happen by any or all of the following methods.

Analytical Verification

Analytical methods are used for factors that cannot be verified after the work is performed without affecting the usability of the product. This includes methods such as failure mode and effects analysis (FMEA), fault tree analysis, or stress/pressure calculations. Analytical methods should be used when it is impractical to perform prototype testing to prove the output; such other factors as time or cost may also prohibit prototype testing. Examples of this type of analysis would include stress calculations on structures or pressure-containing parts, weld strengths, and maximum crush resistance. Properly documented and verified calculations are a common acceptable means of verification (for example, performing an FMEA or a fault tree analysis on a power plant to discover what failure modes would cause a catastrophic failure resulting in injury or death to the operator.)

Prototype Testing

Prototype testing is a second way to verify a new design. This method can be used when the design output cannot be verified by calculations. With this method a prototype of the product is built and tested to verify its functionality and operational limits. The results of these tests should be documented and maintained in the design file.

Comparison to Existing Designs

Another method of verification is to compare the design to existing equipment of a comparable design. If a product or parts of a product are very similar to existing equipment, these areas can be verified based on a comparison of the designs. The design team need only to show a direct relationship between the two designs and document this analysis.

What Is the Requirement of This Element?

This section requires the supplier to verify that the output meets the input requirements. This verification can be accomplished by one or more of the following:

1. Holding design reviews
2. Qualification testing
3. Completing alternative calculations
4. Comparing the new design to similar proven designs

What About the 1994 Version? Design Verification

The 1987 version of ISO 9001 requires design verification by means such as holding and recording design reviews to establish that design output meets design input. In ISO/DIS 9001, this requirement has been expanded to require that "at appropriate stages of design, formal documented review of the design results shall be planned and conducted. Participants at each design review shall include representatives of all functions concerned with the design stage being reviewed as well as other specialist personnel as required. Records of such reviews shall be maintained."

This addition expands the responsibility for design reviews out to departments and other functions which may be affected by decisions made during the design review stage. In typical operations, design reviews are solely the responsibility of the design department. This addition to the standard will require an organization to assess the potential impact on additional departments, such as manufacturing, purchasing, and quality, for inclusion in such reviews.

Implementation Strategy

Using a checklist is one proven method of identifying and verifying design output. This checklist should identify the critical areas of a design and list how each of these areas will be verified as the design evolves. Each of the requirements listed on the user specification should be verified, as should safety-related areas and the portions of the design incorporated to meet regulatory requirements.

The checklist should also identify acceptance criteria for each of the design criteria. Output must be compared to the criteria, and an accept/reject decision made. As each of the areas is verified, the checklist can be completed showing the method used for verification, the accept/reject criteria, and the actual results. If the design is not accepted, the documentation should include the corrective action taken.

With this information in the design file, the final design review can be held with the customer and approval for commercialization gained. Once the transfer takes place, a method to change the design is needed. This is covered in the last area of the design control.

What About the 1994 Version? Design Validation

ISO/DIS 9001 incorporates the requirement of design validation by stating that "design validation shall be performed to ensure that product conforms to defined user needs and/or requirements." A note has also been included stating that "design validation follows successful design verification."

Of all revisions incorporated in ISO/DIS 9001, the addition of design validation within the Design Control element may be the most dramatic. The purpose of validation is to take the requirements of design verification one step further to assure that the final configuration conforms to the needs and requirements as specified by the customer.

For any organization which utilizes prototype testing as a method of design verification, this addition can be met fairly easily if such testing is conducted under simulated conditions. However, in cases where calculations or comparisons are used as methods of design verification, additional activities may be required to meet the intent of design validation.

Design Changes

What Is the Intent of This Element?

This section calls for procedures to be developed to control the design changes. For most companies, this is done through an engineering change (EC) system. The purpose is to ensure that the changes are given the same amount of review and verification as the original design. It would not make much sense for a design to be tested, analyzed, and verified if the changes to that design were not reviewed. A well-tested design could become dangerous or even deadly without design change verification.

What Is the Requirement of This Element?

The requirement of this section is for a process to be developed that will properly control all changes to the design of the product. This procedure should address the following:

1. The identification of design changes should be documented.
2. All design changes should have the same level of analysis and review as did the original design.

Implementation Strategy

In many programs, a change to the original design of a product must be approved by either the engineer who made the original design or by the engineer who is assigned responsibility for the product. A checklist can be developed that will require the designer (who made the change or sustains the product) to sign the engineering change (EC). An EC shows that the change is compatible with the existing design or shows how the change was tested and verified. The process will also require an independent person with proper skills and knowledge to verify and approve the change. A third signature on the sheet will usually be that of the person who entered the change into the system. The last piece of information for inclusion on the form is the effective date of the change, which will show exactly when the change is to take place.

The implementation of this portion of the design control element is usually simple. Most companies have some form of engineering change process in place. For most of these programs, the process should be reviewed to make sure that changes are properly evaluated and that the process is documented.

Summary

The design control portion of the ISO 9001 standard is very comprehensive and complete. The reason the standard is requesting this amount of detail is that the design is the foundation on which all quality is built. A poorly designed product will never be a product of a high quality; customers will not be satisfied with a bad design no matter how well it may be built. Until the quality of design is addressed, manufacturing quality is wasted energy.

Since the ISO 9000 standard is a process-oriented standard, it is imperative the standard effectively address design. Would you want to fly in an airplane that was built to the highest standards, but designed in such a way that the wings fall off in flight?

6

DOCUMENT CONTROL

Document control is one of the eighteen elements that is detailed in both ISO 9001 and 9002. This element is a very traditional requirement found in many quality standards. The basic principle of the element is for management to identify quality records and to develop procedures to control this quality documentation within the company.

Most companies have some sort of system to address the collection, storage, retrieval, and revision of quality documentation. Many companies meet this element to some extent. Most companies, however, do not totally meet the specific requirements. Companies often fall short in defining which documents should be listed and controlled as quality records. Most companies have a well-defined system for controlling prints, drawings, and specifications, but many of these same organizations do not control inspection procedures, test instructions, or operating procedures. This element is somewhat specific as to what documents need to be controlled and provides guidelines as to the method of control.

ISO 9001

4.5 Document control

4.5.1 Document approval and issue

The supplier shall establish and maintain procedures to control all documents and data that relate to the requirements of this International Standard. These documents shall be reviewed and approved for adequacy by authorized personnel prior to issue. This control shall ensure that

a) the pertinent issues of appropriate documents are available at all locations where operations essential to the effective functioning of the quality system are performed;

b) obsolete documents are promptly removed from all points of issue or use.

4.5.2 Document changes/modifications

Changes to documents shall be reviewed and approved by the same functions/organizations that performed the original review and approval unless specifically designated otherwise. The designated organizations shall have access to pertinent background information upon which to base their review and approval. Where practicable, the nature of the change shall be identified in the document or the appropriate attachments.

ISO 9004

17.1 General

The quality management system should establish, and require the maintenance of, a means for identification, collection, indexing, filing, storage, maintenance, retrieval, and disposition of pertinent quality documentation and records. Policies should be established concerning availability and access of records to customers and suppliers. Policies should also be established concerning procedures for changes and modifications in various types of documents.

17.2 Quality documentation

The system should require that sufficient documentation be available to follow the achievement of the required product quality and the effective operation of the quality management system. Appropriate subcontractor documentation should be included. All documentation should be legible, dated (including revision dates), clean, readily identifiable, and maintained in an orderly manner. Data may be hard copy or stored in a computer.

In addition, the quality management system should provide a method of removing and/or disposing of documentation used in the manufacture of products when that documentation has become out of date.

ISO 9001

A master list or equivalent document control procedure shall be established to identify the current revision of documents in order to preclude the use of nonapplicable documents.

Documents shall be re-issued after a practical number of changes have been made.

ISO 9004

The following are examples of the types of documents requiring control:

drawing;

specifications;

blueprints;

inspection instructions;

test procedures;

work instructions;

operation sheets;

quality manual (see 5.3.2);

operational procedures;

quality assurance procedures.

Document Approval and Issue

What Is the Intent of This Element?

This element states that the company should control all documentation relating to the ISO-9001 standard. This control should involve the identification, collection, indexing, filing, storage, maintenance, and disposition of documents. The basic intent of this element is (1) for everyone to have the pertinent revisions of all documentation, and (2) for all appropriate documentation to be identified, collected, stored, and indexed so it can be retrieved and used as needed.

What Is the Requirement of This Element?

This element's requirements center around ensuring that appropriate information reaches the appropriate people at the proper times. The first part of this is document approval. The requirements include the following:

1. A procedure shall be established to control all documents and data that relate to a company's ISO 9001 or 9002 system. (A list of typical documentation is given in ISO 9004).
2. Pertinent documents should be available at all locations where essential operations are being performed.
3. Obsolete documents are promptly removed from all points of issue or use.

What About the 1994 Version? Document Control

The document control element has been updated to address data of different forms such as "hard copy media, or . . . electronic or other media." The standard has further defined the retention of obsolete documentation with requirements for proper identification to preclude unintended use.

Implementation Strategy

One of the simplest implementation strategies is to develop a procedure that identifies controlled documentation. These documents can usually be divided into two types of controlled records: those that are retained and are not changed (for example, test reports, inspection reports, purchase orders), and those that change and should have a revision level (for example, blueprints, drawings, specifications, inspection instructions, policies, procedures).

A systemic means should be documented that would specifically identify the method used to maintain these records. They should be readily retrievable and protected. In addition to these requirements, records that change (blueprints, drawings, specifications, etc.) should have a systematic means available to change the revision level.

Documentation Changes/Modifications

What Is the Intent of This Element?

This section addresses how changes should take place on controlled documents. For the documents to be considered as controlled, a procedure should be developed that will address how they will be updated. In many companies, two procedures will have to be developed. One will cover the engineering change orders (ECOs) to such engineering documents as drawings, bills of material, and specifications; the second will address changes to documents such as operating procedures and manuals. It is the intent of this element for a company to have a means to accomplish the following:

1. Identify the revision level of the document. The revision level should be apparent and easily identified on the document; this will make sure everyone can identify whether it is the pertinent revision.
2. Review and approve changes to documents at the same level as the original document unless specifically designated otherwise.
3. Identify the nature of the change to the document.
4. Maintain a master list that will identify the current revision level.
5. Reissue a document after a practical number of changes have been made.

Changes to a document should be approved at the same level as the original document. Otherwise, the entire intent of a document issued at the highest level of management could be altered through small subsequent changes approved at a lower level. The standard, however, recognizes that there may be certain situations were revisions can be made without the original function/organization having to review the change. A conscious decision must be made here, as the standard states "unless specifically designated otherwise." The decision to allow this activity should not be made in a haphazard manner so as to violate good business practice.

One example is in the initial start-up of a certified program. Many of the operating procedures may be written by the quality assurance department or the designated function that has received the most intensive training. As the system progresses, the educational level of the entire work force is raised with regard to meeting the standard. The activity of meeting such requirements in daily operation and controlling respective procedures may then be shifted to those who own the process.

A second part of this clause is that "the designated organizations shall have access to pertinent background information upon which to base their review and approval." If the proper training has been accomplished and appropriate reference documents are available, it is only logical that the owners of the program become the ones best suited to describe their activities. This, however, must be specifically designated to be in compliance with the standard.

The nature of all changes to a document should be identified. Identifying changes will allow readers to identify quickly what has changed and understand how the change will affect them.

A master list is used so the current revision can be quickly identified. In addition to the current revisions, each of the earlier revisions should be kept for reference. If a question comes up as to how a process was accomplished in the past, the procedure that was in force at that time could be reviewed. This can also work for drawings and prints showing how a part was built at any given point in time.

Documents should be reissued after a practical number of changes have been made. With regard to reissuance, there are two schools of thought, either of which can be found in certified programs. In the first, a document is reissued after a practical number (to be determined by the implementing company) of changes have been made. This allows consolidation of numerous individually identified changes into one issue, including grammatical, spelling, or formatting errors and other revisions that do not affect the intent or function of the document. The second approach adds to this a review of the entire document. This assures that the document still meets the original intent and requirement for which it was generated, and that it remains compatible with other documentation with which it must interface.

What Is the Requirement of This Element?

Once the document is prepared, approved, and issued, the next task is to maintain and update the document as needed. A company should have a documented method to update, review, and approve document updates prior to reissuance. To ensure that information is accurate and compatible, this element requires the following:

1. The changes shall be reviewed and approved by the same functions/organizations that approved the original review, unless specifically designated otherwise.
2. If specifically designated otherwise, the organization having control over the change should have access to the needed information and background for an appropriate decision to be made.
3. Current revision levels of documents should be known. This can be accomplished by maintaining a master listing or through a document control procedure.

Implementation Strategy

A simple method to address this element is to develop a procedure that will identify all the documents that fall into the quality records grouping (as identified by ISO 9004). The procedure should be written to meet the five specific requirements of this section. Revision levels of procedures and policies can be identified by maintaining a master list of this documentation. This list should show the document number, the title, and the current revision level. If these documents are chosen to be retained in a manual, a "master" manual may be designated by the issuing department/organization. Drawings, specifications, and special instructions can be identified from a list maintained either electronically or manually. Any documentation that is controlled with revision levels should have a master file that can be accessed so the current revision level can be identified and maintained.

This is one of the more specific elements, and one of the easiest to meet. Keep in mind that each company must decide what documentation needs to be included in the system. Some companies will have more documentation than is listed in ISO 9004 17.2, whereas others will have less. Each company must decide what is appropriate for its organization.

7

PURCHASING

Purchasing is also one of the eighteen elements detailed in both ISO 9001 and 9002. In general, the purchasing element simply asks the company to ensure that the product being purchased conforms to specified requirements. The standard offers several suggestions as to how this element can be implemented. But, as in every other element, each company must decide what is the most efficient method to assure product quality. The eight areas that need to be addressed are specified in section 9.1 of ISO 9004.

The purchasing element is closely tied to the contract review element. The purchase order (PO) that is issued to a subcontractor is a contract and should go through the same evaluation as did the tender or contract. The only difference with a PO is that the company is issuing, rather than accepting, the contract.

In general terms, this element intends for a company to establish a system to ensure that the appropriate requirements of the purchase order are understood by both the company and the subcontractor before the order is released. It also calls for an evaluation to be performed to determine whether the selected subcontractor has the capability of meeting the requirements. This system should guarantee that the proper information is given to the subcontractor, and that the requirements of quantity, quality levels, and cost are understood, accepted, and met by the subcontractor. The system should also make provisions for determining that the delivered product meets the required quality level described in the order. The basic intent is for the purchasing department to follow good business practices when it comes to purchasing products or services.

In this element, the term *supplier* is used interchangeably to indicate either the company/purchaser or the subcontractor. In each reference to the "supplier," the context of the sentence should be analyzed to determine actually who is responsible for the activity.

ISO 9001

4.6 Purchasing

4.6.1 General

The supplier shall ensure that purchased product conforms to specified requirements.

ISO 9004

9 Quality in procurement

9.1 General

Purchase materials, components and assemblies become part of the company's product and directly affect the quality of its product. Quality of services such as calibration and special processes should also be considered. The procurement of purchased supplies should be planned and controlled. The purchaser should establish a close working relationship and feedback system with each supplier. In this way, a programme of continual quality improvements can be maintained and quality disputes avoided or settled quickly. This close working relationship and feedback system will benefit both the purchaser and the supplier.

The procurement quality programme should include the following elements as a minimum:

a) requirements for specification, drawings and purchase orders (see 9.2);

b) selection of qualified suppliers (see 9.3);

c) agreement on quality assurance (see 9.4);

d) agreement on verification methods (see 9.5);

e) provisions for settlement of quality disputes (see 9.6);

ISO 9004

f) receiving inspection plans (see 9.7);

g) receiving controls (see 9.7);

h) receiving quality records (see 9.8).

9.2 Requirements for specification, drawings and purchase orders

The successful procurement of supplies begins with a clear definition of the requirements. Usually these requirements are contained in the contract specifications, drawings and purchase orders which are provided to the supplier. The procuring activity should develop appropriate methods to ensure that the requirements for the supplies are clearly defined, communicated and, most importantly, are completely understood by the supplier. These methods may include written procedures for the preparation of specifications, drawings and purchase orders, vendor/purchaser conferences prior to purchase order release, and other methods appropriate for the supplies being procured.

Purchasing documents should contain data clearly describing the product or service ordered. Elements that may be included are as follows:

a) precise identification of style and grade;

ISO 9004

b) inspection instructions and applicable specifications;

c) quality system standard to be applied.

Purchasing documents should be reviewed for accuracy and completeness before release.

ISO 9001

4.6.2 Assessment of sub-contractors

The supplier shall select sub-contractors on the basis of their ability to meet sub-contract requirements, including quality requirements. The supplier shall establish and maintain records of acceptable sub-contractors (see 4.16). The selection of sub-contractors and the type and extent of control exercised by the supplier, shall be dependent upon the type of product and, where appropriate, on records of sub-contractors' previously demonstrated capability and performance. The supplier shall ensure that quality system controls are effective.

4.6.3 Purchasing data

Purchasing documents shall contain data clearly describing the product ordered, including, where applicable,

a) the type, class, style, grade or other precise identification;

b) the title or other positive identification, and applicable issue of specifications, drawings, process requirements, inspection instructions and other relevant technical data, including requirements for approval or qualification of product, procedures, process equipment and personnel;

ISO 9004

9.3 Selection of qualified supplies

Each supplier should have a demonstrated capability to furnish supplies which can meet all the requirements of the specifications, drawings and purchase order.

The methods of establishing this capability may include any combination of the following:

a) on-site assessment and evaluation of supplier's capability and/or quality systems;

b) evaluation of product samples;

c) past history with similar supplies;

d) test results of similar supplies;

e) published experience of other users.

9.4 Agreement on quality assurance

A clear understanding should be developed with the supplier on quality assurance for which the supplier is responsible. The assurance to be provided by the supplier may vary as follows:

a) the purchaser relies on supplier's quality assurance system;

b) submission of specified inspection/test data or process control records with shipments;

c) 100% inspection/testing by the supplier;

ISO 9001

c) the title, number and issue of the quality system International Standard to be applied to the product.

The supplier shall review and approve purchasing documents for adequacy of specified requirements prior to release.

4.6.4 Verification of purchased product

Where specified in the contract, the purchaser or his representative shall be afforded the right to verify at source or upon receipt that purchased product conforms to specified requirements. Verification by the purchaser shall not absolve the supplier of the responsibility to provide acceptable product nor shall it preclude subsequent rejection.

When the purchaser or his representative elects to carry out verification at the sub-contractor's plant, such verification shall not be used by the supplier as evidence of effective control of quality by the sub-contractor.

ISO 9004

d) lot acceptance inspection/ testing by sampling by the supplier;

e) implementation of a formal quality assurance system as specified by the purchaser.

f) none—the purchaser relies on receiving inspection or in-house sorting.

The assurance provisions should be commensurate with the needs of the purchaser's business and should avoid unnecessary costs. In certain cases, formal quality assurance systems may be involved (see ISO 9000, ISO 9001, ISO 9002 and ISO 9003). This may include periodic assessment of supplier quality system assurance by the purchaser.

9.5 Agreement on verification methods

A clear agreement should be developed with the supplier on the methods by which conformance to purchaser's requirements will be verified. Such agreements may also include the exchange of inspection and test data with the aim of furthering quality improvements. Reaching agreement can minimize difficulties in the interpretation of requirements as well as inspection, test or sampling methods.

ISO 9004

9.6 Provisions for settlement of quality disputes

Systems and procedures should be established by which settlement of disputes regarding quality can be reached with suppliers. Provisions should exist for dealing with routine and non-routine matters. A very important aspect of these systems and procedures is the provision of improved communication channels between the purchaser and the supplier on matters affecting quality.

9.7 Receiving inspection planning and controls

Appropriate measures should be established to ensure that supplies which have been received are properly controlled. These procedures should include quarantine areas or other appropriate methods to prevent unqualified supplies from being inadvertently used. (See 14.4).

The extent to which receiving inspection will be performed should be carefully planned. The level of inspection, when inspection is deemed necessary, should be selected with overall cost being borne in mind.

In addition, when the decision has been made to perform an inspection, it is necessary to select with care the characteristics to be inspected.

ISO 9004

It is also necessary to ensure, before the supplies arrive, that all the necessary tools, gauges, meters, instruments and equipment are available and properly calibrated, along with adequately trained personnel.

9.8 Receiving quality record

Appropriate receiving quality records should be maintained to ensure the availability of historical data to assess supplier performance and quality trends. In addition, it may be useful and, in certain instances, essential to maintain records of lot identification for the purpose of traceability.

General

What Is the Intent of This Element?

The basic intent of this element is for the development of a documented system that will ensure that purchased product conforms to specified requirements. The ISO 9004 explanation of the standard calls for the company to develop a close working relationship with the subcontractor. This includes establishment of a feedback system. The company should help the subcontractor develop a program of continual quality improvement. The standard calls for development of a system to settle quickly any disputes over quality. According to section 9.1 of ISO 9004, the system should include, as a minimum, the following eight elements:

1. Requirements for specifications, drawings, and purchase orders
2. Selection of qualified suppliers
3. Agreement on quality assurance
4. Agreement on verification methods
5. Provisions for settlement of quality disputes
6. Receiving inspection plans
7. Receiving controls
8. Receiving quality records

With each of these eight areas properly and effectively addressed, the purchasing element will not only meet the requirements of this element but should function in a systematic manner. This should allow for quality improvement in the products and services being purchased.

What Is the Requirement of This Element?

The requirement of this element is specific and simple: the supplier shall ensure that purchased product conforms to specified requirements—no more and no less.

What About the 1994 Version? Purchasing

The first paragraph now includes the word "evaluate" prior to the selection of subcontractors. Although this was implied in the 1987 version of the standard, evaluation of subcontractors is now a specific requirement.

ISO/DIS 9001 has added a paragraph to the purchasing element under verification of purchased product that states, "Where the supplier verifies purchased product at the subcontractor's premises, the supplier shall specify verification arrangements and the method of release in the purchasing documents." In many industry regulated contracts, it is common practice to incorporate third party or source inspection of product at subcontractor's locations. The standard now requires that when such activity is to be performed, purchasing documents must indicate the specifics of the verification arrangements and the method of release on product approval.

Assessment of Subcontractors

What Is the Intent of This Element?

The first requirement of this element is for the company to make an assessment of the subcontractors *before product is purchased.* The intent is for the company to have advance knowledge that the selected subcontractor has the capability to deliver the needed product or service. The product or service should be of an acceptable quality level and deliverable within the desired time window. This assessment can take several forms, ranging from evaluating a company's industry reputation to a formal audit.

Section 9.3 of ISO 9004 (Selection of Qualified Suppliers) lists five methods, one or more of which can be used to qualify subcontractors before the product is ordered:

1. An on-site assessment of the supplier's quality system
2. An evaluation of samples of product
3. The supplier's history with similar supplies
4. Test results of similar supplies
5. Published experience of other users

If one or more of these methods are employed to evaluate the subcontractor, the goods or services received have a higher probability of meeting the agreed-upon quality level than if the product was ordered blind. To gain a further understanding, each of these suggested methods will be explored.

What Is the Requirement of This Element?

The requirements of this element center around the selection and control of subcontractors, along with evaluation of the subcontractor's quality system. Subcontractors should be selected based on (1) the ability of the subcontractor to meet stated requirements, (2) The type of product being ordered, and (3) The past performance of the subcontractor. In addition to this selection criteria, the company is required to maintain records of acceptable subcontractors, and to ensure that quality system controls are effective.

Implementation Strategy

The assessment should be designed to make a judgment about the subcontractor's ability to deliver the product. The company should decide if the quality system followed by the subcontractor is appropriate and will ensure product quality. The key issue in this assessment is what is appropriate for the situation.

In many quality programs, the word *appropriate* will not mean that a subcontractor must have a formal quality program that meets the requirements of ISO 9001 or 9002. Four- and five-man welding, machining, or electronic assembly shops need some type of guideline for conducting business, but probably not a thick quality control manual. In many cases, the manager/owner is doing much of the labor and overseeing the work. In contrast, a large company that employs many people in different departments should have a somewhat formalized program. For the management representative to say, "Trust me, we are making your parts to the highest quality standard," or "trust me, we know what we are doing," is not good enough.

Unfortunately, this is an approach used by many large companies. When arguments such as "The work force is motivated to do good work; we don't have much turnover, so we don't need a quality manual" are made, it is time to dig deeper. One company made the argument that "We have been in business a long time making this product, and we haven't killed too many people with it, so it must be good." Not many people would buy a food product if it was advertised in that way. Why, then, would a company want to buy that manufacturing product?

One of the more common methods used to qualify subcontractors when a company is preparing for ISO 9001 or 9002 certification is to evaluate the existing subcontractor base one at a time. The process qualifies or disqualifies each subcontractor based on that supplier's past performance. Using this method, subcontractors can be "grandfathered" in, provided the past performance has been acceptable. For this process to be accepted, however, specific criteria should be developed that will qualify or disqualify the subcontractor. The rationale of continuing to use a subcontractor just because it has been used in the past will not be accepted by many auditors for ISO 9001 certification. Each subcontractor should be accepted based on specific quality and delivery performance levels, and this evaluation should be documented and made available for auditors who ask how the subcontractor was qualified.

In one company certified to ISO 9001, the acceptance criteria took into account reject rate, on-time deliveries, and cost. Specific criteria for each category were developed that placed the subcontractor into one of three categories—qualified, conditionally qualified, or unqualified—based on the composite scores for all parts delivered over the previous twelve months. This company also rated the subcontractor for each part number it supplied; a subcontractor could have a qualified rating for one part number and be unqualified for a second. The overall subcontractor rating was a composite score based on the individual part ratings. This system was successful in tracking past performance of the subcontractor and was accepted by the certification agency.

If a subcontractor has an acceptable record delivering a specific product, a company can assume that similar product will be delivered at the same acceptable level. For example, assume a company purchases three different castings from one subcontractor. They may approve a subcontractor for delivery of a similar casting without having to requalify the subcontractor for that specific part number. The approval is based on past performance with the three original castings. Once a history is developed for the product, however, the qualification should be based on demonstrated ability to produce that product.

The last method mentioned in the element deals with approval of a subcontractor based on the published experience of other users. This method is occasionally used in conjunction with accepted industry reputation, usually for large companies with outstanding industry reputations. On one project, a customer had a requirement for DC motors that would generate 2,000 sustained horsepower. Only one manufacturer was found who could provide these motors to the project specifications. This subcontractor was a world leader in electric motor technology and had an outstanding reputation all over the world. These motors were off-the-shelf products; approximately twenty-five a day were being produced. This subcontractor was accepted based on its industry reputation and the documented performance of these motors in other installations.

This part of the element intends for the company to make a sound decision regarding which subcontractor should receive a specific order. The ISO 9000 standard intends that these decisions be based on logical evaluations of the company and its performance. The old-boy network approach often taken in the past is not acceptable; the decision should be based on facts instead of long-held misconceptions or a gut feeling. When good decisions are made on a consistent basis, the quality of the final product should become more consistent. And only when consistency is achieved can the quality be improved.

Purchasing Data

What Is the Intent of This Element?

The intent of this section is for the company to ensure that the subcontractor has a complete understanding of what is being ordered. In the ISO 9001 and 9002 standards the data required to ensure this understanding are divided into three types: (1) description, (2) specification, and (3) required system. This understanding may go beyond describing the product and include identifying specific processes and/or equipment that must be used during production.

For the intent of this element to be met, a company should apply the requirements of the contract review element to purchasing.

What Is the Requirement of This Element?

The standard requires the company to provide adequate information in the purchasing documentation to enable the subcontractor to understand exactly what is being ordered. This information is typically divided into three sections as follows:

1. The physical appearance or identification of the product or service (in other words, description of the part by type, class, style, grade, or other precise identification).
2. The parameters in which the activities/personnel must operate, as described through specifications, drawings, process requirements, inspection instructions, and other relevant technical data. These data should also include, where applicable, approval or qualification of product, procedures, process equipment, and personnel.
3. The type of quality system under which the product will be constructed. Typically a specific program (such as ISO 9002, CSA Z299.3, or API Q1) can be referenced in the contract or on the purchase order. This outlines a specific program that must be followed for the product to be considered acceptable.

The last requirement is for the company to review and approve purchasing documentation for adequacy of the specified requirements. This review should occur before the order is released. Once again, the intent of this standard is to ensure that the subcontractor has an in-depth understanding of exactly what is needed and how it should be constructed.

Implementation Strategy

One implementation method for this element is to develop a documented purchase order system. All products and/or services would be ordered using this system. Each product or service should be evaluated to determine what documentation is necessary for the subcontractor. This documentation will ensure an understanding exists between both parties as to what is being ordered. The required information should be included in writing on the purchase order. These requirements should be specific and address the following, (1) physical identification, (2) required activities, and (3) quality system requirements, as applicable.

Off-the-shelf and commercially available items would require purchase order information such as the product's trade name and the supplier's part number or generic title. Purchase orders for custom-built items would include such documentation as specifications and drawings (with current revision levels) to which the product should conform. Specific documentation required with the product and any special testing should be included on the purchase order. Identification, packaging, and labeling requirements should also be included. These specific requirements could be included in addition to more general information such as class, grade, and title.

With either the commercially available or custom-built product, a company may require that the product to be built under a specific quality assurance system or program. Typical programs would include ISO 9001, CSA Z299.3, API Q1, or MIL-STD-9858. If a specific program is required, the program title, number, and issue must be specifically documented in the purchase order. An agreement on which program will be used must be reached prior to releasing the purchase order to the subcontractor.

The purchase order must be accurate and must be reviewed and signed by authorized personnel, because this becomes the contract that governs all aspects of the transaction. In addition, it is the contract that will identify the parameters to which the product will be verified. To verify that this program is working effectively, the requirements of the contract review element of ISO 9001 should also be met.

Verification of Purchased Product

What Is the Intent of This Element?

The intent of this portion of the element is to ensure that the supplier and the customer have the right to verify that product conforms to the requirements of the purchase order. If specified in the contract, the customer should be afforded the right to verify product at the subcontractor's supplier. In other words, if specified in the contract your customer has the right to verify product at your vendor's location. The intent is to verify product acceptability which does not automatically mean that the product must be inspected. The key issue is acceptable product, not inspected product.

In certified programs, the term *verification* has multiple meanings extending beyond the traditional role of incoming inspection. Product verification can take the form of certified test results supplied from a third party. Control charts (indicating a process was in control as the product was being produced) can also be used to verify product; so test results from randomly selected product can be used for verification. In addition, verification of process variables as product was being produced, along with certificates of conformance, could be used for product verification. There are many other forms of verification beyond the examples listed. Whatever method is used, the underlying result must be verification that the product received meets the contract requirements.

What Is the Requirement of This Element?

This element addresses the rights of the customer to verify product where specified in the contract. This is accomplished without relieving the subcontractor of the responsibility for delivering product that conforms to the specifications of the contract. The requirements are as follows:

1. The purchaser shall have the right to verify, either at the source of manufacture or upon receipt, that the product meets the requirements of the contract.
2. Verification by the purchaser does not prevent product from being rejected at a later date if it does not meet the requirements of the contract.
3. Verification of product by the purchaser does not absolve the subcontractor from the responsibility of producing product that meets the contract requirements.

It should be noted that a customer carrying out verification at the subcontractor's facility does not relieve the supplier from the responsibility of delivering acceptable product. It should not be used as evidence to show that a company has adequately assessed the control of quality in the subcontractor's operations. Product quality can be used as an indicator of process control, but verification of acceptable product alone will not ensure effective control of quality by the subcontractor.

Implementation Strategy

Effective implementation requires addressing each of two aspects of this element. The first is to create a boilerplate statement of the rights and responsibilities of the customer and subcontractor on a purchase order. This would include (1) right of access, (2) right of verification at source or verification in-house, and (3) right to reject at subsequent operations. The boilerplate paragraph must specifically state that these activities do not absolve the subcontractor from its responsibility to provide acceptable product. An effective means to implement this is to have the legal department devise a paragraph outlining each of these elements. This paragraph should be applied as standard practice to all purchase orders and/or contracts.

The second aspect is the verification of product samples as a means to control the processes used to produce the product. Keep in mind that successful past performance will *not* guarantee future acceptable performance. With this in mind, several approaches can be taken to help ensure that future product will be essentially the same as the product being used to qualify a process. The first method is to perform an audit of the system. This audit should ensure that there is documentation in place outlining exactly what steps are to be followed to reproduce the parts in the same manner as the examples. Secondly, a contract can be written between the subcontractor and the company that outlines the method to be used when producing the product. The incoming parts can be inspected either by sample inspection or 100 percent inspection. Inspection by sampling might be appropriate in this case. This inspection would ensure that the rest of the product is acceptable.

As mentioned earlier in this chapter, this element parallels the contract review element. The only difference is that the contract review element is used when a company accepts a contract to supply a product or service to a customer. In the case of purchasing, a subcontractor provides a product or service to the company. Each of the elements in the contract review element is present in the purchasing element. Both elements result in a legally binding contract; therefore, both should be closely evaluated and executed.

8

PURCHASER-SUPPLIED PRODUCT

Purchaser-supplied product is another of the eighteen elements detailed in both ISO 9001 and 9002. In many companies, though, this element may sound strange and have little meaning. It refers to how parts supplied by a customer are handled and how they are incorporated into the final product for that customer. This is not a common occurrence for much of the manufacturing industry.

An example that might occur is for a company that custom builds dump trucks. Suppose a customer wants his or her truck to be equipped with a specific type of dump bed; he or she obtains the dump bed and provides it to the company for installation in the truck. The dump bed would fall into the category of purchaser-supplied product. This element, then, addresses what will be required in a program for the care and treatment of such product. The standard is specific on what is required; therefore, no applicable ISO 9004 section parallels this element.

ISO 9001

4.7 Purchaser supplied product

The supplier shall establish and maintain procedures for verification, storage and maintenance of purchaser supplied product provided for incorporation into the supplies. Any such product that is lost, damaged or is otherwise unsuitable for use shall be recorded and reported to the purchaser (see 4.16).

NOTE—Verification by the supplier does not absolve the purchaser of the responsibility to provide acceptable product.

Purchaser-Supplied Product

What Is the Intent of This Element?

The intent of this element is for a company to define purchaser-supplied product for its application(s). The standard defines this generally as "product that is supplied by the customer to be included in that customer's final product." This element requires a company to define how purchaser-supplied product should be handled when it is received, as well as how it will address lost, damaged, or nonconforming product.

This element is not applicable to situations where the product is supplied to a company as standard equipment. For example, suppose an automobile company purchases its standard-equipment headlights from a separate company. The company making the headlights may buy a car from a local dealer that happens to contain headlights it has made. In this situation, the purchaser-supplied product element would not apply. For this element to apply, the customer must supply specific product to the company to be added to an individual piece of product that will be returned to the customer.

So what, then, is the difference between the dump truck bed and the headlights? The main difference exists in the intent of supply. In the case of the dump bed (purchaser-supplied product), the customer has supplied a part for inclusion in a specific unit of product for delivery to that same customer. The customer owns the product and is responsible for its acceptability. In the case of the headlights, the customer is also a subcontractor that has provided product to a company. The ownership of the product is transferred from the customer (now the subcontractor) to the company. The company is not bound to use any of this product in its cars, and the customer's purchase of the car was not directly related to the headlight sale.

Beyond defining purchaser-supplied product, the standard also outlines the need for product evaluation. Product should be handled in an appropriate manner to ensure its quality when it is received back by the customer. Purchaser-supplied product should be adequately maintained to prevent damage or deterioration during storage. If the product is lost, damaged, or unsuitable for its intended purpose, this condition should be recorded and reported to the customer. The last part of the element states that responsibility for the acceptability of the product remains with the customer, even if the product is inspected at the company.

What Is the Requirement of This Element?

The requirements of this element are basic to handling any product. The supplier shall establish and maintain procedures that cover the following:

1. The company should verify the acceptability of customer-supplied product.
2. The product should be stored in such a way as to prevent damage or deterioration during the time it is being stored.
3. The maintenance of the product during the time it is being held in inventory should be defined and accomplished so that the product will not deteriorate.

If the product is lost, damaged, or found to be unsuitable while in the charge of the company, this information must be recorded and reported to the customer.

What About the 1994 Version? Purchaser-Supplied Product

This element has been retitled control of customer-supplied product. The only change was to require documented procedures to address this element if applicable.

Implementation Strategy

When the customer has the option to provide product that will be included in his or her final product, it is the responsibility of the company to take due care to verify the acceptability of the product when it is received. The company shall protect the product in storage and make sure it is included in the customer's final product.

For this to occur effectively, a company should inspect the product as it is delivered to ensure that it is suitable for use. At this time, the product is put in a holding area for protection. The product should also be postitively identified as one designated for inclusion into a specific final product. This issue becomes much more sensitive if the product supplied by the purchaser is similar or identical to product held in inventory. If this is the case, a company should isolate the customer-supplied part to make sure it is not accidentally included in the wrong final product.

Beyond proper storage and identification, a method should be developed to ensure that everyone involved with the project knows what parts have been supplied by the customer. Everyone should know where these parts are located and how they will be combined with the rest of the parts. If this works properly, the customer and company can be assured that the customer-supplied parts will be included in the proper product.

Lastly, a reporting system should be established to monitor the parts and report any that are lost, damaged, or found to be unsuitable for the intended purpose. In any of these instances, the company should keep a record of the situation and notify the customer.

This situation is not common for many companies, but it will occur from time to time. It can prove to be a difficult situation if not properly planned and developed. With a properly planned program, some companies find this situation to be both profitable and satisfying for all parties.

9

PRODUCT IDENTIFICATION AND TRACEABILITY

Product identification and traceability is another of the eighteen elements detailed in both ISO 9001 and 9002. This element addresses two distinct and separate issues: (1) product identification, and (2) product traceability. Applicability of this element is not restricted to hard products. In companies dealing with soft products (such as services or information), the specific service or portion of information provided must be identified at all stages. Companies that deal with hard products should have all components easily identified at each stage of operation.

Traceability has classically been divided into two phases: rearward traceability, and forward traceability. In rearward traceability, the main purpose is to verify receipt of actual desired product. In forward traceability, the product from a group or lot of common products can be tracked to the final end user. In many programs, both phases are required when responsibility or interest promotes what is commonly referred to as "cradle to grave" traceability.

ISO 9001

4.8 Product identification and traceability

Where appropriate, the supplier shall establish and maintain procedures for identifying the product from applicable drawings, specifications or other documents, during all stages of production, delivery and installation.

Where, and to the extent that, traceability is a specified requirement, individual product or batches shall have a unique identification. This identification shall be recorded (see 4.16).

ISO 9004

11.2 Material control and traceability

All materials and parts should conform to appropriate specifications and quality standards before being introduced into production. However, in determining the amount of test and/or inspection necessary, consideration should be given to cost impact and the effect that substandard material quality will have on production flow (see clause 9). Materials should be appropriately stored, segregated, handled and protected during production to maintain their suitability. Special consideration should be given to shelf-life and deterioration control. Where in-plant traceability of material is important to quality, appropriate identification should be maintained throughout the production process to ensure traceability to original material identification and quality status (see 11.7 and 16.1.3).

Product Identification and Traceability

What Is the Intent of This Element?

As stated in the introduction, this element has two unique portions that must be addressed separately. The first area is product identification. The intent is for a company to develop a method to identify parts readily and consistently during all stages of production, delivery, and installation. Product identification allows a worker, at any stage of operation, to identify that the appropriate parts have gone into the assembly. The same concept exists where the product is soft, as in the case of a design file or information gathering. In these instances, proper documentation is assembled into a file to confirm that appropriate stress calculations have been used, that the proper medical procedure has been followed, and so forth.

The second area of the standard deals with traceability. The intent of this element is for a company to evaluate the product or service provided to determine if a traceability program is appropriate. If appropriate, further definition regarding the extent and scope is required, along with specific identification of products/services to be traced.

A traceability program is often deemed necessary when a group of products is built using a common material, process, operation, or operator. If a problem exists on one of the parts, it would be to the company's advantage to have the capability to recall all of the parts affected while limiting the scope of the recall. In the case of an automobile manufacturer, it would be desirable to have the capability of identifying the five hundred cars fitted with brake pads coming from a common lot, in the event that one or more of the pads in that lot exhibit an unacceptable failure. The alternative method would be to recall every car produced within a year or recall a given model to look for the bad brake pads. (Another option is to do nothing and hope the failure will not continue to occur).

In many cases, forward traceability is connected to a rearward traceability program. By having both forward and rearward traceability, a company can monitor and track product in the cradle-to-grave concept.

What Is the Requirement of This Element?

The first requirement of this element is that a company establish a program to identify product at all stages of production, delivery, and installation by using applicable drawings, specifications, or other documentation. The second requirement is for the company to determine if and where a traceability program is applicable. If applicable, the program will include a unique identification by individual product or batch that is recorded by the company.

What About the 1994 Version? Product Identification and Traceability

The only change to this element in the 1994 revision is to require documented procedures for identification and traceability of product where applicable. The verbiage has also changed from specifying typical methods of identification to the statement "suitable means."

Implemenation Strategy

One of the simplest methods to implement product identification is to have part numbers physically applied to individual components when the latter are supplied by subcontractors. When this type of activity is not cost-effective (as with nuts, bolts, watch springs, O-rings, or bulk chemicals) identification can be placed on packaging, labels, or storage bins. An alternative method on some bulk items is identification by manufacturers' markings or physical configuration.

Other approaches allow the product to be identified by methods other than applying a part number, including through such characteristics as color, configuration, or size. An example of this would be a 5/16–18 × 1" grade 8 bolt that can be identified by appearance, measurement, and manufacturer's marking on the head. This type of product would not require individual identification for each bolt in the bin.

As a word of caution, though, reliance on physical configuration or visual clues should not be uniformly applied to all products. The concept of product identification is to ensure that product is readily and consistently identifiable. Each company must determine what is appropriate and effective in a given situation.

The first step in implementing the traceability portion of this element is for the company to determine if a traceability program is applicable. The determination may be due to industry or government regulations or simply found to be good business practice. If it is determined that such a program is necessary, it should be carefully planned, controlled, and documented.

The first question that should be answered is what is the motivation behind the traceability program? If the program is being mandated by industry requirements or by the government, the parameters of the program will usually be defined by the standard or specification imposed. Typical examples are the API 14A standard, Department of Transportation regulations, or Federal Aviation Administration regulations. If a company determines on its own that it is a good business practice to maintain traceability on given products, then additional analysis should be performed to define the scope and detail of the program. To help define the scope of a program, a list of questions should be answered. Typically the questions will include the following:

1. *Why are we doing it?* A common reason for traceability would be in a reactive mode: if a part fails, that part could be tracked to the subcontractor who provided the product. In the proactive mode, if a part failed due to one of the traced factors, it would be desirable to know the number and location of all other parts having the same characteristic. The parts could then be recalled, replaced, or analyzed as necessary. At a minimum, the customer can be notified of the possibility of failure.

2. *What products should be included in the program?* The selection of products for inclusion in the program should be made based on an analysis of the need. A specific cost will be associated with each selection; therefore, a conscious choice should be made about the parts to be traced. The selection of parts will be based on factors such as criticality of the part,

usage, a failure mode and effect analysis, or the probability of part failure.

3. *Should the traceability be forward, rearward, or both?* Rearward traceability usually takes into account the part's physical properties, chemical properties, and manufacturer. The main purpose for the rearward method is to provide product traceability to the subcontractor supplying the part. As noted above, this is a very reactive approach to a failed product. If a company decides that related product should be recalled when a failed product is identified, then forward traceability should be included. This approach is proactive in the sense that the company is going to identify the possibility of failure and do something about the problem. Keep in mind that if the failure is due to something other than one of the critical factors being traced, a recall cannot occur.

4. *What are the critical factors to be traced?* Once the parts are identified, an analysis should be conducted to identify what factors need to be traced. The typical factors that are traced include part number, manufacturer, heat lot, and serial number. In some cases, it may be appropriate to trace such factors as (1) the operator who assembled the part, (2) the machine operation used to make the part, (3) the group in which a part was tested, or (4) how a part was transported. Determining the number and type of factors to be traced on a part will define the complexity of the document retrieval system. If one or two factors need to be traced, the document storage and retrieval process becomes a grouping effort in a file cabinet. If three or more factors are traced on a single part, the retrieval process becomes complex and will cost more.

As an example, assume a gear manufacturer found that a part failed due to improper machining on one of seventeen machines making the same product. The improper parts could only be traced if the identity of which of the seventeen machines made each part was a critical factor that was tracked.

5. *What specific documentation needs to be retained, and in what detail?* Once the critical factors are identified, the next step

is to determine what indicators of acceptability are needed (hardness test results, chemical analysis, functional test results, and so forth). A list should be generated identifying what type of documents are required (such as mill test reports, certificates of conformance, or functional test reports). The list should show the necessary detail for these reports. Keep in mind that storing and retrieving documentation is a costly proposition; having only what is needed will help make a program cost-effective.

6. *How long should the documents be stored? How should the documentation be stored? Who should have access to the information, and how should a request for information be processed? Who will be responsible for the documentation?* The longer the time period of storage is, the higher the cost of the program will be. A decision should be reached regarding how records will be stored. Often original documents must be retained, but in other cases, methods such as electronic storage or microfilm can be used. Whatever the method of storage, the documentation must be readily retrievable, and the method for requests, responsibility, and authority must be defined. Unless responsibility is assigned, no one will take control of the program.

The effectiveness of a traceability program will depend on how well the program is planned and carried out. Many traceability programs fail because of lack of planning, lack of discipline, or lack of consistency. A program must be well planned, well documented, and—most importantly—consistently followed. If any of these elements are missing, the program will not be effective.

10

PROCESS CONTROL

Process control is one of the eighteen elements detailed in both ISO 9001 and 9002. The element is specifically directed toward activities that must be accomplished for a product to be generated. Process control will mean many different and unique activities within different companies, depending on the nature of the company's product. In a company that produces a hard product (such as a fabricated part), process control may refer to such activities as cutting material, folding, welding, riveting, grinding, and painting. These activities would be the ones that must be controlled to satisfy this element.

In a company producing a soft product (such as in engineering), the steps by which a problem is solved, documented, and tested would fall under process control as well as design control. In an engineering company, process control would cover such areas as auto-CAD or other drafting standards, the description of the flow of ideas from pencil sketch to completed design document, or the archiving of engineering software.

ISO 9001

4.9 Process control

4.9.1 General

The supplier shall identify and plan the production and, where applicable, installation processes which directly affect quality and shall ensure that these processes are carried out under controlled conditions. Controlled conditions shall include the following:

a) documented work instructions defining the manner of production and installation, where the absence of such instructions would adversely affect quality, use of suitable production and installation equipment, suitable working environment, compliance with reference standards/codes and quality plans;

b) monitoring and control of suitable process and product characteristics during production and installation;

c) the approval of processes and equipment, as appropriate;

d) criteria for workmanship which shall be stipulated, to the greatest practicable extent, in written standards or by means of representative samples.

ISO 9004

10 Quality in production

10.1 Planning for controlled production

10.1.1 Planning of production operations should ensure that these proceed under controlled conditions in the specified manner and sequence. Controlled conditions include appropriate controls for materials, production equipment, processes and procedures, computer software, personnel, and associated supplies, utilities and environments.

Production operations should be specified to the necessary extent by documented work instructions.

Process capability studies should be conducted to determine the potential effectiveness of a process (see 10.2). Provisions for common practice that apply throughout the production facility should be similarly documented and referenced in individual work instructions. These instructions should describe the criteria for determining satisfactory work completion and conformity to specification and standards of good workmanship. Workmanship standards should be defined to the necessary extent by written standards, photographs and/or physical samples.

10.1.2 Verification of the quality status of a product, process, software, material or environment

ISO 9004

should be considered at important points in the production sequence to minimize effects or errors and to maximize yields. The use of control charts and statistical sampling procedures and plans are examples of techniques employed to facilitate production/process control (see also 12.2).

10.1.3 Verifications at each stage should relate directly to finished product specifications or to an internal requirement, as appropriate. If verification of characteristics of the process itself is not physically or economically practical or feasible, then verification of the product should be utilized. In all cases, relationships between in-process controls, their specifications, and final product specifications should be developed, communicated to production and inspection personnel, and documented.

10.1.4 All in-process and final inspections should be planned and specified. Documented test and inspection procedures should be maintained, including the specific equipment to perform such checks and tests, as well as the specified requirement(s) and/or workmanship standard(s) for each quality characteristic to be checked.

10.1.5 Efforts to develop new methods for improving produc-

ISO 9004

tion quality and process capability should be encouraged.

10.2 Process capability

Production processes should be verified as capable of producing in accordance with product specifications. Operations associated with product or process characteristics that can have a significant effect on product quality should be identified. Appropriate control should be established to ensure that these characteristics remain within specification or that appropriate modifications or changes are made.

Verification of production processes should include material, equipment, computer system and software, procedures and personnel.

10.3 Supplies, utilities and environments

Where important to quality characteristics, auxiliary materials and utilities, such as water, compressed air, electric power and chemicals used for processing, should be controlled and verified periodically to ensure uniformity of effect on the process. Where a production environment such as temperature, humidity and cleanliness, is important to product quality, appropriate limits should be specified, controlled and verified.

ISO 9004

11.3 Equipment control and maintenance

All production equipment, including fixed machinery, jigs, fixtures, tooling, templates, patterns and gauges, should be proved for bias and precision prior to use. Special attention should be paid to computers used in controlling processes, and especially the maintenance of the related software (see 13.1). Equipment should be appropriately stored and adequately protected between use, and verified or recalibrated at appropriate intervals to ensure its bias and precision.

A programme of preventive maintenance should be established to ensure continuing process capability. Special attention should be given to equipment characteristics that contribute to key product quality characteristics.

ISO 9001	ISO 9004

4.9.2 Special processes

These are processes, the results of which cannot be fully verified by subsequent inspection and testing of the product and where, for example, processing deficiencies may become apparent only after the product is in use. Accordingly, continuous monitoring and/or compliance with documented procedures is required to ensure that the specified requirements are met. These processes shall be qualified and shall also comply with the requirements of 4.9.1.

Records shall be maintained for qualified processes, equipment and personnel, as appropriate.

11.4 Special processes

Special consideration should be given to production processes in which control is particularly important to product quality. Such special consideration may be required for product characteristics that are not easily or economically measured, for special skills required in their operation or maintenance, or for a product or process the results of which cannot be fully verified by subsequent inspection and test. More frequent verification of special processes should be made to keep a check on

a) the accuracy and variability of equipment used to make or measure product, including settings and adjustments;

b) the skill, capability and knowledge of operators to meet quality requirements;

c) special environments, time, temperature or other factors affecting quality: d) certification records maintained for personnel, processes and equipment, as appropriate.

11.5 Documentation

Work instructions, specifications and drawings should be controlled as specified by the quality system (see 5.3 and 17.2).

ISO 9004

11.6 Process change control

Those responsible for authorization of process changes should be clearly designated and, where necessary, customer approval should be sought. As with design changes, all changes to production tooling or equipment, materials or processes should be documented. The implementation should be covered by defined procedures. A product should be evaluated after any change to verify that the change instituted had the desired effect upon product quality. Any changes in the relationships between process and product characteristics resulting from the change should be documented and appropriately communicated.

General

What Is the Intent of This Element?

This element is the basic premise on which the entire ISO 9000 standard is built: that the processes by which a product is produced should be effectively planned and controlled. This will help ensure that a consistent product of acceptable quality is produced on an ongoing basis. The philosophy of process control has been the focal point for quality improvement since World War II. These principles are evident in such accepted industry practices as process capability studies and statistical process control.

The intent of the standard is that the following three activities be accomplished: (1) all processes used to produce the product that affect quality should be identified, (2) the production should be planned, and (3) the processes should be maintained within a controlled condition. In general, the standard requires that a company know what it takes to make a product, identify the sequences and equipment to be used in production, and assure that these processes are controlled. The outcome of these activities, if properly carried out, will be processes that are predictable, are repeatable, and work at or near their maximum capability.

The general section of the standard states that "the supplier shall identify and plan the production and, where applicable, installation processes which directly affect quality." The term *installation process* is intended to cover the actual activities required for the product to be installed. The disclaimer is that only those installation activities directly affecting quality are to be controlled, provided that the company producing the product is also installing it.

What Is the Requirement of This Element?

The requirement of this element is composed of three distinct activities:

1. The supplier shall identify the processes used in production and, where applicable, the installation of the product.
2. The supplier shall plan the processes and, where applicable, the installation used in production.

3. The supplier shall ensure that these processes are carried out under controlled conditions.

Controlled conditions are defined as follows:

1. Processes shall have documented work instructions defining the manner of production and installation where, in the absence of such instructions, the quality of the product will be adversely affected. Suitable production and installation equipment shall be used, a suitable working environment will be maintained, and the product shall comply to reference standards/codes and quality plans.
2. Process and product characteristics shall be monitored during production or installation.
3. The processes and equipment, as appropriate, shall be approved.
4. Where appropriate, workmanship standards will be provided in written form or by representative samples.

What About the 1994 Version? Process Control

Although there have been some minor wording changes in this element, the most important change is the requirement for "suitable maintenance of equipment to ensure continuing process capability." This would be the maintenance of equipment such as welding machines, furnaces, and automated processing equipment. The standard is not only to require a company to control its processes but also to maintain its processing equipment.

Implementation Strategy

The strategies for implementation of this element will be as varied as the types of processes used to make a product. Irrespective of the production methods or product type, though, the element of control has some common factors. These common factors are the identification of methods and planning sequences used in production.

The identification and planning for process control usually starts with a process flowchart, which is simply a map showing the steps followed to produce a part. This is a common tool used by manufacturing engineers. At each step, the process is defined, the critical control factors are identified, and a method of monitoring the critical factors is devised and documented. This process continues until each product has a process flowchart showing the factors to evaluate, the method of control, and how the results will be verified. The methods and the sequences are improved, and the evaluation starts over again. This is an area where continuous improvement pays big dividends.

With the implementation and completion of this activity, the identification and planning portion of the element has been met. Keep in mind that only the critical factors need to be controlled. The cost of controlling the critical factors of a process is offset by the savings generated by making quality product; the cost generated by controlling noncritical factors in a process will fall directly to the bottom line.

Beyond the common steps of identification and planning, the diversity in product types and production methods will be most apparent in the different approaches taken toward process control for hard and soft products. The second major difference will be between the manufacturing methods of a job shop and an assembly line.

In the case of a soft product, many of the processes used will actually be methods followed by the operator to accomplish an activity. Examples would include a work instruction that details the proper way to address a customer at a bank, how to process a complaint at a car dealership, or the proper method to archive computer files. With many soft products, work instructions and workmanship standards are used to ensure control. Keep in mind that control, as used in this situation, is the means by which product consistency is achieved. The actual product is a service, information, knowledge, or a solution to a problem; the processes will actually be actions or activities taken by the operator. Consistency of activity will produce consistent output. Each operator should be given the necessary information and direction to achieve a consistent output.

In hard products, the manufacturing is typically divided into one of two basic types, job shop manufacturing or assembly-line manufacturing. Each will have unique methods by which the process can be controlled. There is no set way to apply exactly the same controls on all processes operating in all manufacturing environments; if it were possible, it would have been done long ago. Therefore, the professional must become aware of what types of control procedures work in different manufacturing environments. Some of the process control techniques that generally work well in one manufacturing method may not work well in the other. The control effort should focus on the methods used in production rather than on the product itself.

In an assembly line, parts of a final product are mass produced. Companies that make televisions, automobiles, telephones, and similar high-volume products would employ an assembly line. The manufacture and assembly of pieces are systematically arranged and highly repetitive. The key is that the processes are highly repetitive: an assembly-line worker could work for years making the same gear for a transmission, following the same procedure for every gear made. That gear may then go to an assembler who puts it onto a shaft in a precise sequence, which in turn remains the same for every assembly made.

The sequence of events and the procedures on an assembly line are of the utmost importance. They should be well thought out; if followed on properly maintained equipment, these procedures will produce a serviceable part. This type of manufacturing process is very receptive to statistical analysis. By analyzing the product as it comes off of the assembly line (sampling), it is possible to learn something about the process that produced it and to maintain control of the equipment used to produce these parts.

No process will produce identical parts every time. All parts will vary, but if the process is properly controlled, they will vary in a predictable manner. If the variation becomes unpredictable, then something has gone wrong in the process, and the process is said to be out of control. This may occur because the equipment needs repair, the machine setting is wrong, or the base material is substandard.

By inspecting the *part*, it is possible to monitor the *process*. At this point, process control consists of looking at the average quality of the product, not the quality of each piece that comes off of the line. This is much more reliable and much less expensive than trying to inspect each part. The key here is not to segregate the bad product, but to control the processes that create the product, thereby eliminating or at least controlling the making of bad parts.

There are many other things that influence the process control effort in the assembly line environment. For instance, communication from one machine worker to another may be hard to maintain in a large assembly line atmosphere. Also, communication from one department or factory to another may be necessary in large companies. In a situation like this, process control might consist of a formal communication mechanism being established to ensure that efficient communication takes place. The documentation that would be used to demonstrate process control for an assembly line setting would include the following:

1. Process statistical control charts
2. Detailed work instructions
3. Inspection reports
4. Process variable charts
5. First-piece/last-piece inspection reports
6. Written procedures
7. Detailed workmanship standards

The job-shop method produces small numbers of a product and does not have a highly repetitive process. The worker often works on the product from start to finish with limited written work instructions. Companies using job-shop methods include custom machine shops, welding fabrication shops, or repair shops. Typically, the company makes a small quantity of high-dollar products.

Control in this situation depends heavily on the ability of the operators to know how to perform an activity. If an activity is successfully accomplished several times on a product, then control of that process comes in the form of a trained operator following good workmanship practices.

With this type of environment, there is not enough product to obtain statistical data about the process easily; however, it can be done to some extent. The process itself must be monitored and the step-by-step sequence of events witnessed and recorded. Certifying and training of the assembly personnel to code requirements is a must. Inspection of the product must take place at certain stages of construction by certified personnel. If any of the requirements are unfulfilled, the end product could be worthless.

For example, in the manufacture of a boiler, the item must conform to the American Society of Mechanical Engineers Boiler and Pressure-Vessel Code. That code will demand steel alloys of a specific grade. The raw material for the boiler must be traceable back to the foundry, or it cannot be used. Even if every step of the manufacturing process is followed to the letter and all inspections are conducted according to the codes, the boiler is worthless if one of the required processes is missed or if pieces of documentation are missing. If the foundry process cannot be verified, that metal cannot be used. By the same standard, if the welding processes are not followed precisely or the weld process is correct but not accomplished by certified welders, the boiler is worthless. If inspections are done by uncertified personnel, the boiler again is worthless. In this case, process control could be accomplished by writing a detailed manufacturing, inspection, and test plan. This plan would detail what must be accomplished and what requirements must be met at each step.

In the job-shop environment, it is extremely important that every step of the manufacturing process be closely monitored and recorded. This demands a high amount of verification as compared to an assembly line. The documentation that would be used to demonstrate process control in this type of setting includes the following:

1. Manufacturing, inspection, and test plans
2. Detailed work instructions
3. Inspection reports
4. Process variable charts
5. In-process and final inspection and test reports
6. Written procedures
7. Detailed workmanship standards

In summary, the process control effort on the assembly line will use characteristics of the product to determine the control condition of the process. The job-shop quality effort will use direct verification of the process variables or determine the control status of the processes used to produce the part.

Special Processes

What Is the Intent of This Element?

A special process is defined as a process in which the acceptability of the result cannot be verified by subsequent inspection or test. Deficiencies in the process may only become apparent after the product is in use.

What About the 1994 Version? Special Processes

In the 1994 version of the standard, the term *special process* has further been defined by note as: "Such processes requiring pre-qualification of their process capability are frequently referred to as special processes." Typically, this type of process includes plating, welding, heat treating, chemical treating, or similar processes; these processes should be identified. Special process or operator qualification or monitoring may need to be accomplished to ensure control.

The intent of this element is for a company to identify such special processes. This should be accomplished so the process can be studied and a procedure or specification written that will allow for production of a consistently acceptable product. Following evaluation, the company may determine that operators of these processes need formal training or testing to become qualified to control the process.

The intent is for companies to evaluate processes and determine which ones are special. Then, adequate methods to control the process must be developed. Where required, personnel should be trained to operate the process. To ensure that the process is being properly performed, the process variables should be documented.

What Is the Requirement of This Element?

The requirements focus on qualification and monitoring compliance to procedures. Specifically, they include the following:

1. Continuous monitored and/or compliance with documented procedures is required.
2. The process shall be qualified.

3. The processes shall comply with the requirements of section 4.9.1. (These are the process control requirements discussed earlier in this chapter. One of these requirements is for qualified operators.)
4. Appropriate records will be maintained for qualified processes, equipment, and personnel.

Implementation Strategy

Beyond the information given in the ISO 9004 explanation, it is common for the special processes identified in a company to be controlled by means of an industry standard. As noted earlier, examples of this type of process would include welding, plating, flame spray, heat treating, soldering, and chemical curing of adhesives. Most of these processes have an industry standard and/or specification that provides guidance to process qualification and verification.

An example of this type of process is welding. In many companies, the welding process should be considered a special process if the welds are pressure containing or are holding stressed parts. For the process to be effectively verified and controlled, generally a weld procedure specification (WPS) is developed for a given type and thickness of material. A specific welding process under specific conditions is used. The critical variables (taken from the ASME pressure vessel code or the AWS structural code) are listed on the WPS. The weld procedure specification is then followed, and a test weld is made on the appropriate material. The test coupon is then tested to determine if the procedure specification will produce an acceptable weld. The coupon is subjected to non-destructive and destructive tests to determine if it is strong enough to be accepted. If the tests are passed, the results are placed on a form called a procedure qualification record (PQR).

The PQR is the method and equipment qualification; it indicates that an acceptable weld is possible if the settings used for the test are duplicated by a competent welder. The next step is to test a welder to the WPS. If the WPS is followed and the welder is competent, then the rest results should be acceptable. The process is qualified and verified to produce a good weld, and the operator becomes qualified for that WPS. If the test is failed, it can safely be assumed the operator was at fault.

This is a common method by which special processes and operators are qualified. The qualification will not in itself ensure control, but it will help give assurance of control. In a qualified process performed by a qualified operator, the likelihood of control is greater. The ability of the process to produce an accepted output has been proven, and the operator has shown competency in the method. If the procedures are followed, the result should be acceptable product.

In other cases (such as heat treating), additional material can be processed with the product and then destructively tested. In the case of some types of heat-treated material, one or more pieces of each lot of product are randomly selected and tested destructively. The process is controlled and monitored, and product is tested. In many cases, this is considered acceptable for control of the process.

One last word of caution: if inspection, measuring, or test equipment (or some other reporting device) is used to monitor the process to show control, that device should be in good working order and in proper adjustment. The device should have the needed discrimination and be in proper and documented calibration. The process of calibration is a detailed process that will be discussed in Chapter Twelve (Inspection, Measuring, and Test Equipment). Remember, effective control cannot be determined by a device with questionable accuracy.

11

INSPECTION AND TESTING

Inspection and testing constitute another of the eighteen elements detailed in both ISO 9001 and 9002. Contrary to the present philosophy of many companies today, *quality cannot be inspected into a part. It must be designed and built into the part.* If this statement is true, though, then why would a quality standard address the role of inspection? The answer is that the main role of inspection under this philosophy is one of verification, validation, and data gathering. It is not the traditional role of policeman sorting the good from the bad.

In the traditional role, quality is maintained postmortem. A bad part is produced, the inspector finds it, and a "death certificate" (rejection slip) is filled out and placed in a file with many other death certificates. The inspector has completed his or her job, and no other steps are taken to prevent the recurrence of the defect. In this type of situation, inspection is reactive to defective products being produced. In the business environment of the 1990s, though, this reactive approach has been the fatal blow to many companies.

If inspection is utilized, it should be to gather data for a proactive approach to problem solving. Not only should the inspection be used to identify nonconforming product, it should be used to gather the data needed to identify the root cause of the problem. Inspection should be used to ascertain and monitor the remedy to the cause. This approach is more suited to a quality engineering approach.

Inspection is traditionally used in one or more of the following areas: (1) receiving inspection, (2) in-process inspection, or (3) final inspection. The ISO 9001 standard is a process-oriented standard that allows for inspection to be used as one of several methods to verify product. In the standard the term *verification* can be interchanged with the word *inspection* in most areas.

What About the 1994 Version? Inspection and Testing

ISO/DIS 9001 requires that the quality plan or documented procedures define "the required inspection and testing and the records to be established. . . ." The note regarding the determination of the nature and amount of receiving inspection has been removed as a note and added as a section in the element.

The inspection authority responsible for the release of product must now be identified in the records.

ISO 9001

4.10 Inspection and testing

4.10.1 Receiving inspection and testing

4.10.1.1 The supplier shall ensure that incoming product is not used or processed (except in the circumstances described in 4.10.1.2) until it has been inspected or otherwise verified as conforming to specified requirements. Verification shall be in accordance with the quality plan or documented procedures.

4.10.1.2 Where incoming product is released for urgent production purposes, it shall be positively identified and recorded (see 4.16) in order to permit immediate recall and replacement in the event of nonconformance to specified requirements.

NOTE—In determining the amount and nature of receiving inspection, consideration should be given to the control exercised at source and documented evidence of quality conformance provided.

ISO 9004

12 Product verification

12.1 Incoming materials and parts

The method used to ensure quality of purchased materials, component parts and assemblies that are received into the production facility will depend on the importance of the item to quality, the state of control and information available from the supplier and impact on costs (see clause 9, in particular sub-clauses 9.7 and 9.8).

ISO 9001

4.10.2 In-processing inspection and testing

The supplier shall

a) inspect, test and identify product as required by the quality plan or documented procedures;

b) establish product conformance to specified requirements by use of process monitoring and control methods;

c) hold product until the required inspection and tests have been completed or necessary reports have been received and verified except when product is released under positive recall procedures (see 4.10.1). Release under positive recall procedures shall not preclude the activities outlined in 4.102.a);

d) identify nonconforming product.

ISO 9004

12.2 In-process inspections

Inspections or tests should be considered at appropriate points in the process to verify conformity. Location and frequency will depend on the importance of the characteristics and ease of verification at the stage of production. In general, verification should be made as close as possible to the point of production of the feature of characteristic.

Verifications may include the following checks:

a) set-up and first piece inspection;

b) inspection or test by machine operator;

c) automatic inspection or test;

d) fixed inspection stations at intervals through the process;

e) patrol inspection by inspectors monitoring specified operations.

ISO 9001

4.10.3 Final inspection and testing

The quality plan or documented procedures for final inspection and testing shall require that all specified inspection and tests, including those specified either on receipt of product or in-process, have been carried out and that the data meets specified requirements. The supplier shall carry out all final inspection and testing in accordance with the quality plan or documented procedures to complete the evidence of conformance of the finished product to the specified requirements.

No product shall be dispatched until all the activities specified in the quality plan or documented procedures have been satisfactorily completed and the associated data and documentation is available and authorized.

4.10.4 Inspection and test records

The supplier shall establish and maintain records which give evidence that the product has passed inspection and/or test with defined acceptance criteria (see 4.16).

ISO 9004

12.3 Completed product

To augment inspections and tests made during production, two forms of final verification of completed product are available. Either or both of the following may be used, as appropriate:

a) Acceptance inspections or tests may be used to ensure that items or lots produced have met performance and other quality requirements. Reference may be made to the purchase order to verify that product to be shipped agrees in type and quantity. Examples include screening (100% of items), lot sampling and continuous sampling.

b) Product quality auditing of sample units selected as representative of completed production lots may be either continuous or periodic. Acceptance inspection and product quality auditing may be used to provide rapid feedback for corrective action of product and process. Deficiencies or deviations should be reported, and reworked or repaired. Modified products should be re-inspected or retested.

Receiving Inspection and Testing

What Is the Intent of This Element?

The intent of this element is for the supplier to ensure that incoming products are not used or processed unless they have been inspected or otherwise verified. As discussed in Chapter Seven with regard to purchasing, the methods used to verify product vary widely but include inspection. Because receiving inspection is so widely used in manufacturing today, this method to verify the product is written into the ISO 9001, 9002, and 9003 standards.

If the product is released for urgent manufacturing before verification has occurred, a means must be developed to recall product that is found to be nonconforming. In some companies, a sample is taken of large batches of product as they are received. The material is released to manufacturing as the sample is tested. If the test shows the product is nonconforming, then all finished goods made from this nonconforming product must be recalled for repair, rework, or disposal. This recall system should be in place whenever the product can be released before testing is complete.

Receiving inspection assures management that items received from subcontractors meet requirements of the purchase order. But if this was all a receiving inspector accomplished, soon the inspector could ruin a company. Why? Because a purchase order is just a way of telling a subcontractor what materials, drawings, specifications, and quantities of parts a company needs. Sometimes communication within a company breaks down, and a purchase order may provide a subcontractor with incorrect information. A receiving inspector may see that parts are correct according to the purchase order, but the parts may not be usable for correct production. They could be made from the wrong drawing revision, improper material or heat treatment, or other possible mistakes, all resulting from information not reflected on the purchase order. The receiving inspector must be alert to these potential errors.

The receiving inspector may use a sample of a lot of product to reduce inspection costs. A sampling plan or procedure is a statistical method used to inspect a sample from the lot of product. From this sample, the receiving inspector makes reasonable assumptions regarding lot quality. Typical receiving inspection responsibilities include the following:

1. Parts-count verification
2. Material identification
3. Mechanical dimensions within tolerance
4. Physical properties (hardness, heat treatment)
5. Paint (color, thickness, coverage)
6. Identification (lot number or serial number)
7. Fit (assembly compatibility)
8. Correct threads
9. Drawing revision

Source inspection represents the eyes and ears of a company in its subcontractor's shop. It should be viewed as a method of performing receiving inspection. Problems are always easier to correct when they are detected in a subcontractor's shop rather than when the parts are really needed. Many companies therefore emphasize source inspection as a cost-saving method used to improve shipment schedules. No matter where the product is evaluated and verified, the key issue is the verification; keep in mind that inspection is an expensive method to accomplish this task.

What Is the Requirement of This Element?

This element requires a company to verify that product conforms to specifications before it is used or processed. The verification can take the form of receiving inspection and shall be in accordance with the quality plan or documented procedures.

A second requirement of this element relates to product released for use or processing before the results of the verification process are known. If this activity occurs, a method of positive recall must be in place. If the verification process shows the product is not accepted, then product that has been processed must be recalled.

A note included at the bottom of this section states that a method for determining the amount and type of receiving inspection should be dependent on the amount of control at the source and the documented evidence of quality conformance provided. In other words, if the subcontractor's processes are controlled and documented, receiving inspection of the product may not be needed.

Implementation Strategies

The strategies that can be used to implement this section involve documenting the inspection that is taking place in a company. Most companies have some sort of verification for incoming product. For these companies, the process should be formalized and documented in a procedure. This procedure should provide direction as to the parameters of the program, which should include the following:

1. Define the responsibility for the receiving inspection program.
2. Assign authority for conducting the inspection.
3. Determine what product will be inspected.
4. Define to what extent each part will be inspected.
5. Define how the results of the inspection will be documented.
6. Define when a quality plan will be used in place of an inspection procedure.

Once the receiving inspection method is developed and documented, a choice must be made if material will be released for urgent use before verification is accomplished. If so, a method of positive identification and forward tracking must be in place and followed. If the verification determines the product is not in conformance with the requirements, the product must be recalled and removed from service.

For this program to work, a positive means of tracking must be in place. For a job shop, this tracking system could include a file listing the part number, serial number, and location used for each of the parts in question. If the verification shows the product is out of compliance, the file would show exactly where the parts were used. In an assembly line environment, the questionable parts might be used in assemblies that are numbered sequentially. The parts would be further processed into final assemblies and shipped to the customer. If the parts in question are not accepted, then either the assemblies will go through a general recall or replacement parts will be provided to the customer under warranty. In chemical processing, batch numbers are closely monitored for the reagents included in the batch; in many situations, the final product is isolated until all the testing is complete. Whatever method is used, the important part is that the customer receives a final product that matches the quality specified in the contract.

This requirement has taken many companies by surprise. Some companies have never considered a method of positive identification for recall of product prior to receipt of acceptance results. With these companies, it may be more effective to exempt the possibility from the scope of operations. This can be accomplished by including a simple statement in the appropriate procedure that product will not be released until it has been positively verified. But it is important not to say that product will not be released if in fact it is a common practice. Either release and track the product, or do not allow release.

In-Process Inspection and Testing

What Is the Intent of This Element?

In-process inspection and testing ensures quality during fabrication or assembly. The intent of in-process inspection is to guarantee that if the assembly shop is consistently supplied with good parts from the supplier, the shop will fabricate quality parts or produce quality assemblies. In-process inspection is conducted differently depending on the type of manufacturing method the shop utilizes (job shop or assembly line).

Job shops are used for such low-volume (and usually high-cost) manufacturing as production of offshore oil drilling platforms or supercomputers. Assembly lines are associated with such high-volume (and usually low-cost) manufactured goods as automobiles or microchips. Each manufacturing approach has unique procedures and needs for in-process inspection.

In-Process Inspection and Testing (Job Shop)

An in-process inspector in a job shop ensures that the work performed is in accordance with the correct drawing and/or procedure, and that it is accomplished by qualified individuals. The quality effort in a job shop concentrates on the process used to make the product. If the process was performed by a qualified person following qualified procedures, the product will meet quality standards in most cases. Typical in-process inspection responsibilities are as follows:

1. Ensure that the quality plan is followed and that all inspections are performed as requested by the customer
2. Ensure that defined hold points are performed
3. Ensure that the customer is aware of future hold points and that the parts meet company inspection requirements before the customer's inspection is performed
4. Ensure that correct drawings are used in the shop and that obsolete drawings are removed from the point of issue
5. Determine that correct methods are followed and that current procedures are available at each work station
6. Verify that individuals performing special processes are qualified to do so
7. Verify that equipment and gauges are calibrated
8. Verify that the shop meets quality plan requirements
9. Verify that the individual craftsmen sign their work, when required

In-Process Inspection (Assembly Line)

An assembly line in-process inspector performs either sampling on the line or 100 percent inspection as a checker. Assembly line inspection concentrates on the product characteristics rather than the process variables. A determination can be made as to whether the process is in or out of control by monitoring the product characteristics.

Assembly lines are designed by industrial engineers and quality engineers to ensure that each step on a manufacturing line is easy, fast, and able to maintain good quality. This means that time is spent before production starts to develop quality assembly methods. The parts may be redesigned to make assembly easier, or to prevent handling or assembly damage. Great care is taken to divide each assembly step into a task that can be easily performed by a worker on the line.

With all this care to make the assembly easy while maintaining good quality, what does the in-process inspector do? Many times he or she is a roving inspector, responsible for monitoring the line for problems that may affect quality. This is also an activity that can be delegated to the worker producing the parts. Typical in-process inspection responsibilities include the following:

1. Inspect sample parts from the assembly line
2. Evaluate the product performance during assembly
3. Verify that individuals are using correct assembly techniques
4. Evaluate general appearance of product
5. Evaluate repairs of in-process damage to parts
6. Ensure that design changes are incorporated on assembly line
7. Sample packaging for completeness
8. Verify calibration of test equipment

As noted above, the product is monitored so the inspector can make judgments about the process used to produce it. The main difference in in-process inspection on assembly lines and in job shops is the focus or use of the information. In the job shop, information about the product comes from direct measurement of the process variables and from product inspection. Direct inspection of the product is used as a means to ensure that the latter is accepted. In the assembly line, characteristics of the product are measured to monitor the process by which it was manufactured. Direct product inspection is used to determine if the process is operating within accepted parameters and if it should be adjusted. Acceptability of the product is based on the performance of the process, rather than on direct measurements. This is the basis for statistical process control.

What Is the Requirement of This Element?

This section of the element states four requirements for the product as it is being built:

1. Parts will be tested, inspected, and identified as required by a test plan or a procedure.
2. Process monitoring and control methods will be used to determine if product is accepted.
3. The product will be held until the requirements are met and the product is properly documented, unless a positive recall program is devised.
4. All nonconforming product shall be identified.

Implementation Strategy

The first decision that should be made is what department will have the responsibility of this function. Two schools of thought exist about who should have responsibility. The first proposes that inspection should be a quality control function. With this school of thought, the inspector has special training or skills that enable him or her to find and resolve the root causes of nonconforming products. He or she inspects the product and the paperwork at predetermined hold points; the product is moved to the next station only after the inspector has signed it off. Additionally, the inspector may be present to witness processes or conduct tests. These witness points will be signed off after successful performance. This approach, which is the most common, treats the inspector as a second set of eyes viewing the product objectively and without bias.

The downside to this approach is the inspector may become the QC cop, all but carrying a badge and gun to shoot the worker if rejected product is identified. In one company, a sign hung in the office of the inspection department that said "It is our job to find your mistakes." This approach of the inspector looking over the worker's shoulder fosters a class structure among the work force. An atmosphere of "us versus them" is created. Also, quality is always seen as someone else's responsibility in this scenario. The worker may not feel responsible for the quality of the product, since it has to be "bought off" by the quality control department. No one has sole responsibility for quality, and therefore quality suffers.

The second school of thought is to turn the in-process inspection over to the workers who build the product. Under this approach, the workers are provided with (or might even develop) a quality plan outlining what inspections should be accomplished and at what stage they must take place. Some companies will not allow the worker who built the product to make the inspection; under this approach one of the other workers, a lead man or shop foreman, makes the inspection. Some companies will allow a worker to build, inspect, and accept the product.

The attitude under this philosophy is that if the worker can be trusted to produce the part, he or she should be trusted to accept it. This way the worker becomes responsible for the total quality.

No one else is to blame when the quality is low, and no one else is to be praised when the quality is high. This approach has worked in certified programs as long as operations proceed under controlled conditions. The worker must be provided with appropriate information on which to base decisions, and the functionality of the program be verified by audit.

Once the decision is made regarding who will direct the effort, a quality plan should be developed identifying the inspections to be performed. Hold points are identified, and the acceptance criteria at each are specified along with the method for documentation of the inspection. The quality plan does not necessarily have to be a document titled as such. Identification, acceptance criteria, and hold points may be best documented in a work order router, a checklist, or inspection sheet. The intent is that appropriate areas are addressed effectively to show that there has been some plan established for in-process quality. A procedure should be written providing guidance on methods by which inspected product will be handled, documented, and identified. It also should specify how to process all product, whether accepted or rejected. This program should promote quality of the product, expedite quality improvement, and reduce the probability of nonconforming product reaching the customer.

Final Inspection and Testing

What Is the Intent of This Element?

Final inspection for many companies is the catch-all where the parts and the assembly process can be verified and accepted. The quality plan, test schedule, or test procedure should outline the extent of and the responsibility for final inspection and testing.

In other shops, this activity is viewed as the point for assembling the documentation to prove a product was built using the correct process. One step in this approach is to validate or certify that a quality plan has been followed. This ensures that each manufacturing step has been completed properly and that the correct drawings and procedures are followed by qualified individuals. Final inspection verifies that all the parts requiring certifications or documentation have been checked and that the paperwork is available and accurate.

The final inspection should include a review of plan-and-process sheets to assure the company that all steps were correctly performed. Final inspection should document that all hold points have been satisfied and that customer requirements were properly performed. Typical responsibilities of the final inspector are as follows:

1. Review signed process sheets
2. Verify materials used
3. Inspect the final coating or finish
4. Evaluate completeness of documentation provided to the customer
5. Coordinate final tests with the customer
6. Inspect shipping containers
7. Inspect spare parts

What Is the Requirement of This Element?

The requirements of this element center around the quality plan and/or the inspection procedure. They will focus on the product as well as the documentation of the process used to build it. Both areas will carry the same weight and will include the following requirements:

1. Assure that all the specified inspection and tests have been performed (this will include all receiving and in-process inspections and should include verification of paperwork for these inspections and/or tests)
2. Verify that all final tests and inspections specified in the quality plan and/or inspection procedure were conducted and properly documented
3. Ensure that product is not dispatched until all the required tests and inspections have been satisfactorily completed, documented, and authorized

Implementation Strategy

The first step is to assign responsibility for final inspection. The same arguments that were discussed in the in-process inspection section can be made here. Some successfully operating certified programs have assigned the final inspection activities to the manufacturing department, with audits performed by quality control. More traditional certified programs assign the final inspection activities solely to the quality control department. The decision of assigning responsibility should be made by upper management.

Final inspection should be conducted in accordance with the quality plan for a product or by following a final inspection procedure. This documentation will outline the focus for the inspection. One focus is to perform 100 percent screening as a last-ditch effort to remove as much nonconforming product as can be found. This approach is widely accepted as being no more than 80 percent effective. This means that for every eight parts identified as being nonconforming, two others were inspected and accepted as good when they were actually nonconforming. These are not very good odds.

The second approach is to inspect sample parts to make a value judgment on the entire lot based on the sample. More time can be spent looking over fewer parts. The acceptability of the sample is a statistically accurate reflection of the acceptability of the entire lot. This is a form of statistical quality control called *lot sampling*. In many companies, this is the method of accepting or rejecting final product. With this method, however, a company is resigning itself to the fact that nonconforming product will be sent to the customer.

Inspection and Test Records

What Is the Intent of This Element?

The intent of this element is simply for the supplier to provide documented evidence that the inspection process has been completed. This should also verify that all tests were conducted and the results compared against acceptance criteria. The purpose of this documentation is to demonstrate that the procedures have been followed.

What Is the Requirement of This Element?

The element requires that the supplier maintain documentation proving that the product passed the inspection and test. The inspection and test must have defined acceptance criteria.

Implementation Strategy

The company should identify the method used to retain the inspection test records when a product is finally accepted and/or tested. One method is for the quality plan to outline the test, give the acceptance criteria, and have a place where the results can be documented. This document should be retained so that it may be retrieved as needed. A second method of implementation is for a company to produce a test report file (portfolio or pedigree) that is retained by the supplier. This file would include such information as the test acceptance criteria, test results, certificates, and documentation provided with the parts that make up the final assembly. Decisions specifying the documentation that must be retained should be made based on customer and/or government requirements.

Most standards have been developed in the manufacturing industry. Inspection and testing have typically meant the use of instrumentation or special skills to assess the physical conformance of product to design criteria or specifications. For many soft products, the first response might be that this section does not apply; how would this work in a credit card company, the medical profession, an insurance company, or any other type of service organization? This element is applicable, though, and very well established in most of these types of operations. The challenging part is to determine correctly what activity actually serves as the inspection and test function.

Consider the function of a customer service department for any type of product, either hard or soft. The actual product produced by this department is a service to the customer. Many times, when a customer calls in on the telephone, a recorded message is presented to the customer before the service representative answers. The message states that the call may be monitored by supervisory personnel, or it may be recorded. This monitoring activity is one way to conduct in-process inspection.

The medical profession has established methods of conducting receiving, in-process, and final inspection and testing. When a patient is scheduled for an operation, all manner of criteria must be inspected (blood pressure, heart rate, general physical condition, and so on) before the activity proceeds. In most cases, the physician has secured a second opinion (that is, performed a test) before deciding to conduct the operation. After the operation, the physician will schedule a series of follow-up visits to monitor the progress of the operation against expected results; before closing the case, the patient must return for a final visit. These activities meet the basic intent of the standard regarding receiving, in-process, and final inspection and testing.

12

INSPECTION, MEASURING, AND TEST EQUIPMENT

Inspection, measuring, and test equipment represent one of the eighteen elements detailed in both ISO 9001 and ISO 9002. In most types of manufacturing, specialized precision measuring instrumentation will be used to gauge the acceptability of the product. This instrumentation could range from a tape measure for inspecting the length of an I-beam to a device that measures the change in electrical potential in microvolts. For each type of inspection, measuring, and test equipment, a method must be identified to ensure that the measurements are accurate. The calibrated accuracy of the gauge should be determined by the accuracy required by the measurements. This accuracy is established and measured through a calibration program.

Many companies do not understand or acknowledge the need for a calibration program. Various arguments are made for not having calibrated test equipment (for example, "It's close enough," or "These measurements are not that critical"), but most of these reasons are not true. Usually when inspection, measuring, and test equipment is not calibrated, it can be traced to a lack of understanding of a calibration program and/or a lack of discipline within an organization.

ISO 9001

4.11 Inspection, measuring and test equipment

The supplier shall control, calibrate and maintain inspection, measuring and test equipment, whether owned by the supplier, on loan, or provided by the purchaser, to demonstrate the conformance of product to the specified requirements. Equipment shall be used in a manner which ensures that measurement uncertainty is known and is consistent with the required measurement capability.

The supplier shall

a) Identify the measurements to be made, the accuracy required and select the appropriate inspection, measuring and test equipment;

b) identify, calibrate and adjust all inspection, measuring and test equipment and devices that can affect product quality at prescribed intervals, or prior to use, against certified equipment having a known valid relationship to nationally recognized standards—where no such standards exist, the basis used for calibration shall be documented;

c) establish, document and maintain calibration procedures, including details of equipment type, identification number, location, frequency of checks, check method, acceptance criteria and

ISO 9004

13 Control of measuring and test equipment

13.1 Measurement control

Sufficient control should be maintained over all measurement systems used in the development, manufacture, installation and servicing of a product to provide confidence in decisions or actions based on measurement data. Control should be exercised over gauges, instruments, sensors, special test equipment and related computer software. In addition, manufacturing jigs, fixtures and process instrumentation that can affect the specified characteristics of a product, process or service should be suitably controlled (see 11.3). Procedures should be established to monitor and maintain the measurement process itself under statistical control, including equipment, procedures and operator skills. Measurement error should be compared with requirements and appropriate action taken when precision and/or bias requirements are not achieved.

13.2 Elements of control

The control of measuring and test equipment and test methods should include the following factors, as appropriate:

a) Correct, specification and acquisition, including range, bias, precision, robustness and dura-

ISO 9001

the action to be taken when results are unsatisfactory;

d) ensure that the inspection, measuring and test equipment is capable of the accuracy and precision necessary;

e) identify inspection, measuring and test equipment, with a suitable indicator or approved identification record to show the calibration status;

f) maintain calibration records for inspection, measuring and test equipment (see 4.16);

g) assess and document the validity of previous inspection and test results when inspection, measuring and test equipment is found to be out of calibration;

h) ensure that the environ mental conditions are suitable for the calibrations, inspections, measurements and tests being carried out;

i) ensure that the handling, preservation and storage of inspection, measuring and test equipment is such that the accuracy and fitness for use is maintained;

j) safeguard inspection, measuring and test facilities, including both test hardware and test software, from adjustments which would invalidate the calibration setting.

Where test hardware (e.g. jigs, fixtures, templates, patterns) or

ISO 9004

bility under specified environmental conditions for the intended service.

b) Initial calibration prior to first use in order to validate the required bias and precision; the software, and procedures controlling automatic test equipment, should also be tested.

c) Periodic recall for adjustment, repair and recalibration, considering manufacturer's specification, the results of prior calibration, the method and extent of use, to maintain the required accuracy in use.

d) Documentary evidence covering identification of instruments, frequency of re-calibration, calibration status, and procedures for recall, handling and storage, adjustment, repair, calibration, installation and use.

e) Traceability to reference standards of known accuracy and stability, preferably to national or international standards, or, in industries or products where such do not exist, to specially developed criteria.

13.3 Supplier measurement controls

The control of measuring and test equipment and procedures extend to all suppliers furnishing goods and services.

ISO 9001

test software is used as suitable forms of inspection, they shall be checked to prove that they are capable of verifying the acceptability of product prior to release for use during production and installation and shall be rechecked at prescribed intervals. The supplier shall establish the extent and frequency of such checks and shall maintain records as evidence of control (see 4.16). Measurement design data shall be made available, when required by the purchaser or his representative, for verification that it is functionally adequate.

ISO 9004

13.4 Corrective action

Where measuring processes are found to be out of control or where measuring and test equipment is found to be outside the required calibration limits, corrective action is necessary. Evaluation should be made to determine the effects on completed work and to what extent reprocessing, retesting, recalibration or complete rejection may be necessary. In addition, investigation of cause is important in order to avoid recurrence. This may include review of calibration methods and frequency, training, and adequacy of test equipment.

13.5 Outside testing

The facilities of outside organizations may be used for measurement, testing or calibration services to avoid costly duplication or additional investment, provided that the requirements given in 13.2 and 13.4 are satisfied.

Inspection, Measuring, and Test Equipment

What Is the Intent of This Element?

This element directs a company to establish a program to validate inspection, measuring, and test equipment. The program should determine if the equipment is properly identified, maintained, selected, and calibrated. This standard goes well beyond the traditional approach of using any measuring equipment at hand without knowing if its use is adequate, accurate, repeatable, or calibrated.

The standard was written to provide guidance in developing an acceptable calibration program that meets the ten listed elements of control. It goes beyond inspection, measuring, and test equipment and includes such items as jigs, fixtures, templates, patterns, or test software. Calibration is required on this type of equipment when used as a suitable form of inspection in the production and assessment of the product.

What Is the Requirement of This Element?

The requirements of this element are very specific. The company must control, calibrate, and maintain inspection, measuring, and test equipment, regardless of ownership. It is the *user's* responsibility to ensure that equipment is calibrated.

The standard is specific in identifying ten requirements that must be met for the calibration program to be accepted. The requirement of calibration should also cover test software, fixtures, and jigs where they are used as suitable forms of inspection. These should be verified at appropriate intervals determined by the company. The extent and frequency of checks should be documented.

What About the 1994 Version? Inspection, Measuring, and Test Equipment

With exception of the added requirement for documented procedures to support this element, the only change was to specify "test software" in the body of this element.

Implementation Strategy

This is one element where the implementation strategy is restricted by the standard. The traditional gauge calibration program is one of the more effective methods to meet the intent and requirement of this standard.

A word of warning: *sending the inspection, measuring, and test equipment to a calibration lab and asking them to calibrate it without providing specific information will not meet the requirement of the standard.* This, however, does not mean that a calibration lab cannot be used. What it does mean is that the lab must be directed to calibrate the equipment according to a specific standard or procedure and to a specified acceptance criteria. The key to an acceptable calibration program is for the company to make the decisions about how to direct the calibration process.

It is not acceptable to allow the calibration lab to decide the procedure or standard for calibrating the equipment. The lab should not decide against what acceptance criteria the gauge should be checked, nor should it determine how the equipment is used or the accuracy requirement for each piece of equipment. This information is vital for proper equipment calibration and must be provided by the company. Without specific direction, a calibration lab might calibrate a gauge to $\pm$ 0.001 inch rather than the required $\pm$ 0.00001 inch calibration.

To address this element effectively, a company must take a deliberate approach to the calibration program. The difficult aspect in implementing this element is identifying exactly which pieces of equipment should be included in this program and which pieces, if any, can be excluded. In addition, the extent of calibration with regard to intended use must be determined. For a large number of organizations, the simplest approach is to include all pieces of inspection, measuring, and test equipment. This is an approach that, while assuring that any gauge looked at during an audit will be calibrated, will be very costly. The expense of including equipment in the calibration program, however, is not the determining factor. Each company must determine what applies to its program; the standard states that applicable equipment is that which is used "to demonstrate the conformance of product to the specified requirements," as well as "devices that can affect product quality." The obvious conclusion would be that all equipment is applicable. One proven definition, however, is to include only those pieces of equipment that are used to accept, calibrate, or verify the calibration of product.

In manufacturing, a micrometer may be used to verify rough-cut dimensions prior to further operations. This gives a ballpark feel of product consistency. Later in production, the product will receive a final inspection to verify conformance to specification and product acceptance. Because its activity is merely performed as a manufacturing aid during processing, in this case the micrometer could be excluded from the calibration program.

In another application, a voltmeter may be used to identify simply if voltage is present in a wire, instead of how high it is. In this case, the criteria for calibration is whether the item will detect voltage at the approximate amplitude that is expected in the wire. Again, the calibration accuracy of the equipment must be applicable for the intended use. This same theory can be used on many other types of measurement devices.

The important factor is that the applicability of equipment in the calibration program is readily identifiable and justifiable. Exactly what equipment is included in the program must be obvious and explainable by anyone using the equipment. The reasons for including or excluding equipment must also be obvious and explainable, and the user should be able to describe in which cases and for what purposes the equipment may be used. In the case of equipment used for preliminary checks and on/off situations, it should be appropriately identified. This can be accomplished by placing a sticker on each piece of equipment that says, "Not to be used for acceptance, calibration, or to verify calibration."

Along with the requirements of the standard, good business sense should be used when deciding what equipment to include in the calibration program. Each company should determine the amount of risk it is willing to take regarding continued production of unacceptable materials due to faulty measuring equipment.

For those gauges that are used for product acceptance or calibration of product, a program should be developed to control the gauges, maintain their calibration, and keep them in good working order. This shall be accomplished on gauges even if they are on loan or owned by the customer.

The standard specifies ten requirements that shall be met for a program to be accepted. The remainder of this section will discuss methods that have been used in certified programs to meet these requirements.

1. The company shall determine the accuracy needed for a measurement and select equipment that will have at least that accuracy.

Industry standards require equipment to have an accuracy that is four to ten times the required specification accuracy of the measurement to be taken. In other words, if a part is to be measured to ± 0.003 inches, the measurement instrument should be accurate from ± 0.0007 to ± 0.0003 inches. A part having a required inspection accuracy of ± 0.004 inches would require an inspection instrument having the required accuracy of ± 0.001 to ± 0.0004 inches. The inspector must know the calibrated accuracy of the instrumentation and select the proper tool for the job.

2. Identify, adjust, and calibrate all inspection, measuring, and test equipment that can affect quality. This should occur at designated intervals or before use. The calibration will be against a standard that is traceable to a national standard. If no national standard is used, a decision must be made as to how the calibration will be conducted. This decision should be documented as the basis for future calibration.

This requirement is for a company to identify each piece of equipment individually so it can be easily identified. This can be accomplished by permanently placing a unique serial number or identification number on the tool; an engraved number works well. The next step is to decide at what intervals the calibrations should occur. In one certified program, the intervals were listed as "one year or fifty uses, whichever comes first." This system works well but requires a tracking system that will identify how often a gauge has been used. The tracking system should also identify when the calibration is due.

The standard for the calibration of the gauges should be traceable to a national standard. This means that the certificate of calibration should have the serial/identification number of the standard used to check the calibration of the gauge. The certificate of calibration for the listed standard should also show the serial/identification number of the standard (called a transfer standard) used to check its calibration. If the certification trail were followed from transfer standard to transfer standard, the result would be that the national standard was the first standard in the list. This is what is meant by traceability.

In some cases, no national standard exists. In these instances a company should decide what standard will be appropriate to check the equipment against. In one company that uses radioactive sources to check the density of a fluid in a pipe, the instrumentation is checked with distilled water. This was accepted because the density of distilled water was shown to vary so little that the accuracy of the instrument was four to ten times more accurate than the requirement of the product.

3. The company should develop a documented procedure covering the calibration of all inspection and test equipment. This procedure should include the following as a minimum:
   a. The equipment type
   b. Identification or serial number
   c. Where the equipment is located
   d. How often the equipment is checked for calibration
   e. The method used to check calibration
   f. Definition of the acceptance criteria for each piece of equipment
   g. Actions to be taken when a gauge cannot meet the acceptance criteria

In many cases, the documented procedure can be a spreadsheet covering equipment types or groupings rather than individual pieces. This procedure shall list the specific procedure or industry standard to be followed for the equipment calibration, as well as what to do with equipment that is out of calibration. In one company, this procedure is a spreadsheet that lists a class of equipment (for example, set threaded plug gauge or paint mill thickness tester), details the procedure to follow, and lists the acceptance criteria for each class of equipment. The spreadsheet also identifies the frequency of the calibration and describes the action to take if the equipment is out of calibration.

This sheet covers requirements of all items listed above except for items (b) and (c) (see Appendix II). The company meets these requirements by maintaining a computer file and a paper file that contain all the pertinent information for each piece of calibrated equipment. This file will contain information or usage, specific location, serial number, type, size, standard used for calibration, calibration date, and accuracy. When the file and the sheet are viewed together, all the requirements are met.

4. Decide if the inspection, measuring, and test equipment have the proper accuracy for the measurements that are to be taken with the equipment.

As discussed earlier, the inspector should ensure that instrumentation selected for a measurement is capable of an accuracy of four to ten times the required measurement accuracy. If desired, this can be stated in the procedure covering inspection.

5. The equipment must be identified to show the calibration status.

An easy method is to apply a sticker to the equipment showing when the next calibration is due or if the equipment is out of calibration. The sticker can indicate if the equipment does or does not require calibration before use. In any case, the status of inspection, measuring, and test equipment should be easily identifiable. In one certified program, this status was maintained on a computer file and not shown on the equipment (threaded ring and plug gauges). This was acceptable because the company had in excess of three thousand gauges, and the computer file had to be accessed to find the location of any individual gauge. The calibration information was displayed along with the location when equipment was requested.

6. Maintain the calibration records.

When a gauge is calibrated, a certificate of calibration should accompany the equipment from the lab performing the calibration. This certificate should contain (1) the name and signature of the person performing the calibration, (2) the procedure or specification used to identify how the calibration was performed, (3) the acceptance criteria used, (4) the actual readings encountered, (5) the serial/identification number of the transfer standard used, (6) indication of whether the equipment was accepted or rejected, (7) the date of the last calibration, and (8) the unique identifier of the equipment.

This information can be kept on paper and/or electronically. This same type of certification should be generated for those pieces of equipment that are calibrated in-house. The certification should be retained in the same manner as equipment that is calibrated at an outside calibration lab.

7. If a piece of equipment is found to be out of calibration, a system should be in place that will require the assessment and documentation of the validity of measurements taken since the last time the gauge was calibrated.

This is one part of the element that is very difficult. Two methods can be followed for a company to meet this requirement. The first method, used by one certified program, is for the inspection reports for all products to show the serial number of each gauge used to inspect the part. If a gauge is found to be out of calibration, an assessment is made as to the possible effect of the discrepancy on product accepted with that specific gauge. If the assessment shows the probability of a problem, then the reports are researched, and the specific parts that were checked with that gauge since its last successful calibration are recalled.

A second method is to check the accuracy of the equipment before each use. In one certified program, measuring equipment such as micrometers and calipers are checked on a certified standard before each use. This takes time but will prevent the necessity of having product inspection traceability.

8. Assure that equipment is calibrated, checked, and used in a suitable environment.

In several certified programs, the quality assurance department performs supplier audits of the companies providing calibration services. Part of the audit is to make sure the proper environmental controls are in place for proper calibration to occur. The control parameters (for example, temperature, humidity, and/or pressure) will usually be called out in the procedure or specification by which the gauges are calibrated. In many cases, the certificate of calibration will show the temperature and humidity at the time of calibration. Even when calibration activities are performed in-house, a suitable environment must be provided. This is an area that must be evaluated and not overlooked.

9. The equipment will be properly handled, preserved, and stored in such a way as to maintain the accuracy and its fitness for use.

This requirement will be fulfilled by properly training the inspector and affected work force to care for the equipment and by providing the necessary preservation and storage supplies. A procedure could be written describing the method by which preservation and storage should be accomplished.

10. Protect the equipment (and software if applicable) from adjustments that would destroy the accuracy of the equipment.

For example, this is commonly accomplished by putting hot wax in the calibration screw of a thread gauge so the inspector can visually determine if someone has tampered with the adjustment. For some equipment, lead or other material seals are used to prevent tampering. A method should be decided upon and consistently followed.

The last area addresses templates, fixtures, and jigs. Each one of these should be evaluated. In many cases, a one-time certification will be acceptable. In a company that uses engraved panels, a clear plexiglass overlay is produced that has all the holes and engraving according to the print. When the overlay was first received, it was checked against the print and accepted. Subsequent uses of this overlay require only that it be verified as being the proper revision level.

For each type of equipment a judgment needs to be made about calibration, deciding what is good business and what makes good sense. If common sense and good business practices are followed and the requirements of this element are met, the result should be an effective and efficient calibration program. Proper implementation of this element may require assistance from an expert.

13

INSPECTION AND TEST STATUS

Inspection and test status is also one of the eighteen elements detailed in both ISO 9001 and 9002. The purpose of this element is to ensure that product is identified as to whether it has been inspected and whether it is conforming or nonconforming. Good business practice would dictate that the product be identified at all stages of production. This allows the worker to determine if the part has been inspected and, if so, whether the part passed or failed.

ISO 9001

4.12 Inspection and test status

The inspection and test status of product shall be identified by using markings, authorized stamps, tags, labels, routing cards, inspection records, test software, physical location or other suitable means, which indicate the conformance or nonconformance of product with regard to inspection and tests performed. The identification of inspection and test status shall be maintained, as necessary, throughout production and installation of the product to ensure that only product that has passed the required inspections and tests is dispatched, used or installed.

Records shall identify the inspection authority responsible for the release of conforming product (see 4.16).

ISO 9004

11.7 Control of verification status

Verification status of material and assemblies should be identified throughout production. Such identification may take the form of stamps, tags or notations on shop travellers or inspection records that accompany the product. The identification should include the ability to distinguish between verified and unverified material and indication of acceptance at the point of verification. It should also provide traceability to the unit responsible for the operation.

Inspection and Test Status

What Is the Intent of This Element?

The intent of this element is simply for a company to develop a method of identifying the status of a part with respect to inspections and tests. This allows everyone involved with a product to know if the part has been inspected and whether it was accepted or rejected. This information is critical for the workers who will do further processing on the part. If the product has not been inspected, the parts should not be further processed. If the parts have been inspected and rejected, the parts should be identified and removed from the area where accepted product is held. This will help prevent inadvertent use of rejected product. Only product that has passed the proper tests and inspections and is identified as such should be used.

What Is the Requirement of This Element?

The company must establish and maintain a method to identify the inspection and test status of product, as necessary. This is to ensure that only product that has passed the required inspections and tests continues in production. The element also requires that the authority and responsibility for release of conforming product be determined by the company and proper documentation maintained. These requirements can be outlined as follows:

1. The status of the part should be identified throughout its progression through the required inspections or tests.
2. Identification of inspection results (whether the product found to be in a state of conformance or nonconformance) should be evident.
3. Persons having authority and responsibility to release conforming product should be identified.

Each of these areas must be addressed in a procedure. The procedure must then be followed in practice.

What About the 1994 Version? Inspection and Test Status

The only change for this element in the 1994 version is to add maintenance of inspection and test status during servicing.

Implementation Strategy

Implementation strategies can vary depending on the needs of a company and/or the types of processing. One factor in choosing a strategy would be to decide on a cost-effective, streamlined method to perform identification.

Appropriate methods of identification can be as varied as the organizations that choose to implement the ISO 9000 standard. ISO 9001 itself suggests markings, labels, routing cards, inspection records, physical location, or other suitable means. Within each of these identified methods there are numerous variations, allowing the company a wide range of choices. The only restriction is that the method chosen be appropriate, effective, and understandable. The method must prohibit the processing of nonconforming product.

Three implementation strategies will be reviewed to demonstrate the flexibility of the standard. In one program certified to ISO 9001, physical location was used to identify the acceptance status of product at incoming inspection. Product that met all computerized requirements for ship to stock status was moved directly into the warehouse from the receiving dock without passing through receiving inspection. Product requiring inspection was not released to the warehouse until required inspections were completed. If product was accepted at receiving inspection, it was forwarded to the warehouse. If the product was not accepted, it was placed in a holding area.

The physical location of the parts in the warehouse thus indicated that parts either were ship-to-stock or were inspected and accepted. In either case, the parts were identifiable as ready for further processing. The location of rejected parts in the holding area indicated their status as nonconforming. The procedure identified the incoming inspector as the responsible party to release the product for further processing.

A more traditional approach taken by one company is for a router to follow the product as it progresses through each stage of manufacturing. The router identifies each inspection and test point; each step is signed off upon completion. The inspection and test procedure and the acceptance criteria are listed on the router along with the results of the inspections. Because the router remains with the product, the status can be identified at a glance. In this situation, the procedure identifies the worker as having the authority to make the inspection and release the product for further processing.

In the high-tech world of computer-aided manufacturing and automated inspection, a more sophisticated method of identifying the inspection and test status occurs. The inspection and test results are saved by the computer, and the parts are segregated at some point further down the production line. The identification is kept totally by the computer as part of the test software. This method is also accepted as satisfying the standard's requirements.

This element also lists alternative methods of compliance. They range from physical location to markings, tags, or stamps; they can encompass routers and inspection records, or include computer test files. Every company should be able to find an economic and efficient method to conform with this element.

14

CONTROL OF NONCONFORMING PRODUCT

Control of nonconforming product is also one of the eighteen elements detailed in both ISO 9001 and 9002. It is an element that is common in most manufacturing companies. Whenever an organization is involved in the processing or alteration of a material's form, shape, or state, the potential exists for production of nonconforming product. Additionally, if a company deals with product or raw material supplied from a subcontractor, it will on occasion have to deal with nonconforming product. The issue becomes how to identify and control nonconforming product so it will not continue down the production line and eventually reach the customer.

The element dictates to a company what must be done to address the identification, segregation, disposition, and documentation of the nonconforming product. The focus of any program dealing with nonconforming product should be to prevent the rejected product from reaching the customer. It should identify the presence of a problem and remove the root cause. However the program is devised, these end results must be accomplished for it to be considered effective.

ISO 9001	ISO 9004
4.13 Control of nonconforming product	*11.8 Control of nonconforming material*

ISO 9001

4.13 Control of nonconforming product

The supplier shall establish and maintain procedures to ensure that product that does not conform to specified requirements is prevented from inadvertent use or installation. Control shall provide for identification, documentation, evaluation, segregation (when practical), disposition of nonconforming product and for notification to the functions concerned.

4.13.1 Nonconformity review and disposition

The responsibility for review and authority for the disposition of nonconforming product shall be defined.

Nonconforming product shall be reviewed in accordance with documented procedures. It may be

a) reworked to meet the specified requirements, or

b) accepted with or without repair by concession, or

c) re-graded for alternative applications, or

d) rejected or scrapped.

Where required by the contract, the proposed use or repair of product [see 4.13.1b] which does not conform to specified requirements shall be reported for concession to the purchaser or his

ISO 9004

11.8 Control of nonconforming material

Provision should be made for the positive identification and control of all nonconforming material (see clause 14).

14 Nonconformity

14.1 General

The steps outlined in 14.2 to 14.7 should be taken as soon as indications occur that materials, components or completed product do not or may not meet the specified requirements.

14.2 Identification

Suspected nonconforming items or lots should be immediately identified and the occurrence(s) recorded. Whenever possible, provision should be made as necessary to examine previous production lots.

14.3 Segregation

The nonconforming items should be segregated, wherever possible, from conforming items and adequately identified to prevent further use of them until the appropriate disposition is decided.

14.4 Review

Nonconforming items should be subjected to review by designated persons to determine whether they can be used as they are or whether they shall be repaired,

ISO 9001

representative. The description of nonconformity that has been accepted, and of repairs, shall be recorded to denote the actual condition (see 4.16)

Repaired and reworked product shall be re-inspected in accordance with documented procedures.

ISO 9004

reworked, reclassified or scrapped. Persons carrying out the review should be competent to evaluate the effects of nonconformity on interchangeability, further processing, performance, reliability, safety and esthetics. (See 9.7 and 11.8.)

14.5 Disposition

Disposal of nonconforming items should be taken as soon as practicable in accordance with decisions made in 14.4. Decisions to "pass" an item should be accompanied by authorized concessions/waivers, with appropriate precautions. (See 15.8.)

14.6 Documentation

The steps for dealing with nonconforming items should be set out in documented procedures with examples of the format of markers, forms, and reports (see 17.2).

14.7 Prevention of recurrence

Appropriate steps should be taken to prevent the recurrence of nonconformity (see 15.5 and 15.6). Consideration should be given to establishing a file listing nonconformities to help identify those problems having a common source, contrasted with those that are unique occurrences.

Control of Nonconforming Product

What Is the Intent of This Element?

The intent of this element is for a company to develop a program to quickly identify, segregate, investigate, document, and properly dispose of nonconforming product. The purpose, as stated earlier, is to prevent the nonconforming product from inadvertently being shipped to the customer.

What Is the Requirement of This Element?

This element is very specific as to its requirements. They include the following:

1. Nonconforming product shall be identified.
2. The type and extent of the nonconformance shall be documented.
3. The nonconforming product shall be evaluated.
4. Nonconforming product should be segregated (where practical).
5. A disposition of the nonconforming product shall be made.
6. Notification of the appropriate functions shall be made.
7. Responsibility for review and disposition of the nonconforming product shall be defined.
8. If the product is repaired or reworked, the product shall be reinspected in accordance with documented procedures.

These are simply the minimum requirements for doing business well when addressing nonconforming product. The only requirement that may be new to some companies is the issue of reinspecting the part to documented procedures after it has been repaired or reworked. This inspection should verify that the part now meets the requirements of the specification and that the repair has not adversely affected the integrity of the product.

What About the 1994 Version? Control of Nonconforming Product

Only minor editorial changes were made to this element. Again, the 1994 revision is requiring documented procedures for this element. References to purchaser have been changed to customer and the element now references repair or rework in accordance with the "quality plan" or documented procedures.

Implementation Strategy

The steps that should be followed for this element to be implemented can be quite simple. The first step, after location of a nonconforming product, is identification of the product as nonconforming. This is usually accomplished by the person who found the defect. In many shops, the part is tagged with a red paper tag imprinted with the word *reject*. A form or a report should then be filled out describing the nonconformance. In one certified program, this is accomplished by use of a computer. A part is identified as being rejected, and a report is completed in a computer mainframe; the program assigns a number to be written on the reject tag, and the tagged part is forwarded to the quality control inspection area for processing.

Once the part is identified, it should be segregated so it will not be mistaken for accepted product. This segregation to some companies is a locked holding area to which only appropriate personnel have a key. This will work, but so will a cabinet that has a sign that identifies the product as being rejected. If the product is large, it might be acceptable to leave it where it is and tag it or to move it to a roped-off area outside. The key to this section of the standard is for the part to be identified and segregated if possible to prevent it from being used in further processing.

The next step is for the product to be reviewed and the disposition determined. Traditionally, the method by which this element is met centers around a material review board (MRB). The MRB is a team made up of representatives from the departments that need to provide input on the disposition of nonconforming product. Typically, the group consists of representatives from quality assurance, product engineering, manufacturing engineering, and in some situations a representative from the logistics department. The team meets at predetermined intervals to evaluate nonconforming product and make determinations as to its disposition. These decisions will be documented and the disposition carried out. This is not to say that an MRB is required; depending on the company's operations, numerous other methods may be used if shown to be effective.

In one certified program, the quality control department is responsible for investigating the root cause of the defect. Quality control is also given total authority over the disposition of the nonconforming product. Once the disposition is made, the paperwork is circulated through the appropriate departments and the disposition carried out. Each of the departments that are usually on a MRB evaluate and agree to the disposition before the process is completed.

In any case, the reason for review is to make the proper disposition of the part. According to the standard and in practice, four dispositions can be made:

1. The part is reworked to bring it into conformance with the specification.
2. The part is accepted without repair by an engineering waiver of the specification that is not being met.
3. The part is downgraded to be used in alternative application.
4. The part is scrapped.

One of these decisions should be made so the part can be cycled out of the nonconforming condition and be fixed, used as is, or scrapped. Any of the four will resolve the issue of what to do with the part.

The activities that have occurred from the time the part is identified until the disposition is carried out should be documented. This documentation can take the form of a computer file with areas for appropriate data entry or a printed form that is filled out by hand. It should reflect that the appropriate people were involved in the decision-making process. This documentation also provides additional information about the product to help in determining the cause of the nonconformance and deciding how to prevent recurrence of the problem.

The last (and most important) step is for an investigation to take place to determine the root cause of the nonconformance. Corrective action should be taken to prevent similar defects in the future. This step will take problem-solving skills, training, and common sense. If these are exercised, the logical result will be that problems are effectively identified and solved.

15

CORRECTIVE ACTION

Corrective action is one of the eighteen elements detailed by both ISO 9001 and 9002. A key element in any company is for a continuous quality improvement cycle to be implemented. Every person in a company should be empowered to identify ways in which to improve what they do. This continuous improvement should result in corrective actions being implemented to prevent the recurrence of defective product. This element is tied closely to the control of nonconforming product, as discussed in Chapter Fourteen.

Within this element, corrective actions should stem from two types of investigation. The first is typical of a quality control program: the root cause for defective product is identified, and corrective action is taken to prevent occurrence in the future. The second method is to identify areas where the probability of making bad product exists; the situation is then corrected *before* bad product is produced. The unique part of this element is the requirement for a company to become proactive in its approach to problem solving.

ISO 9001

4.14 Corrective action

The supplier shall establish, document and maintain procedures for

a) investigating the cause of nonconforming product and the corrective action needed to prevent recurrence;

b) analyzing all processes, work operations, concessions, quality records, service reports and customer complaints to detect and eliminate potential causes of nonconforming product;

c) initiating preventative actions to deal with problems to a level corresponding to the risks encountered;

d) applying controls to ensure that corrective actions are taken and that they are effective;

e) implementing and recording changes in procedures resulting from corrective action.

ISO 9004

15 Corrective action

15.1 General

The implementation of corrective action begins with the detection of a quality related problem and involves taking measures to eliminate or minimize the recurrence of a problem. Corrective action also presupposes the repair, reworking, recall or scrapping of unsatisfactory materials or items.

15.2 Assignment of responsibility

The responsibility and authority for instituting corrective action should be defined as part of the quality system. The coordination, recording, and monitoring of corrective action related to all aspects of the organization or a particular product should be assigned to a particular function within the organization. However, the analysis and execution may involve a variety of functions, such as sales, design, production engineering, production and quality control.

15.3 Evaluation of importance

The significance of a problem affecting quality should be evaluated in terms of its potential impact on such aspects as production costs, quality costs, performance, reliability, safety and customer satisfaction.

ISO 9004

15.4 Investigation of possible causes

The relationship of cause and effect should be determined, with all potential causes considered. Important variables affecting the capability of the process to meet required standards should be identified.

15.5 Analysis of problem

In the analysis of a quality related problem, the root cause should be determined before the preventive measures are planned. Often the root cause is not obvious, thus requiring careful analysis of the product or service specifications and of all related processes, operations, quality records, service reports and customer complaints. Statistical methods can be useful in problem analysis (see clause 20).

15.6 Preventive action

In order to prevent a future recurrence of a nonconformity, it may be necessary to change a manufacturing, packing, transit or storage process, revise a product specification and/or revise the quality system. Preventive action should be initiated to a degree appropriate to the magnitude of potential problems.

15.7 Process controls

Sufficient controls of processes and procedures should be imple-

ISO 9004

mented to prevent recurrence of the problem. When the preventive measures are implemented, their effect should be monitored in order to ensure that desired goals are met.

15.8 Disposition of nonconforming items

For work in progress, remedial action should be instituted as soon as practical in order to limit the costs of repair, reworking or scrapping. In addition, it may be necessary to recall completed items, whether these items are in a finished goods warehouse, in transit to distributors, in their stores or already in field use (see 16.1.3). Recall decisions are affected by considerations of safety, product liability and customer satisfaction (see 14.5).

15.9 Permanent changes

Permanent changes resulting from corrective action should be recorded in work instructions, manufacturing processes, product specifications and/or the quality system. It may also be necessary to revise the procedures used to detect and eliminate potential problems.

Corrective Action

What Is the Intent of This Element?

The intent of this element is for a company to develop a program that will systematically reduce the occurrence of nonconforming product. This program should be developed to take a two-pronged approach to quality improvement—reactive and proactive. As stated before, one of the elements that makes the ISO 9000 standard unique and different is that a company must become proactive in its approach to problem solving.

The standard's intent is for a company to identify nonconforming product and to investigate the root cause. This in itself is nothing new for most companies. The element also intends for a company to make systematic and thorough investigations to determine the root cause of multiple instances of the same nonconformance; a corrective action should then be identified, implemented, and documented.

The second phase of corrective action is for the company to develop a proactive approach to investigate and identify potential problem areas and to correct them even before nonconforming product is produced. This aspect of the element is far more difficult for many organizations to implement. In many companies, it is hard to identify the potential for production of bad product.

Once the root cause of the problem (or potential problem) is identified, the next step suggested by the standard is to identify and apply a remedy. The standard then calls for the remedy to be monitored to determine if it is effective. If the remedy is effective, the final step is to modify the procedures relative to any activity that may change due to implementation of the corrective action. The change is the procedures will allow for the corrective action to be uniformly applied.

What Is the Requirement of This Element?

This element has five requirements:

1. Investigate the cause of nonconforming product and solve the root cause

2. Analyze processes and information to eliminate potential causes of nonconforming product
3. Initiate corrective actions to deal with problems in proportion to the risks
4. Apply controls to the corrective actions to make sure they will continue to be effective
5. Document in the procedures the changes in the activities

What About the 1994 Version? Corrective and Preventive Action

The 1987 version of ISO 9001 addressed this element only as Corrective Action. ISO/DIS 9001 has expanded the element title to Corrective and Preventive Action. Although preventive action was addressed in the original issue of the standard, the 1994 revision has pulled all references in the corrective action section and defined preventive action in a section of its own. The section on preventive action states "procedures shall include a) the use of appropriate sources of information such as processes and work operations which affect product quality, concessions, audit results, quality records, service reports and customer complaints to detect, analyze and eliminate potential causes of nonconformities; . . . b) determining the steps needed to deal with any problems requiring preventive action; c) initiating preventive action and applying controls to ensure that it is effective; d) ensuring that relevant information on actions taken including changes to procedures is submitted for management review." Here again the standard is being revised to force a more proactive approach in the prevention of nonconformities in products, processes, and the quality system. The last statement requires that actions taken be submitted to management for review.

Implementation Strategy

The first step of corrective action is to identify the need. As stated earlier, this identification can take the form of reactively evaluating the causes of nonconforming product, or it can evolve to a proactive analysis process. This analysis should evaluate the company's operations and identify ways of preventing the possibility of defective product being generated.

In many companies, corrective action is the result of in-depth evaluations of existing data about bad product. Typically these data include nonconformance reports, inspection reports, customer complaints, and warranty claims. These data are invaluable because they provide information upon which corrective action will be taken.

The typical approach is to evaluate data in an attempt to identify nonconformances that have something in common. The investigation should attempt to identify defects that are caused by the same process, operation, department, and so forth. If a trend can be established, the next step is to identify the root cause; if the root cause can be identified, then corrective action can be implemented. When this cycle takes place, the root cause can be eliminated or controlled. This should reduce the number or severity of the nonconforming products being produced.

Regardless of how an organization chooses to implement this element, the activities must be documented. One proven method uses a form to document the entire process (See Appendix IV). This form should include identification of the department that is assigned the responsibility to investigate the request. The form should include information regarding the problem, specify the response due date, and suggest corrective action. When the corrective action is taken, it should be documented on the form and returned to the originator. The corrective action should then be analyzed to determine that it is effective. If it is effective, the corrective action request is accepted and closed. A log is also maintained to identify all corrective action requests issued and the status (open or closed). This log documents the activities of the program; the status of each request is available at all times. Although corrective action requests may be issued to any department, the responsibility for administration of the program should be specifically assigned.

In one certified program, the activity of tracking and analyzing nonconforming product and administering the corrective action program is assigned to the quality assurance department. The quality assurance manager has sole responsibility for developing and monitoring the program. This program includes a system by which nonconforming product is identified and information about the type and extent of the nonconformance is maintained. This can be accomplished by the system described in Chapter Fourteen (Control of Nonconforming Product). Part of the process of disposition could be for the appropriate experts (such as manufacturing engineers or quality engineers) to evaluate the defect. As part of the disposition process, a determination should be made if the defect is a one-time occurrence or a process error. A corrective action request then is written suggesting ways to prevent this from happening in the future. Unless effective corrective action is taken, the process will continue to produce defective product.

In the proactive approach to this element, many activities and processes need to be analyzed. This analysis identifies areas where improvement of specific activities will reduce the possibility of producing defective product. This program can take one of several approaches, the first of which is for the analysis of existing processes to be relegated to professionals that have special training in this area. Typically this would include manufacturing engineers or quality engineers. The job of these professionals would be to identify areas where the likelihood exists for a process to produce defective product. They would then propose an alternative method for accomplishing the task. Additionally, the responsibility of monitoring the new process would fall to this group, along with all documentation activities.

A second approach is to empower the worker to identify quality problems and develop solutions. In this approach, individuals can be chosen from the work force to form improvement teams. These teams would be taught problem-solving and process improvement tools. Training would also include instruction in team dynamics. The team is allowed to pick an improvement project, and a leader guides the team through the improvement process. The change is documented on the request for corrective action form and monitored to assess its effectiveness.

The third approach is for a company to provide quality improvement training to all employees within a company. Individuals are then allowed to pick improvement projects and make the changes. In one certified company, every individual is empowered to identify opportunities for improving a product or process. The employee can send out a memo to everyone in the company outlining the problem and asking for volunteers to work on the project. The employee is allowed to set up meetings on company time to develop a strategy to deal with the problem and find a solution. After the method to monitor the solution is developed, the team is disbanded. All of this can happen without approval from a supervisor. The only management input consists of having someone from the quality assurance department assigned to each team. This is to ensure coordination of efforts among projects. As with all previously mentioned methods of corrective action, each project is documented on a request for corrective action form to provide a record of the activities conducted.

The key is not so much how the program is structured but that a structure exists. The problem for many companies is that no formal improvement process exists and no corrective action takes place. In the absence of corrective action, a process or product deficiency will continue; in many cases, the discrepancy will increase in severity or frequency. Corrective action is a vital part of any organization's attempt at an improvement cycle focused on customer satisfaction.

16

HANDLING, STORAGE, PACKAGING, AND DELIVERY

Handling, storage, packaging, and delivery constitute another of the eighteen elements detailed in both ISO 9001 and 9002. This element is in support of the design and manufacturing elements. The areas covered are associated with protecting the condition of the material from the time it is received from a supplier through the storage, processing, packaging, and delivery stages.

In many companies this area is not viewed as being as important as areas like design, contract review, or manufacturing. In actuality, though, this area carries as much or more weight when it comes to customer satisfaction. A company can produce the best design and manufacture it perfectly, yet still deliver nonconforming product. If material is damaged while in storage, before delivery to the customer, the result is the same as if the design was inadequate or the parts improperly manufactured. To prevent this, the ISO 9000 standard has included this element, which is emphasized as much as any other element addressed by the standard. By itself this element will not guarantee acceptable product, but it will ensure that good product will not be converted into scrap as a result of improper handling, storage, packaging, or delivery.

ISO 9001

4.15 Handling, storage, packaging and delivery

4.15.1 General

The supplier shall establish, document and maintain procedures for handling, storage, packaging and delivery of product.

4.15.2 Handling

The supplier shall provide methods and means of handling that prevent damage or deterioration.

4.15.3 Storage

The supplier shall provide secure storage areas or stock rooms to prevent damage or deterioration of product, pending use of delivery. Appropriate methods for authorizing receipt and the dispatch to and from such areas shall be stipulated. In order to detect deterioration, the condition of product in stock shall be assessed at appropriate intervals.

4.15.4 Packaging

The supplier shall control packing, preservation and marking processes (including materials used) to the extent necessary to ensure conformance to specified requirements and shall identify, preserve and segregate all product from the time of receipt until the supplier's responsibility ceases.

ISO 9004

16 Handling and post-production functions

16.1 Handling, storage, identification, packaging, installation and delivery

16.1.1 General

The handling of materials requires proper planning, control and a documented system for incoming materials, materials in process and finished goods; this applies not only during delivery but up to the time of being put into use.

16.1.2 Handling and storage

The method of handling and storage of materials should provide for the correct pallets, containers, conveyors and vehicles to prevent damage due to vibration, shock, abrasion, corrosion, temperature or any other conditions occurring during handling and storage. Items in storage should be checked periodically to detect possible deterioration.

16.1.3 Identification

The marking and labelling of materials should be legible, durable and in accordance with the specifications. Identification should remain intact from the time of initial receipt to delivery to the final destination. Marking should be adequate to identify a particular product in the event that a recall or special inspection becomes necessary.

ISO 9001	ISO 9004

ISO 9001

4.15.5 Delivery

The supplier shall arrange for the protection of the quality of product after final inspection and test. Where contractually specified, this protection shall be extended to include delivery to destination.

ISO 9004

16.1.4 Packaging

The methods of cleaning and preserving, and the details of packing, including moisture elimination, cushioning, blocking and crating, should be laid down in written instructions, as appropriate.

16.1.5 Installation

Instructional documents should contribute to proper installations and should include provisions which preclude improper installation or factors degrading the quality, reliability, safety and performance of any product or material.

16.1.6 Delivery

Items with limited shelf-life or requiring special protection during transport or storage should be identified, and procedures should be maintained to ensure that deteriorated items are not put into use. Provision for protection of the quality of product is important during all phases of delivery.

General

What Is the Intent of This Element?

The overall intent of this element is for a company to make conscious decisions about how the product (from raw material to finished goods) is handled and stored. A company should evaluate the methods used to handle the product to ensure no damage occurs during this activity. Product that is stored should be evaluated to determine if special environmental conditions are necessary. Decisions should be made to ensure that product is not damaged or degraded while in storage.

The evaluation should address the methods established for packaging, preservation, and marking. The intent is for a company to make responsible decisions to ensure that the product can be easily identified for any special requirements. The overall intent of the element is for a company to develop procedures that will provide for protection of the product at all stages of storage, production, and shipment. If a part is improperly stored or handled, it could invalidate the results of any final inspection that has been completed; many companies spend a tremendous amount of time and money performing elaborate final inspections only to find out that the accepted product has been damaged beyond repair before it could reach the customer. Poor handling will render the most meticulous and costly inspection an exercise in futility.

In addition to handling, areas such as product identification in stores become a critical issue. Lost or unidentified parts are as bad as damaged parts; either the wrong part reaches the customer or the right part cannot be found when it is time for it to be shipped to the customer, and the sale is delayed or lost. Marking is important to guarantee that the proper material is used in production. This becomes especially important when product cannot be visually identified, as with different grades of steel or different types of chemicals. An airplane wing made out of aluminum of the wrong strength, or a donut that is covered in arsenic instead of powdered sugar, could be costly.

Many products can deteriorate if improperly stored. The atmosphere must therefore be evaluated, and the shelf life of parts must be known and not exceeded. It is common knowledge that ice cream must be kept below freezing or it will be damaged beyond repair. It is less known, however, that some types of exotic epoxies have the same requirement. The proximity of products compared to equipment or other product can be an issue. Elastomers should not be stored close to anything that emits ozone. The ultraviolet rays that are present in sunlight can cause damage to some materials. Even something as simple as storing nickel cadmium batteries next to lead acid batteries will cause deterioration of both products.

The key intent of this element is for a company to recognize that good product cannot be manufactured from improper, damaged, or defective parts. Each company should know the special conditions that exist for the products it maintains. Proper steps should be taken to ensure the integrity of the raw material, parts, and/or finished goods at all stages of production.

What About the 1994 Version? Handling, Storage, Packaging, Preservation, and Delivery

Originally issued as Handling, storage, packaging, and delivery in the 1987 version, ISO/DIS 9001 has expanded this element to include requirements for preservation of the product. This is stated as: "Appropriate methods for preservation and segregation of the product shall be applied when such product is under the supplier's control." To support the original intent of this element, it would be of no benefit to have the most strictly designed and manufactured product if the quality was to be destroyed due to lack of proper preservation.

What Is the Requirement of This Element?

Companies are required to develop a consistent and deliberate approach to the areas of handling, packaging, storage, and delivery. They must develop and maintain documented procedures covering these stages of production, as detailed below.

Handling

The requirement is very simple in this area: the company must provide the means and develop the methods to handle parts without damaging them.

Storage

This portion of the element covers the storage, receipt, dispatch, and evaluation of product in storage. The specific requirements include the following:

1. The company must provide storage areas where the product will be secure from deterioration and damage.
2. The company must have an appropriate method for receipt and dispatch of product from and to storage.
3. The condition of the stock must be assessed at appropriate intervals.

Packaging

The packaging portion of this element also covers preservation and marking. It includes the following requirements:

1. The company shall control packaging, preservation, and marking to the extent needed to ensure conformance to requirements.
2. Control will also extend to the material used for packaging, preservation and marking.
3. The company will identify all parts from the time of receipt until its responsibility ceases.
4. The company will segregate all parts from the time of receipt until its responsibility ceases.
5. The company will preserve all parts from the time of receipt until its responsibility ceases.

Delivery

Once a part is produced and final inspection has been accomplished, the following requirements apply:

1. The company must maintain the quality of the product after final inspection.
2. Where specified by the contract, the company must ensure the product is protected through the delivery at the final destination.

These requirements make good sense and assure that good business is being accomplished. In the final analysis, each of these is important not only to comply with this element but also to ensure the integrity of the product and raw material under the direct control of a company.

Implementation Strategy

The only implementation strategy that can be used for this element is for a company to evaluate the methods it has established to handle and store product. Companies should determine if workers have the proper training and equipment to handle the product in such a way as to prevent damage.

Storage areas should be examined to guarantee that the condition of the product is properly maintained. The product should also be evaluated to determine if special handling and storage conditions are necessary for integrity to be maintained. Special conditions will include items ranging from the marking and packaging of products such as elastomers to the protection of steel parts from moisture. In some locations, the humidity is high and will require desiccant bags or other control efforts to prevent mildew or fungus. Atmospheric conditions (temperature, humidity, salt, sand, dust, and so forth) must be identified, evaluated, and properly addressed.

A procedure should be written describing the method by which product is received from a supplier and accepted into stores. The procedure should also state how product can be issued from storage. The responsibility to receive and dispatch product must be documented.

A method also must be developed to assess the condition of product located in storage. In one certified program, this is accomplished as the parts are cycle counted in inventory or when dispatched to the customer. In many cycle counting schemes, however, the count is performed when the records show zero on hand. Therefore, condition should be assessed at dispatch in addition to cycle count.

The requirement for packaging can be met by developing a standard of performance that describes the method in which product types are usually packaged and preserved. In a certified program a procedure was developed to outline how part groups will usually be preserved and packaged. This procedure gave general information about product types rather than specific products; groups such as elastomers, fabricated parts, electronic components and machined parts were all addressed. The bottom line is that packaging and preservation should prevent damage.

The area of delivery should be addressed when it is part of the contract. Many companies are responsible for the product quality until it is delivered at the customer's location. In this case, proper steps must be taken to ensure that the part is protected during shipment. Keep in mind that the responsibility for product quality cannot be shifted to the shipper under this standard.

In many companies today the areas of handling, packaging, storage, and delivery are viewed as simple issues having less importance than design and manufacturing. In actuality these areas are just as important, if not more so. Therefore handling, storage, packaging, and delivery practices must be properly evaluated and controlled.

17

QUALITY RECORDS

Quality records also represent one of the eighteen elements that is detailed in both ISO 9001 and 9002. Quality records, as defined by this standard, serve three very important purposes. First, they verify that the required activities for the certified program are maintained and followed. Verifying that a company is adhering to the requirements of a standard, specification, or procedure can only be accomplished in two ways. One way would be for someone from the certifying authority to observe every activity regarding the certified program. That person would have to be present at the company twenty-four hours a day, seven days a week to observe everything that happened. This clearly would not work well for most companies. Alternately, the verifying authority can perform periodical audits during which samples of process documentation are verified. This documentation is routinely produced to verify that a procedure is being followed. The auditor can have some assurance that if the paperwork is correct, the procedure most likely was followed.

The second purpose of quality records is to verify the condition of the product at a given point in time. Once an activity has been performed, it can only be verified by relying on the memory of the person who performed or witnessed the event or by reviewing documentation that was generated at that time. Likewise, when the product is no longer available for review at the point of manufacture, the verifying documents (test records or inspection reports) are the only items that remain to provide traceability. This traceability is required for verification that proper (or improper) processing occurred and that the product was either acceptable or nonconforming.

The third purpose for quality records is to provide a history of a part, process, or program. For corrective action to take place, an investigation must usually occur; either the nonconforming product or an evaluation of the output from a process must be reviewed. Many of these investigations will center around reviewing the quality records (drawings, test reports, inspection records, statistical process control charts, product certifications). Without this history, there would be no data to review, and the process would have to run as before until enough data could be generated to analyze. The process would continue to generate nonconforming product while the data were being collected.

ISO 9001

4.16 Quality records

The supplier shall establish and maintain procedures for identification, collection, indexing, filing, storage, maintenance and disposition of quality records.

Quality records shall be maintained to demonstrate achievement of the required quality and the effective operation of the quality system. Pertinent subcontractor quality records shall be an element of these data. All quality records shall be legible and identifiable to the product involved. Quality records shall be stored and maintained in such a way that they are readily retrievable in facilities that provide a suitable environment to minimize deterioration or damage and to prevent loss. Retention times of quality records shall be established and recorded. Where agreed contractually, quality records shall be made available for evaluation by the purchaser or his representative for an agreed period.

ISO 9004

17.3 Quality records

The system should require that sufficient records be maintained to demonstrate achievement of the required quality and verify effective operation of the quality management system.

The following are examples of the types of quality records requiring control:

—inspection reports;
—test data;
—qualification reports;
—validation reports;
—audit reports;
—material review reports;
—calibration data;
—quality cost reports.

Quality records should be retained, for a specified period, in such a manner as to be retrievable for analysis in order to identify quality trends and the need for, and effectiveness of, corrective action. While in storage, quality records should be protected from damage, loss and deterioration due to environmental conditions.

Quality Records

What Is the Intent of This Element?

The intent of this element is for a company to identify and control the documentation generated to support the established program and the product that results. Quality records are retained for verification, monitoring, and analysis. Design control documentation is included in quality records to monitor the process and verify completion of all required activities. Records of control of nonconforming product verify an activity but also provide the data to analyze the process. The intent is that the company identify appropriate records, protect and control them, and provide a means to retrieve them when necessary. The areas in which quality records are required are identified in the standard; the specific documents must be determined by the company.

What About the 1994 Version? Quality Records

The title of this element has been revised to "Control of quality records." Documented procedures are now required along with retention ". . . to demonstrate conformance to specified requirements. . . ." The standard also notes that records can be hard copy, electronic, or other media.

What Is the Requirement of This Element?

This element has seven requirements, which are listed below:

1. Quality records must be controlled. A procedure must be established to identify, collect, index, file, store, maintain, and dispose of quality records.
2. The records retained shall demonstrate the effectiveness of the quality system. These records must not only address the processes involved but demonstrate the achievement of the required quality for the product.
3. Records shall be legible and identifiable to the product involved.
4. Quality records will be stored so that they can be easily retrieved. Efforts devoted to record retention would be in vain

if it were impossible to locate what was needed within reasonable amount of time.

5. Quality records shall be protected from damage while stored. If documented evidence was allowed to deteriorate and become damaged during storage, retention again would serve no valid purpose.
6. Retention periods shall be determined and documented.
7. If the customer requires, records shall be made available to him or her for evaluation for an agreed-upon period of time.

In summary, generating quality records serves no purpose if they are not controlled, accessible, and identifiable. Without documented evidence that all elements of the standard are being met and complied with, verification of compliance becomes a full-time job. Without appropriate documents, the job of monitoring product conformance and improvement activities depends solely upon having the product in hand.

Implementation Strategy

The standard includes a note, "(see 4.16)," in each element where documentation is required. This statement identifies that the documentation being referenced is considered a quality record. In addition to those records specifically identified by "(see 4.16)," records must be retained to demonstrate achievement of the required quality and the effective operation of the quality system. Each company is required to identify applicable records. The element provides the categories, but each company must determine the specifics.

In one certified program, each quality record is noted in a matrix that also specifies the retention location and time. Locations are designated as the engineering print room, the supervisor's office, or a specific department. Some records, such as the design files, are retained for five years after discontinuation of the design; other records, such as in-process inspection check sheets, are retained for only six months. Each individual company determines which records will be included within the required categories and applicable retention periods (See Appendix V).

18

INTERNAL QUALITY AUDITS

Internal quality audits constitute another of the eighteen elements detailed in both ISO 9001 and 9002. This element is included in the standard to ensure that the company continues to monitor the program to the requirements of the standard. Many companies have experienced the "program of the week" philosophy. ISO 9001 and 9002 include the audit element to help prevent the program from falling into this category. For many companies, compliance to the ISO 9000 standard requires an immense amount of up-front work to establish and implement programs; to ensure that this effort is not abandoned, each company is required to monitor the quality system against the requirements of this element.

The quality audit is an inspection of an organization's adherence to the established program. It works in much the same way as a final inspection verifies product conformance to the established specification. Like the inspection of a part, the quality audit must also be well defined. The quality manual that documents the program should be used to set up the audit activity.

The purpose of an internal quality audit is to give management assurance that the established procedures are being followed. Therefore the audit contains a checklist of steps in the procedures that are vital to determining overall product quality. It should be designed to answer three basic questions about the organization being audited:

1. Does the organization have a quality system? A quality system is usually evidenced by the quality manual, operating manual, or quality procedures.
2. Is the quality system being followed? An audit or review of activities is conducted to determine if there is ongoing compliance with the procedures.
3. Is the system effective? Are the results of following the procedures consistent, positive, and meeting the intent of the standard?

Many organizations are familiar with financial and even product audits. The internal quality audit serves basically the same purpose, which is to verify that activities follow written procedures. Financial audits focus on the accounting functions of an organization, and product audits focus on the output produced. The internal quality audit focuses on the processes and programs esablished within an organization to meet a stated purpose.

ISO 9001

4.17 Internal quality audits

The supplier shall carry out a comprehensive system of planned and documented internal quality audits to verify whether quality activities comply with planned arrangements and to determine the effectiveness of the quality system.

Audits shall be scheduled on the basis of the status and importance of the activity.

The audits and follow-up actions shall be carried out in accordance with documented procedures.

The results of the audits shall be documented and brought to the attention of the personnel having responsibility in the area audited. The management personnel responsible for the area shall take timely corrective action on the deficiencies found by the audit (see 4.1.3).

ISO 9004

5.4 Auditing the quality system

5.4.1 General

All elements, aspects, and components pertaining to a quality system should be internally audited and evaluated on a regular basis. Audits should be carried out in order to determine whether various elements within a quality management system are effective in achieving stated quality objectives. For this purpose, an appropriate audit plan should be formulated and established by company management.

5.4.2 Audit plan

The format of the audit plan should cover the following points:

a) the specific activities and areas to be audited;

b) qualifications of personnel carrying out audits;

c) the basis for carrying out audits (e.g. organizational changes, reported deficiencies, routine checks and surveys):

d) procedures for reporting audit findings, conclusions and recommendations.

5.4.3 Carrying out the audit

Objective evaluations of quality system elements by competent personnel may include the following activities or areas:

a) organizational structures;

b) administrative and operational procedures;

ISO 9004

c) personnel, equipment and material resources;

d) work areas, operations and processes;

e) items being produced (to establish degree of conformance to standards and specifications);

f) documentation, reports, record keeping.

Personnel carrying out audits of quality system elements should be independent of the specific activities or areas being audited.

5.4.4. Reporting and follow-up of audit findings

Audit findings, conclusions and recommendations should be submitted in documentary form for consideration by appropriate members of company management.

The following items should be covered in the reporting and follow-up of audit findings:

a) Specific examples of noncompliance or deficiencies should be documented in the audit report; possible reasons for such deficiencies, where evident, may be included.

b) Appropriate corrective actions may be suggested.

c) Implementation and effectiveness of corrective actions suggested in previous audits should be assessed.

Internal Quality Audits

What Is the Intent of This Element?

The intent of this element is for the company to take a proactive approach when assessing the quality program. Not only must the system be monitored, a plan must be developed for a method to conduct this activity. This activity helps management determine if the implemented system is effective in achieving stated quality objectives.

In addition to determining compliance of activities, the program must also assess the effectiveness of the quality system. The intention is to promote continuous improvement of the system. Internal audits should also help prevent the program from becoming stagnant and ineffective. The standard intends for each company to monitor its program internally rather than relying on reviews conducted periodically by a third party agency. The standard identifies the importance of follow-up corrective action with regard to nonconforming conditions. The responsibility of management in addressing such conditions is also addressed.

What Is the Requirement of This Element?

The requirements of this element include the following:

1. The supplier must develop a program in which comprehensive internal audits are planned and documented. These audits should focus on verifying that documented procedures are being followed and that the program is effective.
2. All audits shall be scheduled. This scheduling should be relative to the importance of the activity.
3. Internal audits and corrective action shall be conducted in accordance with documented procedures.
4. The results of the audits shall be documented and brought to the attention of personnel responsible for the activity.
5. Management responsible for the area being audited shall take timely corrective action on any nonconformances noted.

In summary, the company must establish a plan to review systematically the compliance of activities with the procedure and determine the effectiveness of the quality system. The company must determine the status and importance of each activity and schedule audits accordingly.

As with other elements, this program must be documented to address the audit function; this documentation should identify how follow-up actions will be conducted. The audits themselves must also be documented.

The element addresses the responsibility for taking timely corrective action regarding nonconformances identified through the internal audit program. The management of the affected area is charged with the responsibility for correcting nonconformances. This requires the responsible department manager to review the situation and determine the best method to bring the activity into compliance.

What About the 1994 Version? Internal Audits

With some minor wording revisions, the standard has added the requirement for auditing activities to "... be carried out by personnel independent of those having direct responsibility for the activity being audited." This requirement was previously addressed in the management responsibility element.

Implementation Strategy

The formation of an internal quality audit program should be one of the first activities undertaken by the organization. Internal quality audits are a self-analysis (a benchmark tool); they permit a company to determine where it is in relation to where it wants to be. This element is used to verify all other elements of the standard. Implementation strategies will be focused in two areas: the qualified personnel who conduct the internal audit program, and the establishment of the program.

Auditor Qualifications

As first mentioned in Chapter Two (Management Responsibility), personnel involved in verification activities such as audits of the quality system must be properly trained. These auditors should also be independent of those having direct responsibility for the work being performed. There are two methods to accomplish the required training; both methods are described below.

OUTSIDE TRAINING (SEMINARS, COURSES, CONSULTANTS). Many companies are now in business for the sole purpose of providing training programs for the qualification of quality auditors. Although sometimes expensive, this method of acquiring qualified auditors may be effective for organizations who do not have experienced personnel in this activity. *The program should be thoroughly investigated prior to making any commitments.* A good program will include theoretical training on the following:

1. How to set up a schedule
2. How to develop a checklist
3. How to conduct the audit
4. How to follow up and close out any nonconformances

While many good programs exist, a large number of others only result in costing the company several hundred dollars. A good program will include both theoretical and practical training; one of the most important qualifications of an internal auditor comes in practical application. Internal quality auditors should possess certain abilities and attitudes, including (1) freedom from bias, (2) attention to detail, (3) written and oral communication skills, and (4) consistency. Therefore it is important to determine if established programs provide not only the academic foundations for auditor qualification but also the practical application skills. The auditor should exhibit the needed disposition before time and money are spent on formal training.

Many programs will issue a completion certificate that attests to the individual's training. A certificate alone, however, cannot always verify qualification of the individual. The program itself should be evaluated to determine the merit of the certificate. Some certifications require only that a written examination be successfully completed; in these instances, no practical experience was provided or assessed. These types of certifications cannot be relied upon as an indication of an auditor's abilities or skills, although they do attest to a basic understanding of a given body of knowledge.

IN-HOUSE TRAINING. In one program certified to ISO 9001, individuals were selected from cross-functional areas and trained as internal quality auditors. The trainees included shop mechanics, secretaries, planners, product engineering personnel, and manufacturing supervisors. This program yielded several major benefits. First, the audit staff was increased in size. This eliminated the need for a department dedicated to the performance of internal audits. The audit coordination was accomplished through the quality control department while cross-functional teams performed the individual audits.

The second benefit was the variety of auditors, who brought a unique focus to the audits. Written procedures will always be subject to the interpretation of the reader. The understanding of a process that a shop mechanic has, even when it is described in a procedure, may be very different than that of a quality engineer or a planner. This unique understanding helps in determining the companywide effectiveness of a program. What one group may feel is effective may be totally ineffective to another group; such differences should be identified and resolved. The existence of a number of unique views in the program is one of its strong points. Adequate training is also very important. Training is required to maintain the consistency of the program. The areas that must be consistent are the planning activities, checklists, rules of conduct, and the reporting mechanism. This is where in-house training becomes vital.

The third benefit involves responsibility. Widely distributed responsibility for portions of the internal quality audit program reinforces the idea that the ISO 9001 system has companywide ownership instead of being owned solely by the quality assurance department. This becomes apparent when a planner and a secretary are allowed to perform an audit in which the plant manager is held accountable for the management responsibility element of the standard. If the plant manager is held accountable, it becomes evident that every other department will also be held accountable for elements of the standard assigned to them.

A key concern when using auditors from different departments was the consistency in the preparation and conduct of each audit. The integrity and effectiveness of an internal audit program can be jeopardized if it lacks consistency in application. To insure consistency, a formal training program was set up through the quality control department to qualify additional personnel. Appropriate time was spent going through the mechanics of an audit program in a classroom setting, and additional time was dedicated to the actual performance of internal audits. Each trainee was required to participate in three internal audits with qualified auditors who reviewed the trainee's techniques and helped him or her develop basic skills. After this portion of the practical training and assessment was completed, the trainees were qualified to conduct internal audits on their own. Individuals should *never* be allowed into an auditing role without proper practical training so as to ensure consistency in the performance of internal audits.

Established Program

Once the rather nontraditional audit staff was developed in this company, a very traditional program was used to meet the requirements of the standard. Such programs should follow the guidelines set out below.

AUDIT SCHEDULE. An audit schedule should be developed covering each element of the standard. A number will be assigned to each audit to be performed; the team leader and the month for which the audit is scheduled are noted. At the beginning of the year, this schedule should be sent to each department. This is to ensure that there are no surprises regarding audit performance.

Each area should be audited at least once a year, and areas that are determined to be more critical should be audited two or more times a year (see Appendix VI). The industry standard is to audit each element at least annually. Most third-party agencies will require a full cycle of internal quality audits be performed before the certification audit, as well as during each periodical audit cycle. This periodical cycle is one year, although it may be accomplished in more than one visit. Most audit programs therefore will adopt a one-year time frame to assess all areas.

AUDIT CHECKLIST. A checklist should be developed for each activity to be audited, addressing each item covered in the procedure for that activity. A typical checklist is composed of three columns. The first column restates the requirement of the procedure in question form. The second column indicates activity compliance, with either a check mark or yes/no entry. The third column is included to permit auditor notes, which will typically indicate specific items checked or additional comments regarding the activity. The checklist indicates the specific activity to be audited, along with the procedure and revision level to which the activity is checked. The checklist also includes the date the audit is performed and the auditor or team members. (See Appendix VI).

RULES OF CONDUCT. Basic ground rules should be established for how the audit program as a whole, along with each audit, will function. The schedule should be posted at the beginning of the year. Surprise audits should not be conducted; each department should be fully aware of what activities will be audited. Department managers should understand when the audit will be conducted, who will be performing the audit, and how the activity will proceed. If department management finds the times or personnel assigned to be inconvenient, the activities should be rescheduled. An honest effort should be made to use internal audits as an improvement tool instead of a blame-laying, finger-pointing activity.

This is the type of program that is operating in a company certified to ISO 9001. One year into this program a shop supervisor requested additional audits, having discovered that the audits could be used as improvement tools. This is one indicator of an effective audit program.

AUDIT REPORT. After each audit is finished, an audit report should be issued to responsible area management. The audit is copied to the internal audit file. The report should be kept simple using a standard format. In one standard format, the first paragraph identifies the area audited, the applicable procedure, who provided information, and who conducted the audit. A short summary is then included stating the overall effectiveness of the activity. Any nonconformances noted during the audit can be summarized in the body of the report; the required dates for addressing nonconformances and providing responses to the auditor should be clearly stated. The audit report functions as a summary. The audit details are contained in the checklist. (See Appendix VI).

NONCONFORMANCE REPORTS. Each nonconformance identified during the audit should be detailed on a standard form. The form should identify the following:

1. Audit number
2. Notice number
3. Responsible department
4. Department activity audited
5. Responsible auditor
6. Issue date
7. Response due date

A section should be provided detailing the noncompliance. Another section is provided to allow the responsible department to note the corrective action taken in response to the deficiency noted by the auditor. The last section is for notations by the auditor on the acceptability or unacceptability of the response to the nonconformance. If satisfactory, the auditor will verify implementation and close the nonconformance. If unsatisfactory, it should be noted as such and returned to the responsible department for additional considerations. Completed nonconformance notices should be filed with the original audit in the internal audit file. (See Appendix VI).

FOLLOW-UP ON CORRECTIVE ACTION. On occasion, responsible area management will not respond in a timely manner to notices of nonconformance. The internal audit procedure should include a statement explaining that if this happens appropriate levels of management will be notified, up to and including the plant manager if necessary. A form letter can be developed that states the past-due nonconformance notice number, the audit that it resulted from, and when the response was due. The letter should contain a statement that if response is not received within a given period of time, the matter will be forwarded to the next level of management. Although this type of activity requires conscious monitoring by the responsible auditor, it has proven effective in reducing the number of delinquent audit nonconformances in the system. (See Appendix VI).

19

TRAINING

Training, one of the eighteen elements detailed in both ISO 9001 and 9002, is an area that is often overlooked within a company. The basic premise of this element is for a company to identify the knowledge and skill required for an employee to perform a job successfully. Next, the company should identify the knowledge and skill each employee possesses. Finally, it should provide education and training to bridge the gap between the knowledge and skill required for the job and that possessed by the worker.

A well-trained work force is more critical to the successful performance of a company than any other single factor. Sometimes a company may be forced to work from poor or incomplete designs; in such cases, a well-trained work force can compensate for this condition, by making controlled modifications while the product is being produced. If a process is not functioning as expected, a well-trained worker can adjust the process to allow for production of good output. In contrast, a good design produced by capable processes can produce scrap if the processes are controlled by an untrained worker.

ISO 9001

4.18 Training

The supplier shall establish and maintain procedures for identifying the training needs and provide for the training of all personnel performing activities affecting quality. Personnel performing specific assigned tasks shall be qualified on the basis of appropriate education, training and/or experience, as required. Appropriate records of training shall be maintained (see 4.16).

ISO 9004

18. Personnel

18.1 Training

18.1.1 General

The need for training of personnel should be identified and a method for providing that training should be established. Consideration should be given to providing training to all levels of personnel within the organization. Particular attention should be given to the selection and training of recruited personnel and personnel transferred to new assignments.

18.1.2 Executive and management personnel

Training should be considered which will provide executive management with an understanding of the quality system together with the tools and techniques needed for full executive management participation in the operation of the system. Executive management should also understand the criteria available to evaluate the effectiveness of the system.

18.1.3 Technical personnel

Training should be given to the technical personnel to enhance their contribution to the success of the quality system. Training should not be restricted to personnel with primary quality as-

ISO 9004

signments, but should include assignments such as marketing, procurement, and process and product engineering. Particular attention should be given to training in statistical techniques, such as process capability studies, statistical sampling, data collection and analysis, problem analysis and corrective action.

18.1.4 Production supervisors and workers

All production supervisors and workers should be thoroughly trained in the methods and skills required to perform their tasks, i.e. the proper operation of instruments, tools, and machinery they have to use, reading and understanding the documentation provided, the relationship of their duties to quality, and safety in the workplace. As appropriate, operators should be certified in their skills, such as welding. Training in basic statistical techniques should also be considered.

The need to require formal qualification of personnel performing certain specialized operations, processes, tests or inspections should be evaluated and implemented where necessary. Consideration should be given both to experience and demonstrated skills.

ISO 9004

18.3 Motivation

18.3.1. General

Motivation of personnel begins with their understanding of the tasks they are expected to perform and how those tasks support the overall activities. Employees should be made aware of the advantages of proper job performance at all levels, and of the effects of poor job performance on other employees, customer satisfaction, operating costs and the economic well-being of the company.

18.3.2. Application

Efforts to motivate employees towards quality of performance should not be directed only at production workers, but also at personnel in marketing, design, documentation, purchasing, inspection, test, packing and shipping, and after-sales services. Management, professional and staff employees should be included.

18.3.3 Quality awareness

The need for quality should be emphasized through an awareness programme which may include introduction and elementary programmes for new employees, periodic refresher programmes for long-standing employees, provision for employees to initiate corrective actions and other methods.

ISO 9004

18.3.4 Measuring quality

Accurate, definitive measures of quality achievement attributable to individuals or groups may be publicized to let employees and production line supervisors see for themselves what they, as a group or as individuals, are achieving and to encourage them to produce satisfactory quality. Management should provide recognition of performance when satisfactory quality levels are attained.

Training

What Is the Intent of This Element?

The intent of this element is for a company to develop a program that provides a systematic approach to training. The standard calls for this to be accomplished for "personnel performing activities affecting quality." It is to a company's benefit, however, to have this program involve all personnel.

What Is the Requirement of This Element?

The requirements of this element focus on personnel training and qualification. They include the following for all personnel performing activities affecting quality:

1. The company shall identify the training needs.
2. The company shall provide training to address the identified needs.
3. Persons performing specific assigned tasks shall be qualified on the basis of education, training, and/or experience.

What About the 1994 Version? Training

No changes were made to this element in the 1994 version with the exception of the requirement for documented procedures.

Implementation Strategy

The company should first evaluate each job position to determine the skills and knowledge needed to perform the job. The results of this evaluation produce a checklist of necessary skills and knowledge. The items on the list should be specific and measurable; if the list consists of generalities, it will not be useful. When the required knowledge and skills are specifically identified, it becomes much easier to evaluate employee skills and develop a plan to provide specific training to the work force. Being specific becomes critical when addressing deficiencies.

The second area is evaluation of the skills and knowledge possessed by each individual worker. During this evaluation, each worker's training, knowledge, and education should be compared to the list of necessary skills and knowledge. If deficiencies are identified, the company should develop a plan to provide the employee with sufficient training to obtain the skills or knowledge required to perform his or her job.

The last area that the standard addresses is personnel who perform specific, assigned tasks. If a company can show that personnel have the required knowledge, training, and/or experience, then detailed day-to-day work instructions may not be required. The standard will allow a company to strike a balance between training/experience and detailed work instructions. For this reason, documentation of training can be very important.

Implementation of this element can be accomplished by one of several methods. One of the more popular methods used to identify required knowledge and skills is a job description. In a typical job description the educational, training, and experience requirements for the position are listed. This list is usually specific to the position, not the person filling that position. For a company to address this element properly, they must go beyond the point of listing necessary requirements on a job description. The company must evaluate the employee's training and background to identify areas where training may be needed. The results of this assessment should be documented and retained, and the company should provide training in any area where deficiencies were identified. This training should be documented in the personnel file so it can be quickly accessed when desired.

A second approach taken by a certified program was for department managers within each area to develop a training evaluation sheet for every position within their department. The evaluation sheet for each job listed the required education, training, skills, and/or experience a person should possess to perform that job successfully. This information was placed on a training form for that position (see Appendix VII). The next step was to fill out one of these forms for each employee in the company.

The approach was to verify whether the employee had a specific skill or base of knowledge. The supervisor compared the employee's background to the list and verified that the employee had the skill through demonstrated ability, experience, training, or formal education. If this was verified by one or more of the methods, a column was provided for the supervisor's initials. If the employee was deficient in one or more areas, the supervisor wrote an action plan to provide the employee with training. This approach was expanded to include every position within the plant, including upper management. This was the foundation upon which the yearly training schedules were developed for each department.

This approach had a side benefit, as it provided a single place where training for all employees could be documented. This company provided a tremendous amount of training but had no tracking system. With this approach, all training was tracked and documented by the supervisor, who retained the training documentation. If the employee transferred, the documentation was forwarded to the next supervisor. If the employee left the company, this information was provided to him or her. This training evaluation sheet was used to show that each of the requirements of this element were met.

20

SERVICING

Servicing is one of the two elements that is required only by ISO 9001 in the 1987 version. In the 1994 version, however, a company that performs servicing of the product after the sale will certify to ISO 9002 as long as they have no responsibility for the design of the product. Servicing is a contracted activity whereby installation or servicing of a delivered product is provided. The activity may be the installation of the product in the customer's facility. Providing routine maintenance or the repair of a product also falls in this category. In the case of a company that builds boilers, servicing would be applicable if the supplier installed the boiler for the customer as part of the terms of the contract. Servicing may also be the routine preventative maintenance (if performed on a schedule) of the product after the sale. The most obvious example of this situation is a copy machine company that maintains a servicing contract on the equipment once it is in service with the customer.

The controlling factor in determining the applicability of this element is the phrase "specified in the contract." Unless servicing is specified in the contract, this element will not apply to a company.

Standard warranty repair of a product after the sale typically will not fall into the category of servicing. Servicing applies only when special provisions, plans, schedules or details are contained in the contract. When an item is returned under warranty for repair, that repair activity would be covered under one of the normal quality system programs such as the control of nonconforming product. If the required activity falls under the control of one of the other elements of the standard (and is not specified as servicing in the contract), it is not considered servicing.

In summary, there are two qualifying factors to determine the applicability of this element. First, the activity must be specified in the contract. Second, the activities performed must be in addition to the established program regarding the other elements of the standard.

ISO 9001

4.19 Servicing

Where servicing is specified in the contract, the supplier shall establish and maintain procedures for performing and verifying that servicing meets the specified requirements.

ISO 9004

16.2 After-sales servicing

16.2.1 Special-purpose tools or equipment for handling and servicing products during or after installation should have their design and function validated, as for any new product.

16.2.2 Measuring and test equipment used in field installation and test should be controlled (see clause 13).

16.2.3 Instructions for use dealing with the assembly and installation, commissioning, operation, spares or parts lists, and servicing of any product should be comprehensive and supplied in a timely manner. The suitability of instructions for the intended reader should be verified.

16.2.4 Assurance should be provided for an adequate logistic back-up, to include technical advice, spares or parts supply, and competent servicing. Responsibility should be clearly assigned and agreed among suppliers, distributors and users.

16.3 Market reporting and product supervision

An early warning system may be established for reporting instances of product failure or shortcomings, as appropriate, particularly for newly introduced products, to ensure rapid corrective action.

ISO 9004

A feedback system regarding performance in use should exist to monitor the quality characteristics of the product throughout its life cycle. This system should be designed to analyse, as a continuing operation, the degree to which the product or service satisfies customer expectations on quality, including safety and reliability.

Information on complaints, the occurrence and modes of failure, customer needs and expectations or any problem encountered in use should be made available for design review and corrective action in the supply and/or use of the item.

Servicing

What Is the Intent of This Element?

The intent of this element is to ensure that where servicing is specified in the contract, it is performed in accordance with contract requirements. This activity is a key element that should be analyzed during contract review.

What Is the Requirement of This Element?

The requirement of this element is to establish procedures ensuring that servicing is provided in accordance with the contract.

What About the 1994 Version? Servicing

The 1994 version requires documented procedures to address this element when applicable. Such procedures must address the reporting aspect with regard to servicing activities.

Implementation Strategy

Implementation of this element requires a company to establish and maintain procedures for performing and verifying that servicing meets the contract requirements. The complementary section of ISO 9004 provides numerous areas that should be considered in instances where this element applies. Each company should identify if it is involved in servicing activities. To help make this determination, the following questions should be addressed:

1. Does the contract specify activities relating to installation that are the responsibility of the supplier? Does the contract specify activities following installation that are the responsibility of the supplier?
2. Is special equipment used when complying with service requirements of the contract? How is this equipment verified for proper design and function?
3. Is there measuring and test equipment used during field installation and test that requires control?

4. Have special instructions been developed for assembly and installation? Do these instructions include operation, servicing, or spares or parts lists? Are the instructions provided in a manner appropriate to the intended reader?
5. Are the responsibilities for backup defined and understood by the supplier, distributor and user? Does this include technical advice, parts or parts supply, and competent servicing?

Procedures and activities should be developed and maintained to address all areas of servicing adequately and effectively. In summary, if this area is determined to be applicable, it should be established, documented, controlled, and monitored in the same manner as the original contract for the physical product.

21

STATISTICAL TECHNIQUES

Statistical techniques is the last of the eighteen elements detailed in both ISO 9001 and 9002. This element is included to ensure that if statistical methods are being used by a company to control processes or production, the methods are accurate and properly applied.

Statistical techniques, as defined by ISO 9004, can include a large number of methods. These methods can cover a wide range, from market analysis to defect analysis of the product after the sale. Collectively, this variety of methods is termed "statistical quality control." Each of the many methods can have a direct impact on the quality of the finished goods and therefore should be controlled. Statistical process control (SPC) is one of the more popular methods of using statistics in production; SPC should be included in the requirements of this element. Along with these sophisticated methods of analysis, an often overlooked statistical method is statistical sampling. Incoming inspection sampling to a scheme such as MIL-STD-105 E, MIL-STD-414 A, or ISO 2859-1974 should also be included in this element. These statistical methods should be included because they are commonly used in manufacturing.

ISO 9001

4.20 Statistical techniques

Where appropriate, the supplier shall establish procedures for identifying adequate statistical techniques required for verifying the acceptability of process capability and product characteristics.

ISO 9004

20 Use of statistical methods

20.1 Applications

Correct applications of modern statistical methods is an important element at all stages in the quality loop and is not limited to the post-production (or inspection) stages. Applications may be for purposes such as

a) market analysis;

b) product design;

c) reliability specification, longevity/durability prediction;

d) process control/process capability studies;

e) determination of quality levels/inspection plans;

f) data analysis/performance assessment/defect analysis.

20.2 Statistical techniques

Specific statistical methods and applications available include, but are not limited to, the following:

a) design of experiments/factorial analysis;

b) analysis of variance/regression analysis;

c) safety evaluation/risk analysis;

d) tests of significance;

e) quality control charts/cusum techniques;

f) statistical sampling inspection.

NOTE—Attention is drawn to

ISO 9004

the activities of ISO/TC 69, Applications of statistical methods, the activities of ISO/TC 69, Ap- (see ISO Standards Handbook 3, Statistical methods) and IEC/TC 56, Reliability and maintainability, which have published several standard guides (or codes of practice) to assist in this complex sphere.

Statistical Techniques

What Is the Intent of This Element?

The intent of this element is for a company to determine if processes could be improved or properly controlled by the use of statistical techniques. Traditionally these statistical techniques would include statistical process control, process capability studies, design of experiments, statistical sampling, and so forth. The intent of this element is for a company to search out ways to use scientific approaches to quality improvement and control.

Statistical quality control (SQC) is a tool that can vastly improve the process producing a product. Statistical quality control is a method of collecting data from a process to determine if it is running with natural variation or if variation is being induced by an outside cause. The three basic rules upon which SQC is built include the following:

1. Everything varies.
2. The variation that normally occurs in groups of like items is predictable.
3. When the variation in like items becomes unpredictable, an outside force (assignable cause) is acting upon the process.

The predictability of variation is the key to SQC. When data are gathered and placed on a bar graph, if the shape of the distribution looks like a bell curve, no outside force exists. If an outside force is acting on the production process, the distribution will have a different shape. The curve may be skewed or bimodal, either of which indicates that the processes producing these distributions have an outside disturbance acting on them. After determining that outside disturbances exist, the cause of the variation can be located and eliminated. When the disturbance is eliminated, the distribution will return to normal and form a bell curve.

With the variation removed from a process, the product will be produced in a consistent manner. When the output of a process is consistent, the product quality can be improved and the improvement maintained. The first step in gaining real improvement in the output of a process is to obtain consistent output; statistical methods can be used to achieve the needed consistency. Control of the process results in control of the product. If a process is creating a product distribution other than normal, the process is said to be out of control.

The product produced by a process gives the most information about the process. If the product is produced by a process that is out of control, the product distribution will not be normal. Such a process is no longer predictable. Without a predictable process, management becomes reactive rather than proactive. Reactive management (knee-jerk reaction) will traditionally over-respond to a situation. Managers become fire fighters, working on one fire until it is reduced to a point that it is smaller than another. At that time, the attention will shift to the larger fire. If a fire is not completely extinguished, it will smolder for days, weeks, or months until it has sufficient strength to start up again.

Management by reaction ensures that the same problems will have to be solved again and again. Until a process is evaluated and all outside disturbances removed, the process cannot be effectively operated or managed.

The advantage of SQC is that constant evaluations are made allowing consistent corrections to be made. In most processes, variation can be identified and corrective action taken well before production of a bad product. This is the point of total process control. If consistent monitoring is not performed, the process could change drastically between check times. A common example would be to drive a car by looking out the windshield for fifteen seconds. The driver then makes corrections in direction based on the fifteen second analysis. For the next hour, the driver closes his/her eyes and continues driving blind. It sounds crazy to drive a car this way, but many companies try to produce a product by evaluating one piece of product every hour. The process is changed based on that piece of product. To be effective, the process should be continually monitored and adjusted only when the chart shows other than normal variation.

Properly understood and implemented, SQC can drastically improve profitability. This occurs not only through the elimination of scrap, but by allowing a worker to produce product of a higher quality with less effort. SQC allows a process to be improved and ensures that the improvements are maintained.

The intent is not to simply generate numbers for the sake of producing charts that are filed in a desk drawer, decorate walls or fill a file cabinet. In other words, *if the use of statistical quality control does not produce a change in the process, it is an exercise in futility and should be immediately eliminated.* Producing charts and graphs that go unused is an unnecessary overhead expense that should be stopped. The efforts of the people producing this superfluous paperwork could be better spent elsewhere.

What Is the Requirement of This Element?

The requirement is for a company to develop a documented program that will identify adequate statistical techniques to (1) verify the acceptability of process capability, and (2) verify the acceptability of product characteristics. In other words, the standard does not require the use of statistical techniques; each company is required to analyze its processes to determine if statistical analysis or control applies to any given area of that business. A company is also required to ensure that if statistical methods are used, they are appropriate to the situation. The data generated must be properly and effectively used.

What About the 1994 Version? Statistical Techniques

The only change to this element was the requirement for documented procedures when statistical techniques are determined applicable.

Implementation Strategy

The strategies used to meet the requirements of this element can vary widely. They can range from simple applications to extensive and complex measurement and improvement techniques. The key to any implementation is for the selected statistical technique to be properly applied. The focus should be on process improvement and control, rather than generating paperwork just for show.

In one certified program, this element was satisfied by the following policy: "At incoming inspection, appropriate lots of product will be inspected through statistically selected samples. These samples will be selected in accordance with a plan that conforms to MIL-STD-105 D." The procedure specifically called for the "D" revision, which was present at the inspection area, to be used. If no revision level is stated in the procedure, the latest revision is assumed and must be used.

In a different certified program, statistical techniques are one of the more dominant elements. Every batch of material is statistically sampled in accordance with MIL-STD-105 D or MIL-STD-414 A, and the results are recorded. All of the processes used to produce the end product are on X-bar and R charts; the results of final product testing are plotted on a P-chart. Customer complaints are also charted and used as feedback to R & D and manufacturing. Processes are improved through the use of designed experiments.

What makes these applications so successful is not the fact that numbers are being generated. Rather, it is that the numbers mean something. Each method is documented, and the output is used to improve and control the processes. The operators are properly trained in producing and using these charts. The charts and graphs are not viewed as the end result; instead, they are used as a tool to help ensure that each process will operate in a state of control. This will help ensure that product sent to the customer will meet or exceed the customer's expectations.

22

ECONOMICS:
QUALITY-RELATED
COST CONSIDERATIONS

ISO 9004 continues beyond the requirements of ISO 9001 and 9002 to discuss the concept of quality costs and product liability. The standard recognizes that quality goes well beyond the typical idea of being inspected into a part. Rather, it is the result of a well-planned and -executed program. The standard views design as the beginning of quality. Quality continues through conformance to design and culminates in the performance of the product. There are costs associated with good quality and costs associated with poor quality.

Quality of Design

The quality of design is concerned with the specifications for manufacturing. Market research performed by targeting intended buyers will be the initial step in design quality. Also important are the intended functions of the product (such as luxury, style, and longevity), blueprint tolerances, material characteristics, and measurement clearances. In addition to these areas, manufacturing processes, specifications, and procedures are critical.

The cost of the item will increase as the quality of design increases.

For instance, if the design calls for measurement tolerances to be ± 0.0005 inches instead of ± 0.005 inches, then it will cost more to manufacture that part. A product made of top-quality materials designed for extended life will cost more than a product made of lesser quality materials designed for a shorter life expectancy.

Quality of Conformance to Design

This area is the one most often associated with quality control. The greatest influence of quality control has been on a product's conformance to specifications. Quality control deals with whether the processes and procedures outlined in the design phase are being used and effective; conformance of material to specifications is also monitored. Basically, quality of conformance monitors the product and procedures from raw material to shipment of the finished product. This ensures that all aspects of the product and the production process conform to the written specifications.

The cost of the product can actually be *decreased* as the product quality increases by ensuring that product conforms to the written specifications. Failure to hold specified tolerances can cost a company tremendous amounts of money in the form of material costs, rework, shipping, and many other hidden costs. Holding the specified tolerances shown on the blueprint and following the procedures as outlined by a company are not always easy, though, without quality training. The quality of the product is the responsibility of every employee; however, someone must give them direction. That is the job of management, with the help of the quality control department. As the processes are held in control and the employees are trained in proper methods of assembly, defects are reduced, and profits rise.

Quality of Performance

Quality of performance is the result of design quality and quality of conformance. If either the design or conformance quality is not up to par, the quality of performance will suffer. For example, if a product is designed to work under the stresses expected but the tolerances are not held, failure will probably occur early. Also, if a product is not designed to handle the stress to which it will be exposed, no amount of production quality will make it last. Quality control/assurance must be vitally interested in both areas. A company must incorporate a good communication system to allow quality control the information necessary to make changes and corrections that will result in increased performance. Obviously, the term *quality* is not an absolute; quality is a diamond with many facets.

As is stated in the last portion of ISO-9004, the cost of poor quality can be measured and tracked with the traditional approach to quality costs and product liability. Keep in mind that the following topics are from ISO-9004 and are not mandatory or binding. They do, however, contain valuable information on good business practices.

ISO 9001

No equivalent mandatory clauses in ISO-9001

ISO 9004

6 Economics—Quality-related cost considerations

6.1 General

The impact of quality upon the profit-and-loss statement can be highly significant, particularly in the long term. It is, therefore, important that the effectiveness of a quality system be measured in a business-like manner. The main objective of quality cost reporting is to provide means for evaluating effectiveness and establishing the basis for internal improvement programmes.

6.2 Selecting appropriate elements

A portion of total business costs is earmarked for meeting the quality objectives. In practice, the combination of selected elements from this portion of total costs can provide the necessary information for marshalling efforts towards achieving quality goals. It is now common practice to identify and measure "quality costs." Both costs of activities directed at achieving appropriate quality and resultant costs from inadequate control should be identified.

6.3 Types of quality-related costs

6.3.1 General

Quality costs can be broadly divided into operating quality costs (see 6.3.2) and external assurance quality costs (see 6.3.3).

ISO 9004

6.3.2 Operating quality costs

Operating quality costs are those costs incurred by a business in order to attain and ensure specified quality levels. These include the following:

a) Prevention and appraisal costs (or investments)

—prevention: Costs of efforts to prevent failures

—appraisal: Costs of testing, inspection and examination to assess whether specified quality is being maintained

b) Failure costs (or losses)

—internal failure: Costs resulting from a product or service failing to meet the quality requirements prior to delivery (e.g. reperforming of service, reprocessing, rework, retest, scrap)

—external failure: Costs resulting from a product or service failing to meet the quality requirements after delivery (e.g. product service, warranties and returns, direct costs and allowances, product recall costs, liability costs)

6.3.3 External Assurance quality costs

External assurance quality costs are those costs relating to the demonstration and proof required as objective evidence by customers, including particular

ISO 9004

and additional quality assurance provisions, procedures, data, demonstration tests, and assessments (e.g. the cost of testing for specific safety characteristics by recognized independent testing bodies).

19. Product safety and liability

The safety aspects of product or service quality should be identified with the aim of enhancing product safety and minimizing product liability. Steps should be taken to both limit the risk of product liability and to minimize the number of cases by

a) identifying relevant safety standards in order to make the formulation of product or service specifications more effective;

b) carrying out design evaluation tests and prototype (or model) testing for safety and documenting the test results:

c) analyzing instructions and warnings to the user, maintenance manuals and labelling and promotional material in order to minimize misinterpretation;

d) developing a means of traceability to facilitate product recall if features are discovered compromising safety and to allow a planned investigation of products or services suspected of having unsafe features (see 15.4 and 16.1.3)

Quality Cost Concepts

The concept of quality cost has become the starting point for many quality programs. One of the reasons for this intense investigation is that the cost of quality has become staggering. According to Dr. J. M. Juran, the cost of quality may be on the order of ten percent of the economy. This means the amount of potential savings is also staggering. What makes this amount more shocking is that quality costs are only those costs that are related to making an unacceptable product; these costs would go away if the product were made right the first time. A thorough accounting of these costs would determine where the majority of a company's revenue is being lost. When areas of loss are located, corrective action can be taken to eliminate the financial drain.

Quality costs can be divided into four areas, depending on where these costs occur. Quality costs are incurred by the following:

1. Internal failure
2. External failure
3. Appraisal
4. Prevention

If these costs can be identified with precision, they can be eliminated. The first step in the elimination of these costs is to understand each of the areas.

Internal Failure

Internal failure costs are those costs associated with locating the defective product before it is shipped to the customer. These costs include the categories listed below:

Scrap: The total loss in labor, material, production costs, storage, and inspection of material that is defective and cannot be economically repaired.

Rework: The total cost to correct a defective product and make it fit for use (for example, costs of processing, labor, material, and storage).

Retest: The total cost to inspect the product after it has been re-worked.

Downtime: The time, if any, that production is halted due to defective material. In continuous processing mills, this may be a factor because material from one process is directly fed into the next process. If the defective product is produced in the first process, it is removed, and no product is present for the second process to use. This causes downtime for the equipment and labor force (for example, newspaper press halted because of major printing error).

Yield Loss: The cost of lower profit that could be eliminated if the production process were improved. A soft drink company would experience yield loss if the amount of liquid put in the bottle was not controlled. If 50,000 bottles were filled to 32.5 ounces rather than 32 ounces, the cost of production and profit on 781 bottles of the soft drink would be lost.

Disposition: The cost of determining what to do with a nonconforming product. In many cases, this cost would include the cost of a material review board (MRB). An MRB is a group representing management, engineering, and production that makes decision on nonconforming product.

Facilities: The total facility costs of producing a nonconforming product. On the average, if a company produced 5 percent defective product, then 5 percent of the costs of the facilities, administration, and production would be estimated as being used to produce this product.

External Failure

External failure costs are those associated with shipment of defective product to the customer. These costs include the following categories:

Complaint Adjustment: This includes the costs to investigate and adjust the complaint.

Returned Material: This includes the total cost to replace the defective product or refund the purchase price. Also included are costs of storage, return shipment, and disposition of the defective product.

Warranty Cost: This includes all costs associated with servicing and repairing the defective product. For many companies, this cost includes regional repair facilities and repairmen.

Allowances: The cost of discounting a substandard product to a customer (for example, clothing seconds and tire "blems").

Appraisal

Appraisal costs are all costs associated with determining the condition of the product the first time through. These costs include the following categories:

Inspection and Testing: These include the cost of test equipment, material consumed during testing (such as X-ray film or chemicals), labor, facilities, and product consumed during destructive testing.

Maintaining Test Equipment: This includes the costs of calibration and repair of test equipment.

Prevention

Prevention costs are incurred to keep the internal and external failure costs to a minimum. These costs include the categories listed below:

Quality Planning: All costs related to planning and implementing the quality plan for a company or a process. These would include the costs of labor, material, and facilities.

Quality Data Acquisition, Analysis, and Quality Reporting: All costs associated with gathering, analyzing, and reporting on the quality status to middle and upper management.

Process Control: Costs of material, labor, and facilities dedicated to controlling the output quality of the process used to create the product.

Involvement Projects: All costs involved with planning, implementation, and maintenance of projects directed toward improving the output quality of a process.

If 100 percent of the product being produced were defective, the internal and external failure costs would be the total cost of production; the appraisal and prevention costs would be a zero output. As the product approaches 100 percent good quality, the internal and external failure costs decrease. To achieve this improvement, however, the appraisal and prevention costs would rise. Initially, internal and external failure costs will decrease at a greater rate than the appraisal and prevention costs will increase. This results in a good return on investment. As product quality approaches 100 percent good product, the return on investment goes down. At a point near 100 percent, $1.00 invested in improving the product yields a $1.00 reduction in internal and external failures; further improvement will yield a negative return on investment. This point is the economic state of control. Unless industrial requirements force further improvement, a system should be put in place at this point to maintain the process.

Product Safety and Liability

In today's society, litigation over product liability is a common occurrence. The number and size of financial settlements have increased to the point that many companies have gone out of business, and cost to the customer has prevented many products from being sold. Some cities have no doctors who will deliver babies because of the cost of malpractice insurance. In the United States, no aircraft manufacturer produces a two-place aircraft because the cost of product liability insurance doubles the selling price of the airplane. The cost of protection has driven the price of these aircraft beyond what consumers are willing to pay.

The quality control department should play a significant role in reducing the liability exposure of the company. This is accomplished by expanding into every aspect of manufacturing, including (1) engineering, (2) manufacturing, (3) marketing (sales), and (4) warranty. With a quality influence in each of these areas, the liability exposure will be reduced. ISO-9001 and -9002 do an excellent job of specifying good business practices in each of these areas.

Engineering

The responsibility of most engineering departments includes designing, redesigning, and evaluating new and existing products.

Quality control should have an active part in the following functions:

1. Ensuring that safety becomes a formal design parameter.
2. Performance of design reviews for safety at strategic points of the design formation and approval cycle.
3. Ensuring that the design will meet all government and industry safety standards.
4. Review of test data to determine a product's safety and reliability before it is released for production.
5. Review of material and material substitutions to ensure each meets all safety codes.
6. Review of tracking methods for product traceability (this will allow for a rapid and limited recall if the product is determined to be unsafe after it has been produced and sold on the open market).

If quality control is practiced during the design stage of a product, the end result should be a safer product that can be produced efficiently. There should be fewer chances of encountering a product liability suit.

Manufacturing

Manufacturing is where properly followed quality techniques can produce large cost savings. Manufacturing is also the area in which product liability exposure can be reduced. Beyond the cost savings, quality control should be involved in safety to do the following:

1. Ensure that shipped product conforms to specifications, as well as government and industry safety standards.
2. Provide training for workers to meet safety standards.
3. Provide motivation on product safety by explaining why the procedures are necessary.
4. Audit the process to determine that proper checks are made, and that product is accepted or rejected solely on the test results.
5. Provide accurate feedback to upper management on the status of production and product safety.

6. Maintain proper documentation on test results of the product.
7. Maintain calibration of the test equipment.
8. Plan and perform tests, then evaluate test results.
9. Determine if the nonconforming product is fit for use.

Marketing (Sales)

Sales is the area where consumers may get wrong impressions on the use of a product. Quality control should include the following responsibilities:

1. Evaluate sales ads for technical and usage accuracy.
2. Make sure that products are properly packaged and labeled with warnings and remedies.
3. Provide safety information to everyone involved with the product.
4. Evaluate the users' manual for accuracy and proper explanation of the safety procedures to follow when using the product.
5. Ensure the sales force has received proper safety training and is providing this information to the end user.

Warranty

Follow-up on problems will provide information on product performance. Information on how the product is being used and misused by the general public is also obtained. The information on how the product is misused may help in redesigning the product to reduce injuries. The quality control department should be involved in the warranty area in the following ways:

1. Determine if a product failure is induced by engineering or manufacturing.
2. Be involved in investigations involving injury or death to establish if the product is at fault.
3. Ensure that service is performed properly to the customer's satisfaction, and that product is as safe as it was when purchased.

The quality control department is responsible for reducing the liability exposure of the company. If the quality functions are properly performed, many companies will experience a reduction in injury-causing failures. If these failures are controlled, the number of product liability suits will decrease. This reduction in litigation can provide a dramatic cost savings to the company.

Summary

Beyond the ISO 9004 standard, it should be discussed that money is made by not producing bad product. More money will be made from the good product than is saved from not making bad product. In other words, when more product is correctly produced the first time, a company will have a positive, direct, and measurable impact on the bottom line. The results of good quality can be directly measured.

Amazing stories have been documented in the areas of profitability and cost savings through quality improvement. Improving the quality of manufacturing methods, products, and information on a production line has provided tremendous cost savings and improved the quality of the end product.

The following example will demonstrate the potential cost savings and profit enhancement available through the use of quality improvement. ABC Machine and Fabrication is in the business of making threaded unions. Currently, the threaded unions are made and sold in groups of 100. Raw material is purchased, and 100 threaded unions are manufactured and shipped. The cost to produce each threaded union is a combination of parts, direct labor, and overhead. The cost breakdown is as follows:

ABC Machine and Fabrication (ABC) Cost Breakdown

$ 2.00	Parts and material
$ 4.00	Direct labor
$ 4.00	Overhead
$10.00	Delivered cost (cost of doing business)
$12.00	Invoice price per part (20 percent markup)
$ 2.00	Profit per Part (if all parts are accepted)

Cost and Profit on 100 Threaded Unions

$ 200.00	Parts
$ 400.00	Direct labor
$ 400.00	Overhead
$1,000.00	Total cost (to produce 100 parts)
$1,200.00	Invoice amount
$ 200.00	Profit

The total cost of one production run is $1,000.00 and should result in a profit of $200.00 ABC found that 85 out of each 100 threaded unions produced were accepted and 15 were rejected by the customer. If 85 of the threaded unions were acceptable, each accepted threaded union would actually cost $11.76 to produce ($1,000.00/85 = $11.76). The reason for this increase is that the total cost to produce 100 parts ($1,000.00) must be recovered from the revenue produced by the 85 good parts. The cost of parts, labor, and overhead must be recovered from these parts no matter how many (or how few) of the parts can be sold. If the selling price of the threaded unions were $12.00 each, this lot of threaded unions would bring $1,020.00 total revenue and yield a $20.00 profit, as shown below:

$1000.00	Actual cost to produce 85 good parts
$ 1020.00	Invoice (85 parts)
$ 20.00	Total profit

The true cost to produce each acceptable part was increased to $11.76 rather than $10.00, but ABC could only invoice for $1,020.00 (85 parts × $12.00) rather than $1,200.00 (100 parts × $12.00). This resulted in the total profit for this order being $20 instead of the expected $200. A 15 percent reduction in the number of delivered parts resulted in a $0.24 profit per part, a return on investment (ROI) of 2 percent, not 20 percent, and a profit 90 percent lower than expected.

ABC management saw two alternatives to the problem of reduced profits: (1) make more parts with the existing processes to make sure 100 acceptable parts are delivered, or (2) fix the processes to make more of the parts correctly the first time. Both options were explored to determine which would yield the best return. A study was made to determine how many parts should be produced to ensure 100 acceptable parts were made per lot, with the existing process producing 15 percent rejects. ABC discovered that making 118 parts in the current manner would produce 100 good ones. A further cost analysis was conducted to find the profitability of this approach. The results of this analysis are as follows:

Total cost of production	$118 \times \$10.00 = \$1,180.00$
Cost per accepted part	$\$1,180.00 \div 100 = \$11.80$
Invoice price	$\$12.00 \times 100 \text{ parts} = \$1,200.00$
Total part cost	$\$1,180.00$
Total profit	$ 20.00
Profit per delivered Part	$ 0.20
ROI	1.67%

ABC determined that producing more parts did not help the situation. In fact, it resulted in a further decay of the profit per part and had the same effect on the ROI. The overall profit was the same ($20.00) as before; and an investment of $180.00 was required to make the same money. This further eroded the ROI.

The second analysis conducted dealt with making more of the product correctly the first time. ABC ran a comparison of costs and profits assuming that 95 parts had been made correctly the first time. The comparison was as follows:

	85 Good Parts	*95 Good Parts*
Part cost	$ 200.00	$ 200.00
Direct labor	$ 400.00	$ 400.00
Overhead cost	$ 400.00	$ 400.00
Total cost	$1,000.00	$1,000.00
Invoice price	$1,020.00	$1,140.00
Profit	$20.00	$140.00

Cost per accepted part	$11.76	$10.52
Profit per part	$ 0.24	$ 1.40
ROI	2%	14%

The same comparison was made for 98 acceptable parts, with the following results:

	85 Good Parts	*98 Good Parts*
Part cost	$ 200.00	$ 200.00
Direct labor	$ 400.00	$ 400.00
Overhead cost	$ 400.00	$ 400.00
Total cost	$1,000.00	$1,000.00
Invoice price	$1,020.00	$1,176.00
Profit	$ 20.00	$ 176.00
Cost per accepted part	$ 11.76	$ 10.20
Profit per part	$ 0.24	$ 1.76
ROI	2%	17.6%

If through quality improvement the normal production run of 100 yielded 98 acceptable threaded unions, the profit picture would improve dramatically. The cost to run this lot would remain at $1,000.00 as 100 threaded unions were attempted; the cost per threaded union sold would drop to $10.20 each. With the selling price of $12.00 each, this lot would yield $1,176.00. The end result is a $176.00 profit to the company. The total number of threaded unions sold increased by 13, but the profit increased by $156.00. Producing more of the parts correctly the first time would give a disproportionate increase in profit. *A 13 percent increase in the number of parts accepted (98 instead of 85) resulted in an 880 percent increase in profits ($176.00 instead of $20.00).*

Many approaches are used to determine the profitability of a contract; the definition of profit used here is all the dollars that are left over after all the bills are paid. Using this definition, though, how can making 13 percent more product correctly the first time result in an 880 percent increase in profits? The key is in the break-even point for the contract. The cost to produce the lot of 100 parts is a fixed cost. Whether all the parts are acceptable or unacceptable, this cost must be fully recovered before profit is made. For the 100 threaded unions, the break-even point is 83 threaded unions. That is, the entire $12.00 selling price of the first 83 threaded unions sold goes to cover the production cost; no profit is made until at least 84 parts are sold. The entire selling price of all subsequent parts goes to the bottom line as profit. Thus the production cost is recovered on 83 parts, and profit is made on 17 parts. Because the entire invoice price of a rejected part is deducted from the profit, each one has a disproportionate impact on the bottom line.

As an added benefit, if 98 parts were made correctly the first time instead of 85, the production volume would be increased by 13 percent with no additional overhead. The same amount of raw material was purchased, and the same time was spent making 100 threaded unions; no additional workers, machines, or time would be necessary for the 13 percent increase in production. Every company should be interested in increasing production with no increase in production cost. What would the economic effect of a 13 percent increase be in a company that produces parts that sold for $50,000.00 each, if all parts were made right the first time?

Additional profit can be realized by not spending money on producing parts that are defective. In the example of the threaded unions, the assumption was made that the unacceptable threaded unions only cost the amount directly spent on production. In fact, though, there are many indirect costs involved that can be greater and are not as easily identified. When attempting to document these costs, several evaluations should be made. A typical industry assumption is that only one third of the total quality costs are usually identified the first time such an analysis is attempted. This quality cost concept is known as the "iceberg effect." According to this theory, the cost of poor quality can be as much as 20 percent to 40 percent of sales, which is higher than the direct costs (parts and labor only) of producing a bad part.

For a company producing 90 percent acceptable parts, the cost of the 10 percent defective product could be staggering. When one out of ten parts produced is defective, 10 percent of all operating costs are being spent on a bad product. This means that 10 percent of the costs of labor, facility maintenance, floor space, administration, utilities, and insurance have been spent producing bad parts. These costs are usually sizable enough to warrant being aggressively sought out and eliminated. Not only is it good customer relations for a company to improve the quality of the product, it makes good business sense to make more cash and a higher return on every part produced.

23

ROAD MAP TO A THREE-PHASED IMPLEMENTATION

This chapter is presented to provide a generic plan that may be used to structure pursuit of certification to the ISO 9000 series standard. The information and basic guidelines will provide the framework on which the major elements of the program can be based. This guideline assumes a baseline of zero, that is, no documentation, procedures, or formally implemented programs. This chapter may not be required in its entirety for organizations that are familiar with operating to the requirements of government or industry standards.

Familiarity with operating to standards will jump-start an organization in its efforts to achieve certification to ISO 9000. This familiarity, however, may prove to be a hindrance in achieving the actual intent of the standard. This is because the ISO standard is a process-oriented document, while many other quality standards are product oriented. Documentation alone will not assure that the intent of ISO 9000 has been met. Previous generations of existing standards have required volumes of paperwork as a means of substantiating the product, and this knowledge has carried over into the efforts of many companies now pursuing ISO 9000. A program implemented to meet the requirements of the ISO 9000 standard thus can be a paperwork-dominant program. This has been a choice made by the organization, however, and not a requirement of the ISO 9000 standard.

The focus of the implementation process should be directed toward the program rather than at documentation. Many efforts fail because the entire effort is directed toward the generation of written documentation to the exclusion of program implementation. A prevailing philosophy that many companies have followed has been "Document what you do, and do what you document." As previously discussed, many companies have found themselves documenting ill-conceived programs that do not meet the requirements of the standard. Much of the effort is directed toward documenting the program, and little time or effort is spent in evaluating the activity or the relevance of the activity.

The timetable offered is divided into three phases of roughly equal length. The length of each phase depends upon the manpower and financing that a company is willing to devote to the project. A realistic expectation is completion of the entire effort in twelve to eighteen months if a company aggressively pursues the certification, meaning that, each phase will be four to six months long. By no means should this be taken as a hard and fast rule; the length may vary depending on the company. One company in the Midwest has been preparing for the certification audit for five years. The company anticipates it will be ready for the audit in two more years. As a rule, however, implementation will usually take eighteen months for a company of 250 people with no formal program in place.

This chapter is designed to focus on program evaluation, development, and implementation. Documentation efforts and resulting procedures are viewed as secondary; the purpose of documentation is to promote consistency, provide training, give direction, and allow the program to be easily audited. The main focus is to provide a set of guidelines for the development of a program that is viable, consistent, and encompasses all departments. The programs should be developed in such a way that the guidelines become the focal point of all activities. The end result of all the activity is customer satisfaction.

Phase One

Phase one identifies how the program will be defined, determines where the company currently is, and incorporates a media blitz to provide information. As has been said many times, "You can't know where you are going unless you know where you've been." This is the case in attempting certification. The first phase will be characterized by identifying where a company is so it can be directed toward certification.

Determine Management Philosophy

The first and most important issue is determining the management philosophy that will be followed in the pursuit of this certificate. The proper philosophy is for a company to use the implementation effort as an improvement activity. The process of preparing for the certification audit should be viewed as a comparison. The company should compare itself to the operations of a world-class organization; where deficiencies are identified, actions should be taken. With this management philosophy, a company will be open to the changes necessary to bring its operations into compliance with this standard.

Part of this activity calls for a company to make decisions regarding program responsibilities. Will the program be confined to the quality control department, or will the responsibility be divided among the departments that are affected by the elements? While either can be certified, the intent of the standard seems to be for a company to spread responsibility. As has been discussed, giving each department responsibility and accountability for the program will encourage the entire company to feel ownership for the program. This is one of the steps that must occur for a program to be effective.

Management should determine the purpose of the certification effort. If the only purpose is to gain certification, it might be cost-effective to employ a consultant solely for that reason. If, however, this is to be viewed as an opportunity for a company to improve the way it conducts business, the effort should be spread throughout many different departments. Certification should be viewed as a stepping-stone or to show a company that it is on its way. The intent of the standard is to develop a program that changes and improves as better methods are discovered.

Develop the Internal Audit Program

One of the first programs that should be developed is internal auditing. Auditing will become one of the most important activities within a company. In the beginning, the purpose of the audits is for a company to evaluate realistically how it conducts business. In this effort, the audit team should evaluate the company to determine what elements are in compliance, what elements are close to compliance, and what elements are absent.

This activity will cause a rude awakening in many companies. If this activity is properly conducted, the audits should provide an unbiased evaluation of whether a company is meeting the requirements of the different elements of the standard. Beyond determining if the elements are being met, the audit team should make a judgment on the effectiveness of the activity. This determination should be made without bias. The judgment should be on actual activity as it is being performed, not on how the auditor would like to see a program run.

The early audits will also serve as a training program for the audit team and for the individuals audited. Specifically, the audit team will need time to develop its auditing skills. The knowledge of how to prepare for and conduct an audit can be learned from a class, seminar, or book; the skill portion can only be developed by performing audits. The work force involved in the audit will also learn from this activity. Many companies have found themselves in a bad position when professional auditors perform certification audits with people who have never been audited before. This situation occurs when the internal audit program is ineffective and not properly utilized. Internal audits that include people from as many departments as possible allow workers the time and opportunity to learn how to handle an auditor's questions and feel secure in their own response.

Conduct a Companywide Information Blitz

One often-overlooked step in the first stages of the certification effort is to publish good information about what the certification is and how it will benefit the company. This can be accomplished by mass meetings, flyers, small group meetings, or newsletters. The key issue is that in the absence of good information, the void will be filled with rumor and speculation. In most cases, speculation is negative or incorrect and will hurt the effort.

Try to avoid a carnival atmosphere, which will smack of "the program of the month." The typical response to this type of hype is "I've seen them come and I've seen them go, and I'll outlast this one, too." If this is the general response, a company should reevaluate its method of promoting the effort. If a very professional approach is taken to the promotion of this program, though, then the result is usually also professional. The key is to give people information: remember that "good people given good information will make good informed decisions." The alternative approach of "knowledge is power, and power is control" will leave managers with an untrained and uninformed work force. Passing the certification audit with this approach is highly unlikely.

Implementation Teams

An extremely effective method to speed up implementation is the formulation of teams to guide the implementation process. One proven method is to select a certification representative from each department. This person will work as the liaison between the implementation team and the department: an engineer is selected to represent the best interests of the engineering department, a purchasing agent represents purchasing, and so forth. This representative also becomes the chairperson of the elements in which that department has ownership: the engineering representative is the chairperson of the team that is formed to address the design control element, the human resources representative is chairperson over the team that addresses training, and so on.

For this approach to be effective, the implementation of ISO 9001 will involve twenty teams—one for each element. For ISO

9002, eighteen teams will exist. The team should consist of members from departments that are affected by an element. For example, the inspection, measuring, and test equipment element will affect the quality control department, manufacturing, and possibly engineering and purchasing; the team that is developed to address this element needs a representative from each of the departments. This will assure the element is consistently applied and that each of the departments will have the same program. The team will also shorten the time it takes to implement the program.

If these teams are properly coordinated, each element will receive the same intensity of attention at the same time. All programs will be developed, improved, and implemented. The other alternative is for one person or a small group to work on a few at a time. Either way will work; the second method, however, takes longer.

Training team members should be the first step in the team meetings. This training should include the typical areas of team dynamics, brainstorming, and the like. The most important training should concentrate on a common understanding and philosophy of ISO 9000. The training should include evaluation of the standard, element by element, to determine the intent, requirement, management philosophy, and direction for implementation.

This training should specifically teach flowcharting and how to write procedures. Every person involved in the implementation should be familiar with flowcharting. Every process in a company can be shown on a flowchart using three symbols: a circle, a box, and a diamond. The circle is to be used as a start/stop indicator and/or as a connector to the next page. A box is used to describe an activity and to identify who is responsible for that activity. A diamond is used for all yes/no decisions. The question is listed in the diamond, and the activities associated with a yes decision are shown on one side; the activities associated with a no decision are shown on the other side. Be very cautious about adding additional symbols. Flowcharts can become so complex that few people in the organization can understand them, and if they cannot be understood, they are not useful (see Appendix VII).

Determine A Manual Structure

One of the decisions required early in the certification process is how to structure the manual. This decision is totally up to the company. The top-level manual is commonly (and widely accepted as) the quality assurance manual, which contains the quality policies for the program. Below this is a second-level or operating procedures manual, which contains the procedures to be followed to meet the stated policies. The third level usually consists of detailed job instructions. This level may be very extensive but can be scaled down according to the training and experience of the work force.

This structure is common among much of the manufacturing segment today. Each company, however, must decide what is best in a given situation. Several programs that are certified have selected unique manual structures that do not follow a standard convention. The intent of the standard is for a company to improve and have good business practices; it is not forced to do things in a specific format. Be innovative, but keep in mind that the program must be explained and function effectively.

Assign Element Responsibility by Department

As has been described throughout this book, it is highly recommended that the ownership of the elements be spread throughout the entire organization. Each element should be evaluated to determine what department has primary responsibility. That department should be accountable for development and operation in compliance with the procedures. This assignment of responsibility should come from the highest levels of management. The assignment should include management taking responsibility for the first two elements. Management must take the lead in shouldering its responsibility for this standard.

Construct Flowcharts by Element

Flowcharts are used to document a procedure in a form that most people can understand. In one company that is certified to ISO 9001, the process of contract review consumed fourteen pages in a written procedure and took almost an hour to explain to the auditors. Prior to the first periodic audit, the company made a two-page flowchart showing the process and removed all the verbiage; the procedure consisted of the flowchart alone. The procedure was accepted in a flowchart form, and the process was audited in less than ten minutes during the periodic audit.

Flowcharts are very important in helping implementation teams gain understanding of how each process works. Surprisingly, few processes may be totally understood. Each team should start by developing flowcharts of the processes that are in place to meet the element that it is assigned to. Once this is accomplished, comments from everyone involved with the activity should be secured regarding the accuracy of the flowchart. From the chart, an evaluation can be made to determine if the intent and the requirements of the standard are being met.

Proposed changes to the activity should then be reflected in the flowchart. Any change should be discussed and accepted by everyone involved before the activity is actually modified. The flowcharts can then be distributed to document the changed activity. From these flowcharts, the procedures and the work instructions can be written.

Select and Contact the Certification Body

The issuance of the ISO 9000 series standard by the European Community has caused a flurry of activity in the United States. Many American companies are now scrambling to secure certification. This has opened up a phenomenal market for companies providing certification to the standard. Unfortunately, few regulations and minimal control have been established for certification agencies outside the European Community. As of 1993, anyone reading this text can form a company to provide certification to the ISO 9000 series standard (which is not to say that anyone else in the world would recognize that certification). This is probably the most disastrous aspect of the growth in popularity of certification to the ISO 9000 standard in the United States.

Presently there are two categories of companies operating in the certification market. The first are companies that have been in the business of providing third-party inspections and have established a reputation worldwide. These types of organizations, although not exclusively dedicated to program and process evaluation, have experience in performing audits to determine compliance with numerous standards and customer specifications. These companies have completed all of the requirements and are operating within the established guidelines set forth by the International Organization for Standardization. These companies have been accredited by the registration authorities to perform certification activities.

Companies accredited by a registration board can provide certification that will be recognized in the global marketplace. Such agencies have secured reciprocity agreements with many of the countries who recognize ISO 9001 or 9002 certification. A certification issued by one of these agencies will be recognized on a worldwide scale. If a company's intent is recognition in the international marketplace, reciprocity agreements of the certifying agency should be investigated.

The focus of these reciprocity agreements centers on the generally accepted intent and requirements of the standard. ISO standards currently exist for conducting third-party audits and granting certification for companies. These types of agencies have been audited to a standard and must continue operation of their programs within the requirements and guidelines recognized by the International Organization for Standardization. This adds credibility to the agency performing the audit. Extensive training and analysis have been conducted in such companies to ensure that the interpretation of the standard is consistent with the original focus. This ensures that audits performed by different agencies will remain similar and focus on the same intent and requirement.

The other category consists of companies who have entered the certification market as a sideline or have been formed solely for the purpose of providing certification services. An audit performed by one of these companies may be acceptable by all auditing standards issued by the International Organization for Standardization. Without some type of analysis, however, there is no guarantee that the audit will meet these standards.

Many auditing agencies in the second category have been formed by either consultants or professionals who have grown up in very traditional American certification programs. Such programs rely on detailed requirements verified by paperwork. While this philosophy has a long history in the United States, it is incompatible with the philosophy of the ISO 9000 series standard. Even with the best intentions, auditors frequently enter into the analysis of a program with personal bias. Years of operating under this existing American philosophy often influence the perception of the ISO 9000 series standard and its implementation. Therefore, audits conducted under this influence can vary greatly from company to company.

In summary, a company should consciously determine its motive for certification. In making this determination, each company must address the following:

1. What is the rationale for pursuing certification? Is the purpose to gain international recognition, to satisfy one customer, or for improvement of the company?
   (a) For international recognition, an established agency should be considered.
   (b) To satisfy one customer, that customer's input should help in the determination.
   (c) For improvement of the company, an agency with the proper philosophical understanding of the standard should be selected.
2. What is the existing company structure with regard to certification?
   (a) Is there a history of operating to American standards that will make an audit conducted in this manner much less complicated?
   (b) If there is little structure in the company and certification is the final goal, either type would be applicable.
   (c) If there is little structure and the company's goal is to implement a world-class program, an established agency would more than likely be more appropriate.
3. What resources are available to dedicate to the pursuit?
   (a) Certification conducted by major agencies can typically require an investment of $20,000 to $40,000.
   (b) Certification by local, smaller agencies will be considerably less.

There is no certification agency that is perfect for every company. There are, however, many agencies that can prove to be a disaster for most. Careful selection, combined with comments from certified companies, can help ensure that the correct certification body is selected. The company and the certification body will be a team for three years; a productive team can only occur when the company selects the proper certification body. Beware of "Fred's ISO 9000 Certification and Meat Packing Company," because the stakes are tough and the certification usually is not well done. (Sorry about the pun.)

Phase Two

Phase two increases the intensity of the activities introduced in phase one. Work in the second phase involves greater detail and includes more of the work force in the activities. New programs are introduced, and existing programs are modified to comply with the requirements of the standard. Phase two is characterized by change and modification to the way a company conducts business.

Step Up the Propaganda Efforts

During the second phase of the implementation, the more information that can be provided to the work force, the better. Problems are caused by lack of information rather than too much information. Everyone in the organization should know that the engineering department owns the design control element, and that they all have ownership of the document control element. Results of internal audits, including findings and corrective actions, should be broadcast throughout the organization. All program modifications should be highly publicized to increase awareness, and new programs should be advertised to gain support and understanding. The detailed flowcharts that were developed should be published.

The standard can be detailed and defined to the entire work force. The key at this point is to provide information to everyone. During the certification and periodic audits, the auditors will not accept responses solely from management or the quality department. Everyone may be required to answer an auditor's question or explain their part of the program during the audit.

Try to give complete information in a professional manner. Avoid giving the impression that this is another one of those programs that will disappear in a month. One company provided a flyer (on very bright paper) that was called "Hey, John Smith, check it out!!!" Every person in the facility had a personalized sheet with his or her name in the title. This sheet was informational and provided background information on ISO 9000. The flyer gave details on the new programs and provided a schedule of events. When the audits were completed, the findings were published; when the company became certified, the thank-yous were also published. From the very beginning, information is one of the most important tools a company can employ in their efforts to gain certification.

Develop and Publish Detailed Flowcharts

Flowcharting is one tool that, if properly used, can give everyone a better understanding of how a system works. Everyone involved with a process should become knowledgeable about that process. When the auditors evaluate a process such as welding, they will politely invite the manager to stay in the office while they talk to the person with the welding helmet and the rod in hand. If the system can be effectively explained by employees on the shop floor, then the system is probably working.

Flowcharts can be used as training aids, become the instructions that are hung by a work station, or can even take the place of written procedures. As has already been discussed, though, keep the charts simple and use as few symbols as possible.

Develop and Implement the Needed New Programs

Most companies implementing this standard will discover that existing programs need modifications. New programs may also be necessary to meet the intent and requirement of the standard. These programs should be developed by the team assigned to the element. A new program needs to be properly explained to the employees; it should be allowed to operate for as long as possible before the preassessment and certification audits.

Phase two is the time to work out the rough spots in these programs. Information about them can be provided to the workers, and the programs can be audited. This allows everyone involved with a program to become familiar with how it is working and what needs to be changed.

Conduct Formal Internal Audits

A complete series of internal audits should be conducted to determine how the programs will be accepted during the preassessment or certification audit. Most registrars will require at least one complete audit cycle prior to the preassessment.

Completing these audits will yield benefits that go beyond evaluating the program. One very important benefit is that it will allow the auditors time to perfect their auditing skills. This is an important issue because internal auditing will be relied upon heavily to ensure that programs remain in conformance with the requirements of the standard.

A second benefit is that many of the existing programs have not been compared to the ISO 9000 standard by someone other than the implementation team. This should be a fair comparison between the program and the requirement of the standard; the program should be judged to determine if it meets the intent of the standard. The last point in evaluating the program is to determine if the program is operating as documented and if it is effective. Most programs never have this last evaluation.

A third and very important point is that internal audits can be used as a training tool. They teach everyone how audits are performed and what is to be expected. As discussed earlier, auditors will want to discuss programs with the work force rather than with the managers. A worker who has been audited internally will experience less stress during the certification or periodic audits.

Schedule the Preassessment

Deciding which certification body to use is very important. The decision should be made based on the needs of the company. During this phase, a contact should be made to schedule the audit. As of 1993 well-known and reputable certification bodies are scheduling eight to twelve months in advance. This means that it might take twelve months to get a preassessment and certification audit. Make long-range plans; contact the certification body and sign the contracts to have the audit conducted.

When the contracts are signed, an end date exists. All action is then geared toward completion by the examination data. Many companies never schedule the audit and, therefore, are never ready. As mentioned earlier, the management of one company has been preparing for certification for five years. In the beginning, the company thought the certification process would take two years; five years later, it is still saying the process will take two more years.

Conduct Formal System Training

The propaganda should have helped everyone in the facility gain a basic understanding of the standard and the programs that are in place to meet it. Formal training in these areas should follow to ensure that everyone understands the intent and requirement of the standard. Training also teaches employees how the company proposes to meet the requirement.

Intensive system training in two companies yielded a common result: the system was improved by involving everyone. The typical improvement cycle happened when a program was explained and someone in the group said, "It would make things run faster if we would . . ." or "I don't want to start trouble, but we don't do it that way because it won't work like that. What we do is . . ." The program then is documented and formalized. As in all training, everyone learns, even the trainers.

Document the System

As with all quality systems, activities must eventually be documented. The approach taken by this book, which is very different from the approach taken by many other groups, is to provide the vision and direction first, develop the programs and train the people, and—when all of that is complete—document the system. Documentation should be viewed as a means to follow the program consistently and uniformly. It is a source of system training material and a resource to use when auditing the program. In short, *the documentation is supportive information, not an end result.*

Phase Three

In phase three, the company should concentrate solely on honing the implemented programs to maximize their effectiveness. The major portions of each element should be implemented and functioning. All efforts of the company should be directed toward successfully passing the certification audit. If phases one and two have been properly completed, there should be no major adjustments or efforts required during phase three. During this time, the company focuses intensely on familiarity with the program. This provides maximum effectiveness and efficiency in daily operations.

Complete the Preassessment

The preassessment is an entire system audit conducted by the certification body. This activity pays for itself in the information gained about a company's programs. It is the first independent audit most programs will undergo.

This is also the first time the programs will be viewed through the eyes of the certification body. A company may find it has a different view of the standard than the certification body; if this occurs, the company will have time to redirect its efforts to parallel the view of the certification body. In other words, if "black holes" are identified in the programs, a company will have time to resolve these issues before the certification audit.

Publish and Address the Audit Results

Following the preassessment, there will undoubtedly be audit findings that need addressing. Auditors have an uncanny knack for identifying areas in which programs are not as strong as they initially appear. If one supplier out of several hundred is not properly evaluated, the auditor will ask for information on that particular supplier.

The management of the company should keep in mind that findings will occur. That is the job of the auditors, to help find areas that can be improved. If no findings were identified, the full cost of the audit would be lost money. When findings occur, the cost of the audit is offset by the improvement that occurs when the finding is resolved.

A second point is that audit findings should not be considered something to keep under wraps. National security will not be breached if everyone knows the audit findings; they should be distributed to everyone in the facility. When people discover that an activity they are involved with took a finding, they become very interested in helping resolve the issue. Publishing the findings also encourages everyone to follow the system, because bypassing the system could result in an audit finding that will be published plantwide. Everyone becomes publicly accountable for every decision and action.

The purpose of the preassessment is to identify those areas that need further development. Addressing the findings should involve the team that developed the program. The team should meet and develop a solution that will address the finding with as little disruption as possible. Many of the audit findings can be addressed with minor system modifications. If the system modification can be minimized, the changes will be quicker to implement and more widely accepted. If the audit findings were published, the resolution and closure of the findings should also be published.

Continue Training

The requirement for training never goes away. At this phase, though, the training should take on a different perspective. In phase one, the training centered around teaching people about the concept behind the ISO 9000 series. The content was focused on the intent and requirement of the standard, as well as possible implementation strategies.

During phase two, the training centered around the implementation strategies that were outlined to meet the intent of the standard. During that phase, specific tools such as flowchart development and procedure writing were taught. Other quality improvement tools could be taught at this stage, such as team dynamics, brainstorming, and team problem solving. The key at this stage is to provide the information necessary to implement the program.

Phase-three training is characterized by problem solving techniques. At this stage, the majority of the work in developing and implementing new programs or modifying existing programs should be complete. The audit findings need to be evaluated and resolved at this time; for many findings, this will involve conducting team meetings to resolve issues. Training should be conducted for everyone in understanding the changes made in response to the audit findings, and these changes should be documented and implemented as soon as possible. This will allow time for everyone to become comfortable with the modifications.

Final Preparations for Certification Audit

Little or no change to the program should occur in the three months before the certification audit. This time allows everyone to become familiar with the operation of changed or new programs. Only final minor improvements should be made during this time. This is not to say that if a program is not working, it should be allowed to fall on its face. The important factor is for the programs to be functioning. History on the programs is also necessary; the auditors will not approve a program that does not have enough history to show that it is functioning well.

Continue to perform audits and reaudits of the programs. This will ensure that an audit history is available for the certification audit and that the systems have been evaluated by people independent of the operation. Internal auditing will continue providing education for everyone involved with the program. Everyone should learn how the audit process works and how to handle the questions from the auditors. This training will be necessary during the certification audit.

One last activity is to spot-check anything and everything. Take the opportunity to walk into the office of a manager and spot-check that manager's manuals. Stop someone in the hall and start asking questions about how a system works. Go into the inspection area and ask about the gauge calibration program. In other words, spot-check to the point that people beg for mercy, yet know it is for their own good.

Keep everyone informed as the audit approaches, and let everyone know how the company did immediately after the audit. With this approach, everyone will feel part of the program and a sense of accomplishment. Plan a reward when certification is gained. One company had a steak lunch; a second company had watches engraved for everyone with the company logo and the words "We did it—ISO 9001." Plan the reward and make a big deal out of getting the certification, because gaining ISO 9000 certification *is* a big deal.

24

THE 30 MOST FREQUENTLY ASKED QUESTIONS ABOUT ISO 9000

In the year leading up to the writing of this book, I have developed and delivered seminars to more than one thousand people on the ISO standards. I have tried to keep track of the questions that were asked on more than one occasion. This chapter will look at the thirty most frequently asked questions. The answers I will give should not be construed as the only way the question can be resolved. What makes the ISO standard unique is that it is nonspecific as to the exact steps to follow in meeting its intent. My answers are what I found to work in a given situation; they should be viewed as one of many alternative solutions to the question.

1. Why Should a Company Look at Implementing ISO 9000?

This is a question that each person should answer for his or her own specific situation. In the successful certification efforts in which I have been involved, the reasons were twofold: we were getting an increasing number of requests from our customers for this certification (in many cases, certification is customer driven), and my company was starting its quest to develop a TQM environment within both plants. This allowed us to use the standard as a guideline for the development of our system. Gaining certification was viewed as a stepping-stone, or a marker to let us know we were on our way toward TQM. The result of the process was a surprising increase in productivity (revenue per man-hour) in the first year. We also were awarded several multimillion-dollar contracts that were only open to bids by ISO 9001 or 9002 companies. The payoff has been much quicker and more tangible than we expected.

2. How Did You Decide Which Standard (ISO 9001 or 9002) to Pursue?

One of the most misunderstood aspects of the ISO standard is how it is structured. An ISO 9001 program is for any facility that is involved in the design (engineering) of a product and/or servicing of the product after the sale. An ISO 9002 program is for a facility involved in the manufacturing but not the design or service of the product. I have not found many registration organizations that will allow a company involved with design to exempt that function and certify to ISO 9002. In most cases, if you design and/or service the product, your company is ISO 9001 material.

3. Does Certification Require a Full-Time Person to Maintain?

This depends on how you set up the program within your company. In the programs I have helped to develop, the responsibilities for the different elements were distributed throughout the facility. Thus the design control responsibility was given to engineering, purchasing responsibility was assigned to the purchasing department, and so forth. We developed our program to be a true manufacturing system instead of a quality assurance program. With this approach, we found that we did not have to dedicate one person on the payroll solely to maintaining the program. We distributed the responsibility to enough people that the work was easily incorporated into their everyday work load. If all the hours spent by everyone were added, it would probably equal one person's time;

we just decided to distribute the responsibilities and ownership of the program.

4. What Are the Costs?

Costs depend on many factors, including (1) who will be performing the certification audits, (2) the size of the plant, (3) where you are located, and (4) the level to which program controls are currently in place. The major costs a company incurs will come from preparing the audit; the cost to document the system, provide training, perform internal audits, and so on creates the greatest expense. To provide a precise cost estimate would be difficult, but for an average one-hundred-person manufacturing facility with minimal documentation, the cost will in most cases exceed $50,000 ($10,000 to $30,000 would be the direct cost of the registration audit, while the remainder would be the cost to develop the program within a company). The more disciplined the existing programs are, the lower the cost will be.

Appendix I is a checklist that can be used to determine the baseline for a company's quality program. The greater the number of elements that are missing, the higher the cost will be for the implementation.

5. What Are the Expected Man-Hours to Complete?

The answer will depend on the level of documentation and program development of a company. This is not a certification that can be achieved by one person working full-time to bring a plant into conformance. If the ISO program is properly distributed to the departments that are responsible for the functions (in other words, engineering, purchasing, and manufacturing), implementation can be accomplished by one person full-time during the development phase. This person will provide direction much like a product champion does for the introduction of a new product line. This person, however, cannot be totally responsible for the implementation; he or she should direct the efforts of the implementation teams. After the certification is received, the program should run without a full-time, dedicated person. I found that the responsibilities can be distributed throughout the company.

6. What Was the One Activity Associated with Certification That Gave You the Greatest Difficulty?

The activity that gave us the greatest amount of difficulty was coming to the realization that ISO 9000 is a generic standard that goes well beyond the product-oriented specifications of past standards. ISO 9000 is a standard where once the intent of each element is understood, the implementation simply becomes a decision to conduct business in a professional manner. The intent of the standard is for a company to "do good business." This took a long time for me to understand. The second item was that I had to come to the realization that the quality control department could not implement this standard by itself. When we came to the realization that the standard was merely asking for us to do good business in the entire manufacturing process, we got the entire plant involved and accomplished the certification task. I had a hard time accepting the fact that a quality standard could not be developed and controlled by the quality assurance department.

7. With What You Know Now, Would You Do Anything Differently to Achieve Certification?

I would have started the education process much earlier for everyone in the plant. This standard cannot be implemented by one person, or even by the entire quality department. To get the buy-in required will take the education of everyone in the plant very early in the process. This education should involve teaching people what the standard involves, what it is asking for, and how this certification will benefit them. A method should also be developed to inform everyone about the progress of the certification process. Lastly, I would develop implementation teams up front. I would involve people from every part of the work force to develop and implement the areas of the standard that affect them.

8. How Does a Company Get Started?

Beyond what I have already discussed, I would say that the first step is to decide that this is a worthwhile program. The next step is to accept the fact that the standard is valid. Do not waste time arguing that the standard is not valid. When the standard is truly understood, a person quickly discovers that the standard is valid. The standard is asking a company to do good business by doing good engineering, purchasing, manufacturing, and testing. What part of doing good business is not valid?

9. Is There a Certifying Body in the United States?

Yes. You can get publications that list registrars and companies that have been certified. All certification bodies, however, are not created equal. You need to investigate the credentials of the certification body and their reciprocity with other certification bodies and countries. Some companies have found themselves having certifications to ISO 9001 or 9002 that no one recognizes. Ask for their references and letters of agreement before you spend your money.

10. What Exactly Do the Auditors Check?

From my experience, the auditors involved in the certification activities were the best in the field. The first thing auditors check is the objective evidence—some type of documented evidence to show that a procedure has been properly followed. Do not assume that "objective evidence" means massive amounts of paperwork; it might mean only that a purchase order is initialed or signed when it is reviewed, or that an electronic file has a date entered in a field to show that the file has been processed. What the auditors will not accept is the position that "we have conducted business this way for forty years, and we have not killed anyone yet." The stance of "Trust me" will not be accepted. The auditors will look at your program with the following three questions in mind, and they will want objective evidence for the answers:

1. Do procedures properly and completely address the intent of each element of the ISO standard?
2. Are all the activities in the organization following the letter of the procedures?
3. Is the result of following the procedures effectively addressing the area covered by the procedure?

The third question—"Is it effective?"—is the hardest part to grasp. Many old-school quality professionals are under the impression that a company needs only to document what it does. We found that effectively documenting a system that was not working resulted in major findings and a failed audit; we also looked less than professional.

11. Do the Auditors Accept Your Process and Documentation Methods If You Have Data, and How Flexible Are They?

Documentation alone will not guarantee that you will be certified. The ISO standard is focused on the process for which the product is contracted, designed, manufactured, and serviced. It helps if a process is well documented, but you still must understand the intent of the ISO standard and honestly look at your program to see if it meets the intent of the standard. As we all know, an ineffective system that is well documented will not produce a quality product. The system must be documented, must meet the intent of the ISO standard, and *must be effective.*

12. How Should I Handle Existing Mature Products Where Engineering Information Is No Longer Available?

This is a topic you should discuss with the registrar very early in your preparation for an audit. In my experience, we were not forced to go back and recreate paperwork for old designs. We put a date in the design control procedure and stated that all designs after that date would meet the requirements of this procedure. You need to determine very early in the process if this will be accepted.

13. What Is a Preassessment, and Should I Have One?

A preassessment is basically a dry-run audit. In most cases, the registrar that you will use to perform the certification can perform this audit for a fee. It is usually performed around four to six months before the actual certification unit. I would highly recommend that this be performed. As you develop your company's program, you may lose sight of whether a program will satisfy the intent of the standard; this pre-audit will find the "black holes" in your program. Enough time should remain before the certification audit for inadequacies to be fixed.

14. What Activities Were the Most Effective in Getting Ready for the Certification Audit?

The most important skill in the certification process is internal quality auditing. Every procedure must be audited to determine if it meets the intent of the standard, is being performed in accordance with the procedure, and is effective. The certification process consists of professional auditors checking your program, so you must be able to look objectively and honestly at your programs. We also used the internal audit program as a training tool. By interviewing as many people as possible during the internal audits, we allowed the workers to feel more comfortable with the audit process before the ISO auditors arrived. Everyone that is interviewed by the certification team should have been audited by the internal audit team.

15. How Do We Get Started with Our Documentation Process?

After the manual structure is decided, the best way to start is to teach everyone how to make flowcharts. We developed flowcharts with three symbols to show the flow of our work. A circle was the starting point and ending point. A box was an activity and listed who was responsible for that activity. A diamond was a decision marker. Every decision was reduced to a yes or no question. Every diamond had a path; there was one path if the decision was yes, and a different path if the decision was no. We found no need for any other symbols.

The first step in documenting a system, process, or program is to determine how it actually works. You will be surprised to see how systems actually work in your company. When you put the systems on a flowchart, you can appreciate their complexity. The flowchart then can be changed to show how you *want* a process to work. Redesign the flowchart and then document it in a procedure. One idea we had was to use the flowchart as the procedure. You would be surprised how well that works.

16. What Should We Document?

My idea is to provide documentation on anything and everything a person needs to know to perform the assigned job. The intent of the standard is to develop a TQM approach to managing a company. I found that if we tried to document only those things we needed for the ISO program, the manuals were not used, and no one took responsibility for the programs. Giving everyone the procedures they needed to perform a job properly and consistently was helpful. I made sure all of the elements of ISO-9001 were addressed in the manual, and only the procedures for the ISO elements are audited by the registrar. Everyone now has ownership in the program; the procedures manual is followed and updated. This approach has worked well for us.

17. How Far in Advance Should I Schedule My Audit?

As of 1993, the noted registrars are booking audits twelve to eighteen months in advance. You should start to contact registrars as soon as your company decides to plan for certification. If you want certification in the next twelve months, you might find it difficult to get the registrar you want, especially if your company is not located in a major metropolitan area.

18. Do I Have to Have a Quality Assurance Manual?

Surprisingly, the answer is no. I have been involved in a program that has a quality policy and objectives manual as their top-level manual. The second-level manual is a procedures manual that has procedures from all of the departments. This covers those activities that affect two or more departments. The third-level manual contains procedures for activities that affect only one department and are close to the work instructions level. The requirements of ISO 9001 are included in the operating procedures manual and the department procedures manuals. If the day-to-day procedures are being followed, the requirements of ISO 9001 are being met. We developed an index to show what procedures are used to meet each of the elements of ISO 9001; these procedures are the only ones that are audited by the registrar. Many companies have a quality manual because they feel the quality assurance department needs a manual to ensure compliance of its employees. Our registrar accepted this set-up as effective, once it was explained.

19. My Company Is Not Using One of the Twenty Elements. How Can I Be Certified?

One of the programs I helped to develop was for a job shop for heavy equipment. Many of the products had life runs that were as few as twelve and averaged around fifty. At the time we put our quality policy manual in place, statistical techniques did not apply to our operation. If we chose to apply statistical techniques in the future, we would comply with the requirements of ISO 9001 section 4.20. As long as we addressed the element, even if we said that it did not apply to us, our program was accepted. One word of caution: most registrars will take a dim view of a company stating that fifteen of the twenty elements of ISO 9001 do not apply to their organization. The maximum number of elements that I have seen listed as not applying in a certified program was three: purchaser-supplied product, servicing, and statistical techniques. Before the decision is made to exempt any element from your program, you probably should discuss this with your registrar. Get his or her input in this area as you develop your program.

20. How Did Your Company Justify the Cost?

The company for which I worked was in the situation that its customers were asking for this certification. One of our competitors had already been certified, and we found that countries like Canada were demanding certification before allowing a company to bid on contracts. We had also made a commitment to develop a TQM culture within the company. Upon seeing the trend in the market toward requiring ISO certification and having a competitor that was certified, we did not have trouble gaining support for the ISO program. Keep in mind, though, that upper management will look for a return on the investment. We found that the cost of certification was well worth the effort and the investment. We increased productivity by 30 percent in terms of dollars of revenue per man-hour worked.

21. How Is a Company Scored under the Dutch Scheme?

Under the Dutch scheme, a company is scored on a scale of 0 to 100 on each of the elements, and the scores from each of the elements are averaged. A company will pass or fail based on the following criteria:

1. All elements must be successfully addressed.
2. No single element score is below 65 percent.
3. The average of all of the elements is not below 70 percent.

22. How Is a Company Scored under the British Scheme?

Scoring under the British scheme is very different from the Dutch scheme. Findings are put into one of two categories, depending on the severity of the finding.

A Category 1 finding is issued when the finding is so severe an entire element is not effective; any Category 1 finding causes a company to fail the audit. This finding is issued for one of the following reasons:

1. One entire element has not been addressed.

2. No objective evidence can be found to show the procedures covering one element are being followed.
3. The procedures are being followed, but the element is not effectively being addressed, or following the procedures will not meet the intent of the element.
4. So many minor (Category 2) findings have been identified in one element that, in the opinion of the auditors, the effectiveness of that entire element is questionable. I have not been able to determine the number of Category 2 findings that are necessary to automatically make a Category 1 finding. This is an area where the auditors must make a judgment call.

A Category 2 finding is a minor problem. This problem shows a mistake but does not indicate a complete breakdown of that element. This type of finding would be if one out of twenty documents did not have some piece of information required by the procedure. It will not indicate the system is ineffective unless the number of minor findings indicates a lack of control. These findings will not cause a company to fail an audit; however, the company must agree to corrective action before the auditors leave. The corrective action will be followed up by the auditors.

23. How Often Will the System Be Reaudited By the Registrar?

The entire system will be reaudited annually. Some of the registrars will audit the entire system once a year, while others will audit a little over one-half of the system every six months. Both parties will know in advance what elements are being audited. I have found that the type of objective evidence the auditors look for cannot be quickly manufactured, so surprise audits are not necessary. The auditors will not be fooled by a large amount of paperwork; the effectiveness of a program is not ensured by mountains of paper. One auditor has stated that large amounts of paperwork warn him that the element is suspect, and he will therefore dig very deep in that area. He knows that if an element is weak, many people will try to baffle the auditors with lots of paper.

24. How Long Is the Certification Valid?

Certification is presently valid for three years unless surrendered or revoked. After three years the registrar will make a new certification audit, and the process of periodic audits begins again. This might change, as the certification process is so new as of 1993 that very few companies have made it to the three-year recertification. You should watch for changes in the standard in the next few years.

25. How Long Should I Plan to Take to Develop a Certifiable Program?

I am constantly asked this question. The only answer I can give is to ask, how dedicated is your management? If upper management is willing to dedicate finances and people, the time frame to implement the program will be shorter. Typically, an implementation from kickoff to certification will take approximately two years. This appears to be acceptable to most management, and most of the work can be effectively accomplished in this time frame. Try to avoid the disastrous decision of obtaining certification in the next ninety days. Most companies will need to develop and implement several new programs to meet the elements of the standard; allow time for a properly structured program to be developed. Ample time is also necessary for an implemented program to mature. I have found it is better to take the time to develop and implement a program properly rather than try to fix it later. In most companies, later never comes, and they are stuck with programs that are ineffective at best and counterproductive at worst. Keep in mind that a hastily conceived program, in many cases, is a Category 1 finding waiting to happen.

26. If My Company Is Currently Certified, How Will the 1994 Version of the ISO 9000 Series Standard Affect It?

Companies currently certified will have to re-certify at some point under the 1994 version of the standard. The approach taken by one of the world's leading registrars is that, at the first periodical audit following formal issuance of the 1994 version, minor nonconformities will be raised against the requirements of the 1994 version (any nonconformities of this nature would not jeopardize the validity of the issued certificate). Subsequent periodical audits will be performed based on the requirements of the 1994 version, upon successful completion of the audit to this version, a revised certificate will be issued.

This appears to be the common approach taken by most registrars; however, each company should check with its individual registrar for verification.

27. What Are the Major Changes With the 1994 Version?

1. Where the 1987 version of the standard made gains in redirecting the intent of a quality system standard from identification and prevention of nonconforming product to customer satisfaction, the 1994 version continues to encourage progression away from an inspection of heavy organization to the development and control of processes to ensure customer satisfaction. References throughout the standard now include not only product nonconformances but also those that occur with processes and the quality system.

2. A company performing the servicing of the product after the sale but with no design responsibility will certify under ISO 9002 with the 1994 version.

3. References to supplier's management with responsibility for quality now include the term "executive." This statement appears to further elevate the importance of executive level involvement in the quality system.

4. The 1994 version requires that a quality manual be developed to include or reference the documented procedures that form part of the quality system.

5. Formal documented review of the design results are required to be planned and conducted. The standard now requires the participation of representatives of all functions concerned with the design stage being reviewed. Design validation is required to be performed to ensure that product conforms to defined user needs and/or requirements. This is in addition to the requirement of design verification.

6. Where the supplier chooses to carry out verification of purchased product on the subcontractor's premises, the arrangement specifics and the method release must be documented in the purchasing documents.
7. Process control requirements have been updated to include the maintenance of equipment to ensure continuing process capability.
8. The importance of preventive action has been stressed further by the 1994 version by updating the element title to Corrective and *Preventive* Action and including an entire section on procedures for such.
9. Preservation has been added to the element of handling, storage, packaging, and delivery.

28. What Was the Process for Revising the ISO 9000 Series Standard?

Recommendations by the technical committee (TC 176) were prepared and put into a draft international standard form. The recommended revisions were presented in draft form to member countries in early 1993 for comments and a vote for or against ratification. The draft standard was referred to as ISO/DIS 9000 through ISO/DIS 9004. The member countries evaluated the standard and, in September 1993, voted to accept the content of the modifications to the ISO 9000 standard. The modified standard will be issued in the spring of 1994 with the U.S. version being issued through the American National Standards Institute in late spring of 1994. Although minor editorial changes are expected between the ISO/DIS 9000 series standard and the ISO 9000 1994 revision, no major content or requirement changes are anticipated.

Upon formal issuance, the final version of the 1994 ISO 9000 series standard can be purchased through the American National Standards Institute at 11 West 42nd Street, New York, NY 10036.

29. When Does a Company Have to Certify to the 1994 Version Instead of the 1987 Version?

It appears that most registrars are following the general rule that audits and certification to the 1994 standard will be required three months after the formal issuance of the standard. Before that time, audits may be conducted to the 1987 or 1994 version at the company's and registrar's discretion. As previously stated, all companies will be required to certify to the 1994 version at the first periodical following the three-month grace period after issuance. This may not be correct for all registrars, so companies involved in certification activities should contact their registration representative. It is highly recommended that companies preparing for certification address the requirements of the 1994 revision of the standard.

30. When Can We Expect the Standard to Be Revised Again?

Because revision to the ISO 9000 series standard is scheduled on a five-year cycle, the next anticipated, formal revision issue should occur in 1999. The evaluation and voting process should occur through 1998, with the revisions either approved or rejected by the member countries late that year.

APPENDIX I

QUALITY EVALUATION FORM

Completed By:	QUALITY	Page
	EVALUATION	1 of 25
Date:	FORM	

Area:
    MANAGEMENT RESPONSIBILITY
	Requirement:
	    ISO 9001 para 4.1	

Questions	Comply	Comment
Are quality policies and objectives defined and documented?		
Is the policy understood, implemented and maintained at all levels?		
Is the responsibility, authority and interrelation of all personnel who manage, perform and verify work affecting quality defined?		
Are in-house verification requirements identified with adequate resources provided and trained personnel assigned?		
Are verification activities carried out by personnel independent of those having direct responsibility for the work being performed?		
Has a management representative been appointed who has defined authority and responsibility for ensuring the requirements of the standard are implemented and maintained?		
Does management review the quality system at appropriate intervals to ensure continuing suitability and effectiveness?		
Are records of management reviews maintained?		

Completed By:	QUALITY	Page
	EVALUATION	2 of 25
Date:	FORM	

Area: QUALITY SYSTEM		Requirement: ISO 9001 para 4.2	
Questions	Comply		Comment
Is a documented quality system established and maintained?			
Are there documented quality system procedures and instructions?			
Are documented quality system procedures and instructions effectively implemented?			

Completed By:	QUALITY	Page
	EVALUATION	3 of 25
Date:	FORM	

Area: CONTRACT REVIEW	Requirement: ISO 9001 para 4.3	
Questions	Comply	Comment
Are procedures established and maintained for contract review? Are contracts reviewed to assure: - requirements adequately defined and documented? - requirements differing from the tender are resolved? - supplier has the capability to meet contractual requirements? Are records of contract reviews maintained?		

Completed By:	QUALITY	Page
	EVALUATION	4 of 25
Date:	FORM	

Area: DESIGN CONTROL	Requirement: ISO 9001 para 4.4	

Questions	Comply	Comment
Are procedures established and maintained to control and verify design of the product to ensure that that the specified requirements are met?		
Are the responsibilities for each design and development activity identified?		
Are design and verification activities planned and assigned to qualified personnel equipped with adequate resources?		
Are organizational and technical interfaces between different groups identified and the necessary information documented, transmitted and regularly reviewed?		
Are design input requirements identified, documented and the selection reviewed for adequacy?		
Are incomplete, ambiguous or conflicting requirements resolved with those responsible for drawing up the requirements?		
Is design output documented and expressed in terms of requirements, calculations and analyses?		
Does design output: - meet design input requirements? - contain or reference acceptance criteria?		

Completed By:	QUALITY	Page
	EVALUATION	5 of 25
Date:	FORM	

Area: DESIGN CONTROL	Requirement: ISO 9001 para 4.4	
Questions	Comply	Comment
- conform to appropriate regulatory requirements? - identify those characteristics of the design that are crucial to the safe and proper functioning of the product? Is design verification planned, established, documented and assigned to competent personnel? Does design verification establish that design output meets design input requirements? Are procedures established and maintained for the identification, documentation and appropriate review and approval of all changes and modifications?		

Completed By:	QUALITY	Page
	EVALUATION	6 of 25
Date:	FORM	

Area:
  DOCUMENT CONTROL
	Requirement:
	  ISO 9001 para 4.5	

Questions	Comply	Comment
Are procedures established and maintained to control all documents and data that relate to the requirements of the program?		
Are documents reviewed and approved for adequacy by authorized personnel prior to issue?		
Are pertinent issues of appropriate documents available at all locations where operations essential to effective functioning of the quality system are performed?		
Are obsolete documents promptly removed from points of issue or use?		
Are changes to documents reviewed and approved by the same functions/ organizations that performed the original review and approval unless specifically designated otherwise?		
Do designated organizations have access to pertinent background information upon which to base review and approval?		
Where practicable, is the nature of the change identified in the document or appropriate attachments?		
Is a master list or equivalent document control procedure established to identify current revision of documents?		
Are documents reissued after a practical number of changes?		

Completed By:	QUALITY	Page
	EVALUATION	7 of 25
Date:	FORM	

Area: PURCHASING	Requirement: ISO 9001 para 4.6	
ʿQuestions	Comply	Comment
Does supplier ensure that purchased product conforms to specified requirements?		
Are sub-contractors selected on the basis of their ability to meet sub-contract requirements including quality?		
Are records of acceptable sub-contractors established and maintained?		
Are quality system controls effective?		
Do purchasing documents clearly describe the product ordered?		
Are purchasing documents reviewed and approved for adequacy prior to release?		
When specified in the contract, does the purchaser have the right to verify at source or on receipt that purchased product conforms to specified requirements?		

Completed By: Date:	QUALITY EVALUATION FORM	Page 8 of 25
Area: PURCHASER SUPPLIED PRODUCT		**Requirement:** ISO 9001 para 4.7

Questions	Comply	Comment
If the purchaser supplies product, are there procedures established and maintained for the verification, storage and maintenance of the product provided for incorporation into the supplies? If product is lost, damaged or is otherwise unsuitable for use, is it recorded and reported to the purchaser?		

Completed By:	QUALITY	Page
	EVALUATION	9 of 25
Date:	FORM	

| Area: | Requirement: |
| PRODUCT IDENTIFICATION/TRACEABILITY | ISO 9001 para 4.8 |

Questions	Comply	Comment
Where appropriate, are procedures established and maintained for identifying the product from applicable drawings, specifications or other documents, during all stages of production, delivery and installation? If traceability is a specified requirement, do individual products or batches have unique identification? Is identification recorded?		

Completed By:	QUALITY	Page
	EVALUATION	10 of 25
Date:	FORM	

Area: PROCESS CONTROL	Requirement: ISO 9001 para 4.9	

Questions	Comply	Comment
Is production that directly affects quality identified and planned?		
Where applicable, are installation processes identified and planned?		
Are these processes carried out under controlled conditions?		
Is continuous monitoring and/or compliance with documented procedures implemented to assure conformance to specified requirements for special processes?		
Are special processes qualified?		
Do special processes conform to all requirements of process control?		
Are records maintained for qualified processes, equipment and personnel as appropriate for special processes?		

Completed By:	QUALITY	Page
	EVALUATION	11 of 25
Date:	FORM	

Area: INSPECTION AND TESTING	Requirement: ISO 9001 para 4.10	
Questions	Comply	Comment
Is incoming product inspected or otherwise verified prior to use or processing?		
Is verification in accordance with quality plans or documented procedures?		
If incoming product is released for urgent use, is it positively identified and recorded to permit immediate recall and replacement in the event of nonconformance to specified requirements?		
Is in-process inspection and testing conducted in accordance with required quality plans or documented procedures?		
Is product held until required inspection and tests have been completed or necessary reports have been received and verified?		
Is nonconforming product identified in-process?		
Does final inspection assure that inspections and tests specified for product receipt or in-process inspections have been carried out and that the data meets specified requirements?		
Are final inspections carried out in accordance with quality plans or documented procedures?		

Completed By:	QUALITY	Page
	EVALUATION	12 of 25
Date:	FORM	

Area: INSPECTION AND TESTING	Requirement: ISO 9001 para 4.10	
Questions	Comply	Comment
Do final inspections complete the evidence of conformance of the finished product to the specified requirements?		
Are all final inspections completed prior to the product being released for despatch?		
Is all associated data and documentation available and authorized as required by quality plans or documented procedures prior to product being released for despatch?		
Are inspection and test records established and maintained?		

Completed By:	QUALITY	Page
	EVALUATION	13 of 25
Date:	FORM	

Area: INSPECTION, MEASURING & TEST EQUIPMENT	Requirement: ISO 9001 para 4.11	

Questions	Comply	Comment
Is inspection, measuring and test equipment controlled, calibrated and maintained to demonstrate the conformance of product to specified requirements?		
Is equipment used in a manner which ensures that measurement uncertainty is known and is consistent with the required measurement capability?		
Are measurements and accuracy requirements identified?		
Is appropriate inspection, measuring and test equipment used?		
Is all inspection, measuring and test equipment that can affect product quality identified, calibrated and adjusted at prescribed intervals or prior to use?		
Are calibrations against certified equipment having a known valid relationship to nationally recognized standards?		
If no standard exists, is the basis for calibration documented?		
Are calibration procedures established, documented and maintained?		
Do calibration procedures include details of equipment type,		

Completed By:	QUALITY	Page
	EVALUATION	14 of 25
Date:	FORM	

Area: INSPECTION, MEASURING AND TEST EQUIPMENT	Requirement: ISO 9001 para 4.11

Questions	Comply	Comment
identification number, location, frequency of checks, check method, acceptance criteria and the action to be taken when results are unsatisfactory?		
Is inspection, measuring and test equipment capable of the accuracy and precision necessary?		
Is inspection, measuring and test equipment identified with a suitable indicator or approved identification record to show calibration status?		
Are calibration records maintained for inspection, measuring and test equipment?		
If inspection, measuring and test equipment is found to be out of calibration, is the validity of previous inspection and test results assessed and documented?		
Are environmental conditions suitable for calibrations, inspections, measurements and tests that are carried out?		
Is accuracy and fitness for use maintained during handling, preservation and storage of inspection, measuring and test equipment?		

Completed By:	QUALITY	Page
	EVALUATION	15 of 25
Date:	FORM	

Area: Requirement:
   INSPECTION, MEASURING AND TEST EQUIPMENT   ISO 9001 para 4.11

Questions	Comply	Comment
Is test hardware and software safeguarded from adjustments that would invalidate the calibration setting?		
If test hardware (jigs, fixtures, templates, patterns) or test software is used for inspection, is it checked to verify acceptability for product verification?		
Is the extent and frequency of such checks established and records maintained as evidence of control?		
Is measurement design data available when required for verification that it is functionally adequate?		

Completed By:	QUALITY	Page
	EVALUATION	16 of 25
Date:	FORM	

Area: INSPECTION AND TEST STATUS	Requirement: ISO 9001 para 4.12	
Questions	Comply	Comment
Is the inspection and test status of product identified with regard to inspections and tests performed? Is the identification of inspection and test status maintained as necessary throughout production and installation to ensure that only product that has passed required inspections and tests is despatched, used or installed? Are records maintained to identify the inspection authority responsible for the release of conforming product?		

Completed By:	QUALITY	Page
	EVALUATION	17 of 25
Date:	FORM	

Area: CONTROL OF NONCONFORMING PRODUCT	Requirement: ISO 9001 para 4.13	
Questions	Comply	Comment
Are procedures established and maintained to ensure that product that does not conform to specified requirements is prevented from inadvertent use or installation?		
Does control provide for the identification, documentation, evaluation, segregation, disposition of nonconforming product and for notification of functions concerned?		
Is the responsibility for review and authority for the disposition of nonconforming product defined?		
Is nonconforming product reviewed in accordance with documented procedures?		
Is nonconforming product classified as reworked, accepted, re-graded or scrapped?		
If required by the contract, is the proposed use or repair of nonconforming product reported for concession to the purchaser?		
Are records of concession maintained?		
Is repaired and reworked product re-inspected in accordance with documented procedures?		

Completed By:	QUALITY	Page
	EVALUATION	18 of 25
Date:	FORM	

Area: CORRECTIVE ACTION REQUEST	Requirement: ISO 9001 para 4.14	

Questions	Comply	Comment
Are procedures established, documented and maintained for - investigation of cause of nonconforming product and corrective action, - analysing records to detect and eliminate potential causes of nonconforming product, - initiating preventative actions to deal with problems, - ensuring effectivity of corrective actions taken, - implementing and recording changes in procedures resulting from corrective action?		

Completed By:	QUALITY	Page
	EVALUATION	19 of 25
Date:	FORM	

Area: HANDLING, STORAGE, PACKAGING AND DELIVERY	Requirement: ISO 9001 para 4.15

Questions	Comply	Comment
Are procedures established, documented and maintained for handling of product?		
Are methods and means provided to prevent damage or deterioration from handling?		
Are procedures established, documented and maintained for storage of the product?		
Are secure storage areas or stock rooms provided to prevent damage or deterioration of product pending use or delivery?		
Are appropriate methods for authorizing receipt and despatch to and from storage stipulated?		
Is product in storage assessed at appropriate intervals to detect deterioration?		
Are procedures established, documented and maintained for packaging of product?		
Is the packing, preservation and marking controlled to ensure conformance to specified requirements?		
Is product identified, preserved and segregated from time of receipt until responsibility ceases?		

Completed By:	QUALITY	Page
	EVALUATION	20 of 25
Date:	FORM	

Area: HANDLING, STORAGE, PACKAGING AND DELIVERY		Requirement: ISO 9001 para 4.15
Questions	**Comply**	**Comment**
Are procedures established, documented and maintained for the delivery of product? Are arrangements made for the protection of the quality of the product after final inspection and test? If specified by contract, does protection extend to delivery to destination?		

Completed By:	QUALITY	Page
	EVALUATION	21 of 25
Date:	FORM	

Area: QUALITY RECORDS	Requirement: ISO 9001 para 4.16	
Questions	Comply	Comment
Are procedures established and maintained for identification, collection, indexing, filing, storage, maintenance and disposition of quality records?		
Do quality records demonstrate achievement of required quality and effective operation of the quality system?		
If pertinent, does this include sub-contractors records?		
Are records legible and identifiable to the product involved?		
Are records readily retrievable?		
Are records stored to minimize deterioration or damage and prevent loss?		
Are retention times established and recorded?		
Are records available for purchaser review if required by contract?		

Completed By:	QUALITY	Page
	EVALUATION	22 of 25
Date:	FORM	

Area: INTERNAL QUALITY AUDITS	Requirement: ISO 9001 para 4.17	
Questions	Comply	Comment
Is there a planned and documented internal audit program?		
Are audits scheduled on the basis of activity status and importance?		
Are audits and follow-up actions carried out in accordance with documented procedures?		
Are results of audits documented and brought to the attention of the personnel having responsibility in the area audited?		
Does management personnel responsible for the area take timely corrective action on deficiencies found by the audit?		

Completed By:	QUALITY	Page
	EVALUATION	23 of 25
Date:	FORM	

Area: TRAINING	Requirement: ISO 9001 para 4.18	
Questions	Comply	Comment
Are procedures established and maintained for identifying training needs and providing training of all personnel performing activities affecting quality? Are personnel performing specific assigned tasks qualified on the basis of appropriate education, training, and/or experience? Are records of training maintained?		

Completed By:	QUALITY	Page
	EVALUATION	24 of 25
Date:	FORM	

Area:
  SERVICING
	Requirement:
	    ISO 9001 para 4.19	

Questions	Comply	Comment
Where servicing is specified in the contract, are procedures established and maintained for performing and verifying that servicing meets specified requirements?		

Completed By:	QUALITY	Page
	EVALUATION	25 of 25
Date:	FORM	

Area: STATISTICAL TECHNIQUES		Requirement: ISO 9001 para 4.20	
Questions	**Comply**	**Comment**	
Where appropriate, are procedures established for identifying adequate statistical techniques required to verify the acceptability of process capability and product characteristics?			

APPENDIX II

QUALITY POLICY

FACILITY POLICY

1.0.0 STATEMENT OF POLICY

The principal factor in the successful performance of the ABC
Corp. is the incorporation of quality into all our services,
products and equipment.

Our policy is to always attain, and wherever possible, exceed
the standards expected by our customers. This can only be
achieved by developing, establishing and maintaining a
Quality Management System that encompasses all of our
personnel and activities.

The Quality Program, as described in this manual, has been
approved by all levels of management for issue and
implementation within the company. The purpose of this
program is to assure that all products, services and
equipment provided will meet or exceed the requirements
specified by our customers, by appropriate controlling
documents and as set forth by corporate management.

The Quality Manager, who reports directly to me, is hereby
assigned the responsibility and the authority to organize,
maintain and administer the Quality Program and to assure its
effective implementation. Further, all ABC Corp. employees
are given the responsibility and authority to identify
problems, implement solutions to those problems, and to
control further processing of affected product. This
includes preventing shipment of nonconforming, deficient or
unsatisfactory materials or products, until satisfactory
corrective action has been taken.

Each department is required to implement the Quality Program
in its area of responsibility. The Plant Manager shall
resolve any conflicts which cannot be resolved by the Quality
Manager and department managers. Resolution of such
conflicts shall always be in accordance with the requirements
of the controlling documents and this Quality Program Manual.
I fully support and approve this program.

_____   _____

Plant Manager   Date

MANAGEMENT RESPONSIBILITY

1.1.0 Scope

This document outlines management responsibility criteria that the ABC Corp. must identify and address for compliance with ISO-9001 "Quality Systems - Model for Quality Assurance in Design/Development, Production, Installation and Servicing."

1.1.1 References

- ISO-9001 "Quality System - Model for Quality Assurance in Design/Development, Production, Installation and Servicing," Part 4.1 Management Responsibility

- ABC Corp. Quality and/or Departmental Manual

1.1.2 Management Policy, Objectives and Commitment to Quality

The principal factor in the successful performance of ABC Corp. is the incorporation of quality into all our services, products and equipment.

ABC Corp. policy is to always attain the standards required by the customer. This can only be achieved by the establishment and maintenance of a quality system that encompasses all ABC Corp. personnel and activities. The quality system, as described in this manual, has been approved for issue and implementation within ABC Corp. The purpose of this program is to assure that all services, products and equipment provided by ABC Corp. comply with the requirements specified by the customer and by the appropriate controlling quality documents in the system's Quality Assurance manuals.

1.1.3 Appointed Management Representative

The Quality Assurance Manager, who reports directly to the Plant Manager, has been appointed as the management representative who will organize, maintain and administer the quality system and assure its implementation. This includes organizational freedom to identify problems, affecting implementation of solutions to those problems, and to control further processing and prevent shipment of non-conforming, deficient or unsatisfactory materials or products until satisfactory corrective action has been taken.

1.1.4   ABC Corp. Organizational Chart

Exhibit 1 (Organizational Chart) identifies the departments and departmental managers that are responsible for the quality in services, products or equipment.

1.1.5   Job Descriptions

The following are job descriptions for departmental managers whose departments affect the quality of the services, products or equipment at ABC Corp.

- Plant Manager
  The Plant Manager is responsible for all activities at ABC Corp. The Plant Manager reports directly to the ABC Corp. Board of directors.

- Engineering Manager
  The Product Engineering Manager is responsible for the manufacturing design of parts and equipment manufactured at ABC Corp. The Product Engineering Manager reports directly to the Plant Manager.

- Quality Assurance Manager
  The Quality Assurance Manager is responsible for monitoring the quality system at ABC Corp. This includes responsibility for managing of the various quality departments and for quality related activities that these departments perform. The Quality Assurance Manager reports directly to the Plant Manager.

- Production Control Manager
  The Production Control Manager is responsible for all activities in the Production Control Department. The Production Control Manager reports directly to the Plant Manager.

- Manufacturing Manager
  The Manufacturing Manager is responsible for manufacturing or equipment assembly at ABC Corp. The Manufacturing Manager reports directly to the Plant Manager.

1.1.6   Other Management Responsibilities

Management has other responsibilities that are documented in ABC Corp. quality assurance and departmental manuals. These include but are not limited to

- quality system review by management
- records on management review of the quality system
- responsibility and authority of all personnel for inspection and testing during production and prior to shipment.
- inspections, tests and in-house monitoring to verify product integrity.

MANAGEMENT RESPONSIBILITY

ATTACHMENT 1

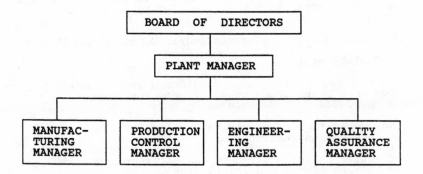

QUALITY SYSTEM

1.2.0   Scope

This document outlines quality system criteria that ABC Corp. must identify and address for compliance with ISO-9001 "Quality Systems - Model for Quality Assurance in Design/Development, Production, Installation and Servicing."

1.2.1   References

- ISO-9001 "Quality Systems - Model for Quality Assurance in Design/Development, Production, Installation and Servicing," Part 4.2   Quality System

- ABC Corp. Quality Assurance and/or Departmental Manual

1.2.2   Quality System

ABC Corp. shall establish and maintain a documented quality system as a means of ensuring fitness for purpose in ABC Corp. products. This includes:

- the preparation of documented quality system procedures and instructions

- effective implementation of the documented quality system procedures and instructions.

1.2.3   Meeting Fitness for Purpose

In meeting fitness for purpose, ABC Corp. gives consideration to the following activities

- the preparation of quality plans and Quality Assurance manuals in accordance with specified requirements

- the identification and acquisition of any controls, processes, inspection equipment, fixtures, total production resources and skills that may be needed to achieve the required quality

- the updating, as necessary, of quality control, inspection and testing techniques, including the development of new instrumentation

- the clarification of standards of acceptability for all features and requirements, including those which contain a subjective element

- the compatibility of the design, production process, installation, inspection and test procedures and applicable documentation

- the identification and preparation of quality records.

1.2.4   ABC Corp. Manual Structure

ABC Corp. has a documented quality system which includes two (2) levels of Quality Assurance procedure manuals. These manuals include

- ABC Corp. Quality Assurance Manual

- Departmental Operation Manuals.

1.2.5   ABC Corp. Quality Assurance Manual

The ABC Corp. Quality Assurance Manual is the top-level manual that details the criteria that ABC Corp. will follow for compliance to the ISO-9001 standard and also documents interdepartmental activities.

It is the responsibility of the Plant Manager to assure that this manual is reviewed on an annual basis.

It is the responsibility of the Plant Manager to assign controlled copies of the Quality Assurance Manual to personnel that perform quality-related functions. Personnel shall be copied on initial section/procedure issuance and subsequent revision.

1.2.6   ABC Corp. Departmental Operation Manual

The ABC Corp. Departmental Operation Manuals are the lower level manuals that describe specific intradepartmental procedures.

These manuals further define departmental responsibilities of activities outlined in the Quality Assurance Manual or document intradepartmental activities not defined or documented in the Quality Assurance Manual.

It is the responsibility of the Department Managers to issue and control respective departmental operation manuals.

1.2.7   Verification of the Implementation of the Quality System

The Quality Department shall perform internal auditing as specified further in the ABC Corp. Quality Assurance Manual. This internal quality auditing of ABC Corp. departments shall further verify the implementation of the quality system.

ATTACHMENT 2

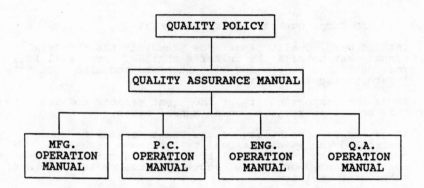

CONTRACT REVIEW
1.3.0   Scope

This document outlines contract review criteria that ABC
Corp. must identify and address to comply with the
ISO-9001 "Quality Systems - Model for Quality Assurance in
Design/Development, Production, Installation and Servicing."

1.3.1   References

- ISO-9001 "Quality Systems - Model for Quality Assurance in
  Design/Development, Production, Installation and
  Servicing," Part 4.3 Contract Review

- ABC Corp. Quality Assurance and/or Departmental Manual

1.3.2   ABC Corp. Contract Review

ABC Corp. shall establish and maintain procedures for
contract review and for the coordination of these activities.

Each contract shall be reviewed by ABC Corp. to ensure that:

- the requirements are adequately defined and documented

- any requirements differing from those in the tender
  are resolved

- ABC Corp. has the capability to meet contractual
  requirements.

Records for contract review shall be maintained.

DESIGN CONTROL

1.4.0   Scope

This document outlines design control criteria that ABC Corp.
must identify and address to comply with the ISO-9001
"Quality Systems - Model for Quality Assurance in
Design/Development, Production, Installation and Servicing."

1.4.1   References

- ISO-9001 "Quality Systems - Model for Quality Assurance in
  Design/Development, Production, Installation and
  Servicing," Part 4.4 Design Control

- ABC Corp. Quality Assurance and/or Departmental Manual

1.4.2   ABC Corp. Design Control

ABC Corp. shall establish and maintain procedures to control
and verify the design of the product to ensure that fitness
for purpose is achieved.

1.4.3   Design and Development Planning

ABC Corp. shall establish procedures that identify the
responsibility for each design and development activity.
Procedures shall describe or reference these activities and
shall be updated as the design evolves.

The design and verification activities shall be planned and
assigned to qualified personnel equipped with adequate
resources.

Organizational and technical interfaces between different
groups shall be identified and the necessary information
documented, transmitted and regularly reviewed.

1.4.4   Design Input

Design input requirements relating to the product shall be
identified, documented and their selection reviewed by ABC
Corp. for adequacy.

Incomplete, ambiguous or conflicting requirements shall be
resolved with those responsible for drawing up these
requirements.

1.4.5   Design Output

Design output shall be documented and expressed in terms of the requirements, calculations and analyses.

Design output shall:

- meet the design input requirements

- contain or reference acceptance criteria

- conform to appropriate regulatory requirements whether or not these have been stated in the input information

- identify those characteristics of the design that are crucial to the safe functioning of the product.

1.4.6   Design Verification

ABC Corp. shall plan, establish, document and assign to competent personnel functions for verifying the design. Design verification shall establish that design output meets the design input requirement by means of design control activities such as:

- holding and recording design reviews

- undertaking qualification tests and demonstrations

- conducting alternative calculations

- comparing the new design with a similar proven design, if available.

1.4.7   Design Changes

ABC Corp. shall establish and maintain procedures for the identification, documentation and appropriate review and approval of all changes and modifications.

DOCUMENT CONTROL

1.5.0   Scope

This document outlines document control criteria that ABC
Corp. must identify and address to comply with the ISO-9001
"Quality Systems - Model for Quality Assurance in
Design/Development, Production, Installation and Servicing."

1.5.1   References

- ISO-9001 "Quality Systems - Models for Quality Assurance in
  Design/Development, Production, Installation and
  Servicing," Part 4.5 Document Control

- ABC Corp. Quality Assurance and/or Departmental Manual

1.5.2   Document Approval and Issue

ABC Corp. shall establish and maintain procedures to control
all documents and data that relate to the requirements of
ISO-9001. These documents shall be reviewed and approved for
adequacy by authorized personnel prior to issue. This
control shall ensure that

- the pertinent issues of appropriate documents are
  available at all locations where operations essential to
  the effective functioning of the quality system are
  performed

- obsolete documents are promptly removed.

1.5.3   Document Changes/Modifications

Changes to documents shall be reviewed and approved by the
same functions/organizations that performed the original
review and approval unless specifically designated otherwise.
The designated organizations shall have access to pertinent
background information on which to base their review and
approval. Where practical, the nature of the change shall be
identified in the document or the appropriate attachments.

A master log or equivalent document control procedure shall
be established to identify the current revision of documents
to preclude the use of non-applicable documents.

Documents shall be re-issued when changes are made that
affect purpose, implementation or scope of activity
controlled by that document.

PURCHASING

1.6.0   Scope

This document outlines purchasing criteria that ABC Corp.
must identify and address to comply with the ISO-9001
"Quality Systems - Model for Quality Assurance in
Design/Development, Production, Installation and Servicing."

1.6.1   References

- ISO-9001 "Quality Systems - Model for Quality Assurance in
  Design/Development, Production, Installation and
  Servicing," Part 4.6 Purchasing

- ABC Corp. Quality Assurance and/or Departmental Manual

1.6.2   Purchasing

ABC Corp. shall establish and maintain procedures to ensure
that purchased products conform to specified requirements.

1.6.3   Assessment of Subcontractors

ABC Corp. shall select subcontractors on the basis of their
ability to meet subcontract requirements, including quality
requirements. ABC Corp. shall establish and maintain records
of acceptable subcontractors. The selection of
subcontractors, and the type and extent of control
exercised by ABC Corp., shall be dependent on the type of
product and, where appropriate, on records of subcontractors'
previously demonstrated capability and performance.

ABC Corp. shall ensure that quality system controls are
effective.

1.6.4   Purchasing Data

Purchasing documents shall contain data clearly describing
the product ordered, including, where applicable:

- the type, class, style, grade or other precise
  identification

- the title or other positive identification, and applicable
  issue of specifications, drawings, process requirements,
  inspection instructions and other relevant technical data,
  including requirements for approval or qualification of
  product and procedures.

ABC Corp. shall review and approve the purchasing documents
for adequacy of specified requirements prior to release.

1.6.5   Verification of Purchased Product

Where specified in the contract, ABC Corp. shall be afforded the right to verify at the source or on receipt that the purchased product conforms to specified requirements. Verification by ABC Corp. shall not absolve the supplier of the responsibility to provide acceptable products nor shall it preclude subsequent rejection.

When ABC Corp. elects to conduct verification at the subcontractor's plant, such verification shall not be used by ABC Corp. as evidence of effective control of quality by the subcontractor.

PURCHASER SUPPLIED PRODUCT

1.7.0 Scope

This document outlines the criteria ABC Corp. shall identify and address to comply with the ISO-9001 "Quality Systems - Model for Quality Assurance in Design/Development, Production, Installation and Servicing."

1.7.1 References

- ISO-9001 "Quality Systems - Model for Quality Assurance for Design/Development, Production, Installation and Servicing," Part 4.7 Purchaser Supplied Product

- ABC Corp. Quality Assurance and/or Departmental Manual

1.7.2 Purchaser Supplied Product

ABC Corp. shall establish and maintain procedures for verification, storage and maintenance of such. These procedures will be at a minimum, equivalent to those for ABC Corp. standard inventory documented in ABC Corp. Quality Assurance and/or Departmental Manual. Any such product that is lost, damaged or is otherwise unsuitable for use shall be recorded and reported to the Purchaser.

Verification by ABC Corp. does not absolve the purchaser of the responsibility to provide an acceptable product.

PRODUCT IDENTIFICATION AND TRACEABILITY

1.8.0   Scope

This document outlines what criteria ABC Corp. shall identify
and address to comply with the ISO-9001 "Quality Systems
- Model for Quality Assurance in Design/Development,
Production, Installation and Servicing."

1.8.1   References

- ISO-9001 "Quality Systems - Model for Quality Assurance in
  Design/Development, Production, Installation and
  Servicing," Part 4.8 Product Identification and
  Traceability

- ABC Corp. Quality Assurance and/or Departmental Manual

1.8.2   Product Identification and Traceability

Where appropriate, ABC Corp. shall establish and maintain
procedures for identifying the product from applicable
drawings, specifications or other documents, during all
stages of production, delivery and installation.

Where, and to the extent that, traceability is a specified
requirement, individual product or batches shall have a
unique identification. This identification shall be recorded
in ABC Corp. records.

PROCESS CONTROL

1.9.0   Scope

This document outlines what process control criteria ABC Corp. shall identify and address to comply with the ISO-9001 "Quality Systems - Model for Quality Assurance in Design/Development, Production, Installation and Servicing."

1.9.1   References

- ISO-9001 "Quality Systems - Model for Quality Assurance in Design/Development, Production, Installation and Servicing," Part 4.9 Process Control

- ABC Corp. Quality Assurance and/or Departmental Manual

1.9.2   ABC Corp. Process Control

ABC Corp. shall establish and maintain procedures to identify and plan the production and, where applicable, installation processes which directly affect quality and shall ensure that these processes are carried out under controlled conditions. Controlled conditions may include the following:

- documented routing instructions defining the steps of production and installation, where the absence of such instructions would adversely affect quality, use of suitable production and installation equipment, suitable working environment, compliance with reference standards/codes and quality plans

- monitoring and control of suitable process and product characteristics during production and installation

- the approval of processes and equipment, as appropriate

- criteria for workmanship which shall be stipulated, to the greatest practical extent, in written standards or by means of representative samples.

1.9.3   Special Processes

All special processes shall be qualified and shall also comply with the requirements stated in 1.9.2 above.

1.9.4   Process Control Records

Records shall be maintained for qualified processes, equipment and personnel, as appropriate.

INSPECTION AND TESTING

1.10.0 Scope

This document outlines the inspection and testing criteria
that ABC Corp. shall identify and address to comply with the
ISO-9001 "Quality Systems - Model for Quality Assurance in
Design/Development, Production, Installation and Servicing."

1.10.1 References

- ISO-9001 "Quality Systems - Model for Quality Assurance in
  Design/Development, Production, Installation and
  Servicing," Part 4.10 Inspection and Testing

- ABC Corp. Quality Assurance and/or Departmental Manual

1.10.2 Receiving Inspection and Testing

In determining the amount and nature of receiving inspection,
consideration will be given to the control exercised at the
source and the documented evidence of quality conformance
provided.

1.10.3 In-Process Inspection and Testing

ABC Corp. shall:

-   inspect, test and identify the product as required by the
    quality plan or documented procedures

-   hold the product until the required inspection and tests
    have been completed or necessary reports have been
    received and verified.

-   identify non-conforming products

1.10.4 Final Inspection and Testing

ABC Corp. shall conduct all final inspection and testing in
accordance with the quality plan or documented procedures to
complete the evidence of conformance of the finished product
to the specified requirements.

No product shall be released for shipment until all
activities specified in the quality plan or documented
procedures have been satisfactorily completed.

1.10.5 Inspection and Test Records

ABC Corp. shall establish and maintain records which give
evidence that the product has passed inspection and/or test
with defined acceptance criteria, where applicable.

INSPECTION, MEASURING AND TEST EQUIPMENT

1.11.0 Scope

This document outlines the inspection, measuring and test equipment criteria that ABC Corp. must identify and address to comply with the ISO-9001 "Quality Systems - Model for Quality Assurance in Design/Development, Production, Installation and Servicing."

1.11.1 References

- ISO-9001 "Quality Systems - Model for Quality Assurance in Design/Development, Production, Installation and Servicing," Part 4.11 Inspection, Measuring and Test Equipment

- ABC Corp. Quality Assurance and/or Departmental Manual

1.11.2 ABC Corp. Inspection, Measuring and Test Equipment

ABC Corp. shall control, calibrate and maintain inspection measuring and test equipment, whether owned by ABC Corp., on loan, or provided by the purchaser, to demonstrate the conformance of the product to the specified requirements. Equipment shall be used in a manner which ensures that measurement uncertainty is known, and is consistent with the required measurement capability.

ABC Corp. shall

- identify the measurements to be made, the accuracy required and select the appropriate inspection, measuring and test equipment

- identify, calibrate and adjust all inspection, measuring and test equipment and devices that can affect product quality

- establish, document and maintain calibration procedures

- ensure that the inspection, measuring and test equipment is capable of the accuracy and precision necessary

- identify calibration status of inspection, measuring and test equipment and maintain calibration records

- ensure that the environmental conditions are suitable for the calibrations, inspections, measurements and tests being carried out

- ensure adequate handling, preservation and storage of inspection, measuring and test equipment

- safeguard inspection, measuring and test equipment from
  adjustments which would invalidate the calibration
  setting.

When test hardware; i.e., jigs, fixtures, templates,
patterns, or test software, is used as suitable forms of
inspection, they shall be checked to prove that they are
capable of verifying the acceptability of the product prior
to release for use during production and installation and
shall be rechecked at prescribed intervals. ABC Corp. shall
establish the extent and frequency of such checks and shall
maintain records as evidence of control. Measurement design
data shall be made available, when required by the purchaser
or his representative, for verification that it is
functionally adequate.

INSPECTION AND TEST STATUS

1.12.0 Scope

This document outlines inspection and test status criteria that ABC Corp. must identify and address to comply with the ISO-9001 "Quality Systems - Model in Quality Assurance in Design/Development, Production, Installation and Servicing."

1.12.1 References

- ISO-9001 "Quality System - Model for Quality Assurance in Design/Development, Production, Installation and Servicing," Part 4.12 Inspection and Test Status

- ABC Corp. Quality Assurance and/or Departmental Manual

1.12.2 ABC Corp. Inspection and Test Status

The inspection and test status of the product shall be identified. This identification shall be maintained, as necessary, throughout production to ensure that only product that has passed required inspections and tests is dispatched, used or installed.

Records shall identify responsible authority for release of conforming product.

CONTROL OF NONCONFORMING PRODUCT

1.13.0 Scope

This document outlines the control of nonconforming product criteria that ABC Corp. must identify and address to comply with ISO-9001 "Quality Systems - Model for Quality Assurance in Design/Development, Production, Installation and Servicing."

1.13.1 References

- ISO-9001 "Quality Systems - Model for Quality Assurance in Design/Development, Production, Installation and Servicing," Part 4.13 Control of Non-Conforming Product

- ABC Corp. Quality Assurance and/or Departmental Manual

1.13.2 ABC Corp. Control of Nonconforming Product

ABC Corp. shall establish and maintain procedures to ensure that product that does not conform to specified requirements is prevented from inadvertent use or installation.

1.13.3 Nonconformity Review and Disposition

The responsibility for review and authority for the disposition of nonconforming products shall be defined.

Nonconforming products shall be reviewed and disposition determined in accordance with documented procedures.

Where required by the contract, nonconformances shall be reported for concession to the purchaser or his representative. Documentation shall be maintained.

Repaired and reworked products shall be re-inspected in accordance with documented procedures.

CORRECTIVE ACTION

1.14.0 Scope

This document outlines the corrective action criteria that ABC Corp. must identify and address to comply with the ISO-9001 "Quality Systems - Model for Quality Assurance in Design/Development, Production, Installation and Servicing."

1.14.1 References

- ISO-9001 "Quality Systems - Model for Quality Assurance in Design/Development, Production, Installation and Servicing," Part 4.14 Corrective Action

- ABC Corp. Quality Assurance and/or Departmental Manual

1.14.2 ABC Corp. Corrective Action

ABC Corp. shall establish, document and maintain procedures for a corrective action system that will incorporate the following elements.

- investigation of the cause of nonconforming products and corrective action needed to prevent recurrence

- analysis of Quality Assurance parameters and documents to detect and eliminate potential causes of nonconforming products

- initiation of preventative actions to deal with problems to a level corresponding to the risks encountered

- application of controls to ensure that corrective actions are taken and that they are effective

- implementation and update of procedures resulting from corrective action.

These procedures shall be detailed in the Corrective Action Program documented in Quality Assurance and/or Departmental Procedures.

Authority and responsibility for administration of the corrective action program shall be assigned to the Quality Assurance Department.

HANDLING, STORAGE, PACKAGING AND DELIVERY

1.15.0 Scope

This document outlines handling, storage, packaging and delivery criteria that ABC Corp. must identify and address order to comply with ISO-9001 "Quality Systems - Model for Quality Assurance in Design/Development, Production, Installation and Servicing."

1.15.1 References

- ISO-9001 "Quality Systems - Model for Quality Assurance in Design/Development, Production, Installation and Servicing," Part 4.15 Handling, Storage, Packaging and Delivery

- ABC Corp. Quality Assurance and/or Departmental Manual

1.15.2 ABC Corp. Handling, Storage, Packaging and Delivery

ABC Corp. shall establish, document and maintain procedures for:

- control of handling to prevent damage or deterioration

- secured/controlled storage areas or stockrooms to prevent damage or deterioration of the product, pending use or delivery

- controlled packaging, preservation and marking processes to the extent necessary to ensure conformance to specified requirements

- protection of the quality of the product after final inspection and test

QUALITY RECORDS

1.16.0 Scope

This document outlines quality records criteria that ABC
Corp. must identify and address to comply with the ISO-9001
"Quality Systems - Model for Quality Assurance in
Design/Development, Production, Installation and Servicing."

1.16.1 References

- ISO-9001 "Quality Systems - Model for Quality Assurance in
  Design/Development, Production, Installation and
  Servicing," Part 4.16 Quality records

- ABC Corp. Quality Assurance and/or Departmental Manual

1.16.2 Procedure

ABC Corp. shall establish and maintain procedures for
identification, collection, indexing, filing, storage,
maintenance and disposition of quality records.

Quality records shall be maintained to demonstrate
achievement of required quality and the effective operation
of the quality system. Subcontractor quality records shall
be an element of the data when applicable.

Retention times of quality records shall be established and
recorded as necessary.

INTERNAL QUALITY AUDITS

1.17.0 Scope

This document outlines internal quality audit criteria that ABC Corp. must identify and address to comply with the ISO-9001 "Quality Systems - Model for Quality Assurance in Design/Development, Production, Installation and Servicing."

1.17.1 References

- ISO-9001 "Quality Systems - Model for Quality Assurance in Design/Development, Production, Installation and Servicing," Part 4.17 Internal Quality Audits

- ABC Corp. Quality Assurance and/or Departmental Manual

1.17.3 ABC Corp. Internal Quality Audits

ABC Corp. shall conduct a comprehensive system of planned and documented internal quality audits to verify whether quality activities comply with planned arrangements and to determine the effectiveness of the quality system.

Audits shall be scheduled on the basis of the status and importance of the activity.

The audits and follow-up actions shall be carried out in accordance with documented procedures.

The results of the audits shall be documented and brought to the attention of the personnel having responsibility in the area audited. The management personnel responsible for the area shall take timely corrective action on the deficiencies found by the audit.

TRAINING

1.18.0 Scope

This document outlines training criteria that ABC Corp. must identify and address to comply with the ISO-9001 "Quality Systems - Model for Quality Assurance in Design/Development, Production, Installation and Servicing."

1.18.1 References

- ISO-9001 "Quality Systems - Model for Quality Assurance in Design/Development, Production, Installation and Servicing," Part 4.18 Training

- ABC Corp. Quality Assurance and/or Departmental Manual

1.18.2 ABC Corp. Training

ABC Corp. shall establish and maintain procedures for identifying the training needs and provide for the training of all personnel. Personnel performing specific assigned tasks shall be qualified on the basis of appropriate education, training and/or experience, as necessary. Appropriate records of training shall be maintained when applicable.

SERVICING

1.19.0 Scope

This document outlines servicing criteria that ABC Corp. must identify and address to comply with the ISO-9001 "Quality Systems - Model for Quality Assurance in Design/Development, Production, Installation and Servicing."

1.19.1 References

- ISO-9001 "Quality Systems - Model for Quality Assurance in Design/Development, Production, Installation and Servicing," Part 4.19 Servicing

- ABC Corp. Quality Assurance and/or Departmental Manual

1.19.2 Servicing

Currently, servicing is not within the scope of activities conducted by ABC Corp.. However, should future situations require or where servicing is specified in the contract, ABC Corp. shall establish and maintain procedures for performing and verifying that servicing meets the specified requirements.

STATISTICAL TECHNIQUES

1.20.0 Scope

This document outlines statistical techniques criteria that ABC Corp. must identify and address to comply with the ISO-9001 "Quality Systems - Model for Quality Assurance in Design/Development, Production, Installation and Servicing."

1.20.1 References

- ISO-9001 "Quality Systems - Model for Quality Assurance in Design/Development, Production, Installation and Servicing," Part 4.20 Statistical Techniques

- ABC Corp. Quality Assurance and/or Departmental Manual

1.20.2 ABC Corp. Statistical Techniques

Where appropriate, ABC Corp. shall establish procedures identifying adequate statistical techniques required for verifying the acceptability of process capability and product characteristics.

APPENDIX III

GAGE CALIBRATION MATRIX

GAGE CALIBRATION MATRIX

DESCRIPTION	INTERVAL	CAL SPEC	TOLERANCE
HARDNESS TESTER	1 YEAR	ASTM E18-89 or ASTM E10-84	ASTM E18-89 or ASTM E10-84
DIAL INDICATORS	2 YEARS	NAVAIR 17-20MD-11	NAVAIR 17-20MD-11
RING STANDARDS	2 YEARS	NAVAIR 17-20MD-31	NAVAIR 17-20MD-31
SPRING TESTER	3 YEARS	INTERNAL PROCEDURE #6	INTERNAL PROCEDURE #6
SURFACE PLATE	5 YEARS	CAL SHOP PROCEDURE #20	CAL SHOP PROCEDURE #20
GAGE BLOCKS	3 YEARS	CAL SHOP PROCEDURE #31	CAL SHOP PROCEDURE #31
MICROMETERS	1 YEAR	INTERNAL PROCEDURE #2	INTERNAL PROCEDURE #2
SONIC THICKNESS GAGE	1 YEAR	MANUFACTURER'S SPECS	MANUFACTURER'S SPECS
CALIPERS	1 YEAR	INTERNAL PROCEDURE #4	INTERNAL PROCEDURE #4
HEIGHT GAGE	1 YEAR	INTERNAL PROCEDURE #1	INTERNAL PROCEDURE #1
STRAIGHT STANDARDS	3 YEARS	INTERNAL PROCEDURE #3	FED STD GGG-C-105C

APPENDIX IV

CORRECTIVE ACTION REQUEST

CORRECTIVE ACTION REQUEST

REPORT NUMBER: _____

PREPARED BY: _____
ASSIGNED TO: _____
DATE ISSUED: _____
DATE DUE: _____

DESCRIPTION: _____
_____
_____
_____
_____
_____

SUGGESTED CORRECTIVE ACTION: _____
_____
_____
_____

CORRECTIVE ACTION TAKEN: _____
_____
_____
_____
_____

EFFECTIVITY DATE: _____

COMPLETED BY: _____ DATE: _____

ANALYSIS OF CORRECTIVE ACTION: _____
_____
_____

REVIEWED BY: _____ DATE: _____

QA-100   REV. 1

APPENDIX V

QUALITY RECORDS MATRIX

QUALITY RECORDS MATRIX

DOCUMENT	LOCATION	RETENTION PERIOD
Management Review Records	QA Manager's Office	1 year
Employee Qualification/ Training Records	Supervisor's Office	·Term of Employment
Contract Review Records	Customer Service	1 Year

Test Reports
    Trouble Reports
    Data Acquisition Reports
    Certified Test Report
    Diskette
	Manufacturing Test Office	2 Years

Material Test Reports
    Chemical Analysis
    Physical Analysis
    Heat Treat Certs
    NDE Reports
	Print Room	3 Years

Approved Suppliers List	Computer	Part Life
Calibration Records	QC Office	1 Calibration Int.
Corrective Action Requests	QA Office	1 Year
Nonconformance Reports	Computer	1 Year
Design Drawings	Print Room	Life
Internal Audit Reports	QC Office	1 Year
Inprocess Checksheets	Group Leader's Office	2 weeks
Receiving Inspection Reports	QC Office	2 Years

APPENDIX VI

INTERNAL AUDIT DOCUMENTS

INTERNAL AUDIT SCHEDULE

Approved: _____

Date: _____

	JAN	FEB	MAR	APR	MAY	JUN	JUL	AUG	SEP	OCT	NOV	DEC
Management Review		X					X					
Contract Review			X									
Design Control						X						
Document Control	X											
Purchasing				X								
Purchaser Supplied Product									X			
Identification/Traceability					X							
Process Control											X	
Inspection and Test								X				
Inspection, Measuring and Test Equipment						X						X
Nonconformance Control			X							X		
Corrective Action									X			
Handling, Storage, Packaging and Delivery										X		
Quality Records		X										
Internal Audits				X				X				
Training					X							
Servicing	X											
Statistical Techniques							X					

Completed By:	INTERNAL QUALITY		Page
Date:	AUDIT CHECKLIST		1 of 2

Subject:	Corrective Action Requests		

Question	Comply	Std	Comments
Is the QA Manager responsible for the generation of Corrective Action Requests?		QA-15A	
Are departments assigned Corrective Action Requests responsible for analysis and execution?		QA-15A	
Is the purpose of the Corrective Action Request to provide a means of identifying, investigating and documenting response to correct the causes of quality related problems and measures taken to eliminate or minimize the recurrence of a problem?		QA-15A	
Are Corrective Action Requests issued from data collected through the Nonconformance Program, Internal Audit Program and through data gathered by the Quality Control Dept?		QA-15A	
Do Corrective Action Requests attempt to eliminate the root cause?		QA-15A	
Are preventative actions planned and taken to prevent recurrence?		QA-15A	
Does the QA Manager review and close-out Corrective Action Request on completion?		QA-15A	

Completed By:	INTERNAL QUALITY		Page	
Date:	AUDIT CHECKLIST		2 of 2	

Subject: Corrective Action Requests			
Question	Comply	Std	Comments
Do responses indicated measures taken and record changes?		QA-15A	
If the response is not acceptable, does the QA Manager indicate so on the form?		QA-15A	
If response is not accep-table, does the QA Manager indicate so on the form?		QA-15A	
If response is not accep-table, is it returned for additional processing?		QA-15A	
Is form QA-110 Rev. 1 used?		QA-15A	
Are files maintained in the QA Office?		QA-07C	

AUDIT NUMBER	INTERNAL AUDIT NONCOMPLIANCE NOTICE	NOTICE NUMBER

Assigned To: _____

Procedure Number: _____

Auditor: _____

Issue Date: _____

Response Date: _____

Description of Noncompliance:

_____

_____

_____

_____

Corrective Action:

_____

_____

_____

_____

Supervisor/Manager: _____

Date: _____

Review of Corrective Action:

_____

_____

Closed By: _____

Date: _____

QA-202 Rev. C

APPENDIX VII

TRAINING RECORDS

NAME: J.Q. Engineer
POSITION: QC Engineer   DEPARTMENT: Quality Control

EDUCATION

TYPE	MAJOR	SCHOOL	DATE
TECHNICAL	Inspection	City Junior College	1970
ASSOCIATE	Quality Control	City Junior College	1972
BA/BS	Mechanical Engineering	State University	1975
MA/MS			

PROFESSIONAL CERTIFICATION

CERTIFICATION	NUMBER	AGENCY	DATE
Auditor	AAA-123	The Quality Society	1978
Engineer	AAA-456	The Quality Society	1983

JOB SKILLS

SKILL	D/A	EXPERIENCE	EDUCATION	VERIFIED
Blueprint Reading	X			TBC
Quality Techniques			State Univ.	TBC
Statistics			State Univ.	TBC
Auditing		4 Years		TBC
Knowledge of Welding				
Communication Skills	X			TBC
Mechanical Inspection			City Jr College	TBC
Manufacturing Experience		12 Years		TBC

D/A = Demonstrated Ability

CONTINUING EDUCATION

SUBJECT	AGENCY	HOURS	DATE
Computer Training	In-House	8	7/87
Supplier Certification	The Training Co.	40	3/90
ISO-9000	Consultants, LTD	36	8/90
Internal Auditing	In-House	16	4/91
Statistical Problem Solving	State Univ.	36	1/92

APPENDIX VIII

FLOW CHART

Appendix VIII

Internal Audit Flow Chart

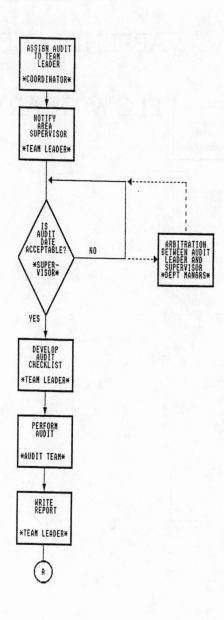

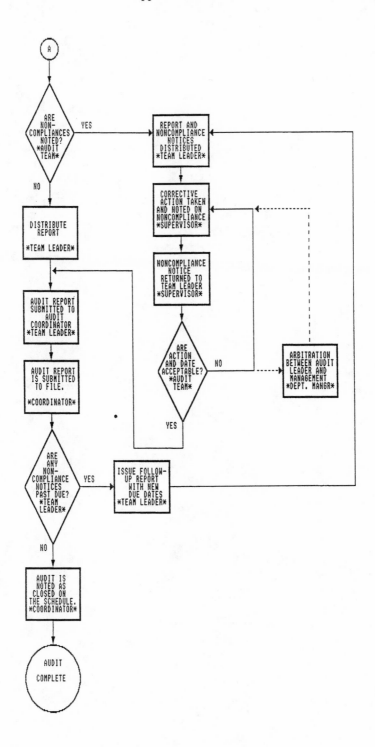

INDEX

ABOUT THE AUTHOR

Kenneth L. Arnold has been in the quality assurance field for over fifteen years. He holds an A.A.S. in Aviation Maintenance from the Spartan School of Aeronautics, a B.S. in Technical Education from Oklahoma State University, and an M.A. in Business Administration from Norwich University. He is certified by the American society for Quality Control as a Certified Quality Engineer (CQE) and a Certified Quality Auditor (CQA).